ISBN: 9781313898584

Published by:
HardPress Publishing
8345 NW 66TH ST #2561
MIAMI FL 33166-2626

Email: info@hardpress.net
Web: http://www.hardpress.net

PSYCHOLOGY

GENERAL INTRODUCTION

BY

CHARLES HUBBARD JUDD

PROFESSOR OF EDUCATION AND DIRECTOR OF THE
SCHOOL OF EDUCATION OF THE UNIVERSITY OF CHICAGO

SECOND COMPLETELY REVISED EDITION

GINN AND COMPANY

BOSTON . · NEW YORK · CHICAGO · LONDON
ATLANTA · DALLAS · COLUMBUS · SAN FRANCISCO

𝕿𝖍𝖊 𝕬𝖙𝖍𝖊𝖓𝖆𝖚𝖒 𝕻𝖗𝖊𝖘𝖘
GINN AND COMPANY · PRO-
PRIETORS · BOSTON · U.S.A.

PREFACE TO THE SECOND EDITION

This revised edition has been very largely rewritten. The emphasis which was laid on motor processes in the volume when it appeared in 1907 has been more than justified by recent developments of "behaviorism" in psychology. The present edition goes further than did the first in working out the doctrines of functional psychology, especially in so far as these use motor processes in explaining mental organization.

The doctrine of attitudes which was presented in the first edition has been much expanded.

The applications of psychology have been elaborated, especially through a new chapter on mental hygiene.

The view with regard to the importance of consciousness in evolution which was set forth in my paper before the American Psychological Association in 1909 has been adopted as a guiding principle in this volume. In keeping with this view, the chapter on volition has been wholly rewritten, and several earlier sections have been largely worked over.

Perhaps the simplest method of economizing the time of those who are interested merely in the new parts will be to enumerate the chapters which are not greatly modified. These are Chapters I, II, III, V, VIII, IX, X, XI, XIV, and XVII. The remainder of the volume includes liberal revisions. Chapters IV, VI, VII, XII, XV, and XVI are new or very largely so. The book has been freed so far as possible from technical controversial discussions, with the result that some chapters, notably Chapter XIII, have been reduced.

Many new obligations have accumulated since the first edition appeared. Those who have used the book in class or have read it in individual study have in many instances sent to the author helpful criticisms. All of these have been kept in mind in the revision and are here gratefully acknowledged.

C. H. J.

CHICAGO, ILLINOIS

PREFACE TO THE FIRST EDITION

There is very general agreement as to the main topics which must be treated in a textbook on psychology. There is, however, no accepted method of approaching these topics, and, as a result, questions of emphasis and proportion are always matters of individual judgment. It is, accordingly, not out of place for one to attempt in his preface to anticipate the criticism of those who take up the book, by offering a general statement of the principles which have guided him in his particular form of treatment. This book aims to develop a functional view of mental life. Indeed, I am quite unable to accept the contentions or sympathize with the views of the defenders of a structural or purely analytical psychology. In the second place, I have aimed to adopt the genetic method of treatment. It may be well to remark that the term " genetic " is used here in its broad sense to cover all that relates to general evolution or individual development. In the third place, I have attempted to give to the psychological conditions of mental life a more conspicuous place than has been given by recent writers of general textbooks on psychology. In doing this I have aimed to so coördinate the material as to escape the criticism of producing a loose mixture of physiology and introspective description. In the fourth place, I have aimed to make as clear as possible the significance of ideation as a unique and final stage of evolution. The continuity running through the evolution of the sensory and motor functions in all grades of animal life is not, I believe, the most significant fact for psychology. The clear recognition of this continuity which the student reaches through studies of sensation and habit, and even perception, is the firmest possible foundation on which to base an intelligent estimate of the significance of human ideational processes. The clear comprehension of the dominant importance of ideational processes in man's life is at once the chief outcome of our study and the complete justification for a science of psychology, distinct from all of the other special disciplines which deal with life and its variations. The purpose of this book may therefore be stated in terms which mark as sharp a contrast as possible with much that has been said and written of late regarding the advantages of a biological point of view in the study of consciousness. This work is intended to develop a point of view which shall include all that is given in the biological doctrine of adaptation, while at the same time it passes beyond the biological doctrine to a more elaborate principle of indirect ideational adaptation.

In the preparation of this book I am under double obligation to A. C. Armstrong. As my first teacher in psychology, he has by his broad sympathies and critical insight influenced all of my work. Furthermore, he has given me the benefit of his judgment in regard to all parts of this book while it was in preparation. Two others I may mention as teachers to whom I am largely indebted. The direct influence of Wilhelm Wundt will be seen at many points in this book. As the leader in the great advances in modern psychology, especially in the adoption of experimental methods, and as the most systematic writer in this field, he has left his impression on all who have worked in the Leipzig laboratory to an extent which makes such a book as this in a very large sense of the word an expression of his teaching. Finally, I am indebted to William James. I have received instruction from him only through his writings, but take this opportunity of acknowledging his unquestioned primacy in American psychological thought and the influence of his genius in turning the attention of all students to the functional explanations of mental life which it is one of the aims of this book to diffuse.

My colleagues, Dr. R. P. Angier and Dr. E. H. Cameron, read the manuscript and gave me many valuable suggestions which have been incorporated into the text. Mr. C. H. Smith assisted me in the preparation of the figures.

C. H. J.

New Haven, Connecticut

CONTENTS

tension. Various forms of attention. Sympathy with fellow beings.
Sympathy involved in all recognition of objects. Illusion due to
muscular tension. Such muscular tensions common to many experiences. All consciousness a form of sympathetic attention. Attitudes
as related to higher processes of recognition.

Sensory experience always complex. Sensation combinations or
fusions. Space not a sensation, but a product of fusion. Tactual
space as a simple example of fusion. Subjective and objective
space. Perception and training. Development of spatial arrangements in the course of individual experience. Vision and movement as aids to touch. Tactual percepts of the blind. Wundt on the
tactual perception of the blind. Lotze's local signs. Inner tactual
factors. Space not attached to any single sense. General conclusions regarding tactual space. Auditory recognition of location.
Influence of movements in auditory experience of position. Qualitative differences and localization. Distance of sounds recognized
only indirectly. Unfamiliar sounds difficult to locate. Visual space
and optical illusions. Effects of practice. Percepts always complex.
Contrast. Common facts showing size to be a matter of relations.
Physiological conditions of visual perception. Psychological statement. Photographic records of percepted movements. Relation
between size and distance. Definite optical relation between the
distance and the size of an object and the size of the retinal image
from this object. Berkeley's statement of the problem of visual
depth perception. Experiments on binocular vision. Difference
between the images in the two eyes. Stereoscopic figures and
appearance of solidity. Retinal rivalry. Factors other than those
contributed by the two eyes. Aërial perspective. Geometrical perspective and familiarity. Shadows. Intervening objects. Depth a
matter of complex perception. Relation to movements. General
movements as conditions of fusion of retinal sensations. Space
a system of relations developed through fusion. Movement and
mechanical laws. Perception of individual objects. Mere coexistence of sensations no explanation of unity in the percepts of
objects. Range of fusion determined by practical considerations.
Changes in percepts through repetition. Parallel development of
perception and habit. Time as a general form of experience. Experimental determination of the scope of "the present." Scope of
"the present" and its varying conditions. Time relations in verse
and related systems of experience. Time arrangement as conditioned by the rhythmical changes in nervous processes. Perception
more than the flux of sensations. Discussions of perception.

is related to education. Early scientific studies of behavior purely external. Purely external investigations not ' productive. Recent investigations and their stress on introspection and analysis of movement. Analysis of the form' of movement. Concept of organization as fundamental in all psychological studies.

Hygiene a suggestive term for psychology. Relation of psychological hygiene to physiological. Coördination of bodily activities. Control of excessive stimulations. Perceptual analysis. Perceptual synthesis. Dangers of specialization. Control of perceptual attitudes. Control of attitudes as a case of volition. Rules of wholesome ideation. Economy of mental effort. Preparation as aid to memory. Organization the key to all correct thought. The domination of thought by some leading idea. Language of great importance in furnishing central ideas. The ineffectiveness of a detached verbal idea. Higher organization as a cure for verbalism. Self-directed organization as the goal of the higher mental life.

Psychology a basis of scientific thinking about human conduct. Design in art as a psychological fact. Freedom in art. Architectural harmony analogous to musical rhythm and harmony. Literary art and psychological laws. Prose rhythms as related to the personal organization of writers. Verse another example of the same type. Literary content controlled by psychological laws. Feeling and intuition. Many of the social sciences predominantly objective in their methods. Introspective psychology and its limited support to social science. Interrelation of psychology and social science. Human evolution psychical. An hypothesis to explain the break between man and the animals. Spencer's application of psychology to sociology. Relation of educational practices to scientific psychology. Psychology as a preparation for the intelligent diagnosis of particular situations which arise in educational practice. A curve illustrating the process of learning. Significance of a "plateau" in development. Other examples of the same type of development. Motor habits intermittent. School training in its relation to the stage of development attained by the mind. Significance of scientific studies often indirect. Expression as an essential condition of mental life. Psychology historically a part of philosophy. Relation of psychology to philosophy closer than that of any of the special sciences. Psychology and logic. Psychology and æsthetics. Psychology and ethics. Psychology and metaphysics.

LIST OF ILLUSTRATIONS

PSYCHOLOGY

CHAPTER I

THE SCOPE AND METHODS OF PSYCHOLOGY

Psychology a study of conscious processes. " The understanding, like the eye, whilst it makes us see and perceive all other things, takes no notice of itself; and it requires art and pains to set it at a distance, and make it its own object." [1] Thus did one of the earliest English psychologists point out the distinction between ordinary experience and the scientific study of mental processes. A man may be afraid, or enthusiastic, or lost in reverie; in each case his mind will be full of emotions and ideas, but he will not be led by the intensity of his experiences to make them subjects of analysis and explanation. Indeed, the more he is absorbed in the experience itself, the less likely he is to psychologize about himself. We all have the raw materials for a science of mental processes within us, but we require special motives to lead us to that careful study of these processes which gives rise to the science of psychology.

The motive of wonder. The motives which have led men to make a scientific study of their conscious processes are numerous and varied in character. Perhaps the most common of these motives is to be found in the exceptional and baffling experiences through which one passes from time to time. I think I hear a voice, but find on examination that no one spoke. I try to grasp an object, but find that for

[1] John Locke, Essay concerning Human Understanding, Bk. I, chap. i, sect. 1.

my sense of touch the thing is not what it seems to be for my sense of vision. Such experiences as these require some explanation, and even the most superficial observer is likely to become interested, at least for the moment, in their interpretation. Popular psychology seldom gets beyond this examination of striking and unique experiences ; consequently the notion has gained wide currency that psychology is devoted entirely to the investigation of occult phenomena.

Discovery of individual differences as motive. Interest in exceptional experiences is hardly a sufficient motive, however, to lead to long-continued systematic study. It is to be doubted whether psychology would ever have developed into a serious science unless other more fundamental motives had arisen to turn the attention of men to the examination and explanation of their conscious processes. The more fundamental motives began to appear as far back as the time of the Greeks. These early thinkers found themselves in bitter intellectual controversies. Given the same facts and the same earnest effort to use these facts in the establishment of truth, the Greeks found that two individuals often arrive at opposite conclusions. This made it clear that like facts may lead in two different minds to entirely different processes of thought. So striking were the individual differences that early thinkers despaired of finding any general laws. Gradually, however, as the way in which men remember and the way in which men relate their ideas were studied, it became apparent that back of the seeming variety there are certain common forms of consciousness, certain fundamental laws of mental activity which can be discovered and systematically arranged into a science of mental life. To this task the Greek philosophers set themselves with enthusiasm, though with inadequate methods, and out of their efforts arose the earliest schools of serious psychological investigation.

Differences between experience and physical facts. Another fundamental motive appeared early in the modern period as a direct outgrowth of the discovery that there is a disparity between the facts discovered by physical science and the direct testimony of consciousness. Thus Sir Isaac Newton discovered that he could break up white light into all the colors of the rainbow. Conscious experience of white light is, on the contrary, absolutely simple and unanalyzable. Even among the students of physical science there had never been any hesitation up to the time of Newton in assuming that external white light is just as simple as human consciousness of whiteness. The ancients had a definite explanation of vision which shows that they explicitly believed in the simplicity of external white light. Light was for them a series of particles emanating from the object and entering the eye. When they saw white, they believed that the experience was due to white particles in the eye, and that these white particles came from a white body. All was uninterrupted likeness from the physical object to consciousness. Such an explanation of white light as that offered by the ancients was rendered utterly untenable by Newton's discovery. When further investigations led physicists to define light and other forms of physical energy as modes of vibration, the breach between conscious experience and external reality became so wide that men felt compelled to study conscious experience as well as physical facts. It is noteworthy that the period during which Newton and his successors were making their discoveries in physics was a period of the profoundest interest in psychological problems.

Place of consciousness in evolution. As reënforcements to the impetus given to psychological study by discoveries in physics, new motives for such study arose with the development of physiology, and especially with the establishment of the biological doctrine of evolution. Every highly developed function of an animal is recognized in biology as having its relation to the struggle for existence. If an animal can run well, we find this ability serviceable in saving the animal from enemies, or in helping it to procure food. If an animal has keen vision, we find that the animal depends on this sense in the essential activities of life. With such facts clearly before us, we cannot escape the question, What part does consciousness play in the economy of life ? From the lower forms of animal life up to the highest, we find a steady increase in the scope of intelligence. In the highest animals we find mental evolution carried so far that intelligence is very often of more significance than any other single function or even group of functions. Certainly this is true of man. The digestive functions of a man differ very little from those of the higher animals ; the muscles and bones and organs of circulation in man are very much like those of his near relatives in the animal kingdom. In matters of intelligence, on the other hand, man has never been in any doubt as to the wide difference between himself and even the highest of the animals. Man lives in a world of ideas from which animals are excluded by their lack of intelligence and by their lack of that means of social intercourse which is the possession of man alone, namely, language. Furthermore, in his dealings with the physical world man discovered the use of tools through which he has been able to reshape his environment. Man has, in short, through his conscious activities, attained to a mode of struggle for existence which is unique. We cannot understand and explain human life and human institutions without studying the facts and laws of consciousness, without raising the question of the relation of consciousness to all of man's other attributes.

The first method of psychology. The methods of psychological investigation have progressed with the rise of each new motive for the study of conscious life. At first, the method was one of direct self-observation. This method is known as introspection. When one has an emotion, others may see its external expressions, but only the man himself can observe the conscious state which constitutes the emotion. In looking inward and observing this conscious state, one is said to introspect.

The early psychologists were so impressed with the importance of introspection that they regarded it as the sole method of collecting facts for their science. They thus seriously limited the scope of their studies. Mental processes are fully understood only when the relations of these inner events to the outer world are taken into account. When a man meets his friend and greets him, the psychologist is interested not only in the inner fact of conscious recognition but also in the impression made on the eye, for it is in this impression that recognition originates ; furthermore, the psychologist must study the bodily activities of greeting which follow recognition. Indeed, the most productive discoveries of modern psychology have come from a study of the setting in which conscious processes belong.

Nervous processes as conditions of consciousness. Thus we see that among the facts which are not open to introspection but are of importance in explaining consciousness are the processes which go on in the organs of sense and in other parts of the nervous system. One cannot introspect brain processes, but much light has been thrown on the way in which men think by a study of both the structure and action of the brain.

Studies of behavior. Another type of indirect or non-introspective investigation which has of late been cultivated with very great advantage to psychology deals with the facts of human and animal behavior. Here, as in the examination of the nervous activities, it is possible to discover certain stages of development and to relate these to the well-recognized general fact that there are progressive stages of intelligence in the animal kingdom.

If these and other modes of indirect study of mental life are judiciously added to introspective observations of one's own conscious processes, psychology loses nothing of its directness, and it gains much in breadth.

Overemphasis of slower forms of mental activity through introspection. A further advantage which is secured by recognizing that introspection is not the only possible method of collecting psychological facts is that the experiences most directly open to introspection are thrown into a truer perspective by the combination of indirect and direct examination. The student who depends solely on introspection will give the largest share of his attention to that which is in the foreground of consciousness, usually to some complex mental process which passes slowly across the stage of consciousness. He will often give undue weight to some single experience because it is so clear, adopting this clear experience as typical, and depending upon it for the explanation of many of the less obvious facts of mental life. For example, when one hears a word and stops to consider deliberately the conscious process by which he interprets the word, he is very likely to experience a series of memory images which follow upon the word and give it meaning. Thus, let the reader ask himself what he thinks of when he sees the word " house." The more carefully he searches in his consciousness, the more he becomes aware of trains of memory images. Many psychologists having made this introspective observation set it down as a general fact of all mental life that the process of recognition always consists in the revival of trains of memory images. If the skeptical observer ventures to say that he does not find in his ordinary recognition of words such attendant trains of memory images, he is reproved for incomplete introspection. When we come to the problem of recognition of words in our later discussions, this question will be taken up in detail, and it will be shown that what is needed is not a formula borrowed from the more elaborate, easily introspected case, in which recognition is slow and long drawn out. What is needed is a formula derived from a study of habit. When we become very familiar with an object we are less and less likely to attach to it trains of images ; we respond to it promptly and skillfully without waiting for a full picture to be developed in the mind. So it is also with words. The more familiar the word, the less the mind delays and pictures its meanings. This example shows that psychology must not adopt as its chief bases for explanation the long-drawn-out mental processes which furnish the most content for introspection.

Experiment in psychology. When psychology is recognized as a broad science, dealing with many facts related to consciousness as well as with consciousness itself, it will be understood why recent studies in this field have made liberal use of experimental methods. Experiment became a conspicuous method in psychology about fifty years ago. Prior to that time the observations of psychologists were limited by the opportunities of personal experience.

Let us see the advantages of deliberate experimentation by canvassing an example. A psychologist is studying memory. He notes, when he tries to recall objects which he has observed, that there is a certain incompleteness in his mental reproduction and that this incompleteness becomes increasingly impressive with the passage of time. He will hardly fail to find out by this sort of self-observation much that will help him in describing his processes of memory. Suppose, however, that he wishes to find out with definiteness the law which memory exhibits in its decay, or suppose that he wishes some final decision as to the best way of examining groups of objects in order that he may carry away a complete and permanent memory of them. He will find it advantageous for this more complete study to arrange the objects with a view to the questions which he wishes to answer. He will observe the objects during a fixed period, and after a known interval will submit his memory to a definite test. This illustration is sufficient to show that there are advantages in the precise control of the conditions of observations, which is the first step in experimentation. If, now, the psychologist adds certain aids in the way of apparatus which will make it easy to record the time intervals and to present the matter to be memorized in absolutely uniform fashion, it will be recognized at once that the more fully developed and precise method of investigation leads to a degree of accuracy in ascertaining the facts which is otherwise quite impossible. The experimental method also makes it possible for observers remote from one another to collect their observations under the same conditions, so that they can compare their results and generalize the information which they have gathered.

There has been much discussion as to the exact place of experiment in psychology, some holding that it is the only true scientific method, others holding that it is very limited in its application. Those who are most devoted to experimental methods have sometimes gone so far as to assert that experimental psychology is a separate discipline. Those who criticize the method point out that the profounder emotions, such as intense sorrow, and the higher forms of abstract thought, such as are involved in a scientific discovery, cannot be produced and modified at will. Both extreme positions are to be avoided. Carefully prearranged observation under controlled conditions, wherever this is possible, is the true ideal of scientific psychology. Where experiment is not possible, other forms of observation must and should be employed.

Explanation at variance with mere observation. It may be well, both for the sake of defining the scope of psychology and for the purpose of illustrating its methods, to call attention to the fact that this science, like other sciences, frequently brings out in its explanations facts which seem to run counter to direct observation. Thus, before we study any of the physical sciences, we observe that the surface of the earth about us is apparently flat. As we progress in science we come on facts which are incompatible with the notion that the earth is flat. We note all these observations and compare them, and finally accept as our general scientific conclusion the statement that the earth is spherical and not flat, as it seems to ordinary observation. Again, we do not hesitate to accept the dictum of science that the earth is moving at a tremendous rate, although we do not observe the movement directly. These illustrations go to show that scientific conclusions are broader in scope than single observations, and frequently so different from the single observations as to constitute essentially new facts.

×

FIG. I. Diagram for use in demonstration of the blind spot (see page 10)

When we leave physical science where we have learned easily to accept the results of inference, and turn to psychology, we do well to remember that earlier generations less trained in the methods of science found it difficult, indeed quite impossible, to substitute inferences about the shape and motion of the earth for the facts of sense experience. We should therefore be prepared by the consideration of these analogies to recognize the necessity of comparison and interpretation in our psychology and to overcome our own hesitation in accepting psychological inferences as substitutes for introspective observations.

A simple mental experience which offers an excellent opportunity for the application of the principle of inference is as follows : Let an observer close one eye and look with the open eye at the printed page before him. He will undoubtedly observe what seems to be an uninterrupted series of impressions coming to him from all parts of the page. This is, however, quite as incomplete a description of the facts as is the description of the earth's surface based upon direct observation. To demonstrate this, let the observer close or cover the left eye and look steadily with the right eye at the small cross in Fig. 1. Now let him move the book backward and forward from seven to eight inches in front of his face until the black circle disappears. He will thus discover that a certain part of the page is not yielding an uninterrupted series of impressions. The explanation of the facts here involved cannot be obtained through introspective observation, for it depends on the structure of the eye, there being in the sensory surface of the eye an area that cannot receive impressions. This is the area where the optic nerve leaves the eye. This illustration should prepare the student to find in the science of psychology many statements about the nature of his conscious processes which he cannot expect to verify by a simple process of observation. Observation is indispensable, but the scientific understanding of consciousness requires an elaborate interpretation of all the facts which can be obtained.

Subdivisions of psychology. Psychology as a science dealing in a broad way with conscious processes and with the conditions and results of these processes has proved to be most fruitful in its applications. Wherever human nature is to be influenced, whether it be in the writing of an advertisement or in convincing a jury, the psychology of the process is worth understanding. If the study of the process can be made exact through experimentation and comparison, applications will be the safer and more effective. There has been in recent years a vigorous cultivation of psychology in all its possible forms and in all its possible applications. Thus, there is a psychology of animal consciousness. There is a psychology of the child's consciousness, especially cultivated by those who wish to ascertain the laws of mental development which underlie education. There is a psychology of abnormal human minds known by the special name of psychiatry. There is a psychology of the products of human minds when they act in social groups, as in the development of language, customs, and institutions. This is called social psychology or folk psychology. Certain other lines of subdivision are sometimes drawn. Thus, experimental psychology has sometimes been marked off from other forms of investigation. Physiological psychology has also been treated as a separate science. Finally, it is not uncommon to meet such titles as the psychology of art, or of literature ; the psychology of religion, of the crowd ; and so on through a long list of highly differentiated specialties.

Some confusion has resulted because of the tendency of psychology to break up into so many minor disciplines. The confusion disappears, however, as soon as one recognizes that in methods and subject matter all the special psychologies are merely parts of the general science. The explanation of the subdivisions is partly historical. As new interests or new methods have asserted themselves, the traditions of the earlier stage of psychology have often resisted the innovation to such a degree that a new discipline was for a time necessary to accomplish the development of the science. In addition to these historical reasons, the breadth of human interests in the study of experience is so great that the mastery of any single phase of mental life involves a concentration somewhat more pronounced than that which is required in many sections of the physical sciences.

Summary and definition of psychology. The special departments of psychology cannot all be fully treated in a general course, such as that which is to be given in the following chapters. Much can be touched upon only by way of illustration. The general treatment must confine itself to

the establishment of broad principles applicable in greater
or less degree to all of the special fields. With this necessity of general exposition in mind, the statement with which
this introductory chapter began may be amplified as follows :
The legitimate function of a course in general psychology
is to consider the typical processes of mental life with reference to their internal constitution and also with reference to
their external conditions ; to examine these processes with
the aid of experiments and observations from both the introspective and impersonal points of view; and, finally, to relate
consciousness to the other phases of life, especially to human
and animal behavior, and also to external reality in such a
way as to furnish the basis for an adequate understanding
not only of individual consciousness but also of the experience of all conscious beings.

Definitions of certain general psychological terms. In this
statement and throughout the chapter the terms "consciousness," "mental life," and "experience" have been used without any effort to define them. Complete critical definitions
of these terms presuppose a knowledge of the results of
psychological study, for it is the function of psychology to
ascertain the characteristics of consciousness. In the meantime there is no danger of confusion in the preliminary use
of the terms. Consciousness is what each one of us has
when he sees and hears, when he feels pleasure or sorrow,
when he imagines or reasons, or decides to pursue a line of
action. Experience is a general word which may conveniently be used to cover the same group of facts. Stones do
not experience impressions or emotions. Man, on the other
hand, lives in a world of experiences. His inner life is not
made up of objects, but of experiences of objects. Whenever we think, or remember, or try to understand an object
presented to the senses, we have an experience. As pointed
out in the discussion of introspection, conscious processes
may be distinguished from other facts by the possibility of

self-observation or introspection, by which method alone these conscious facts can be directly observed. Facts of external reality are open to general observation by many different individuals; conscious experiences are purely personal, open to introspective observation only. We sometimes express the contrast between the facts of conscious experience and the facts of external reality by the use of the terms "subjective" and "objective." Whatever belongs exclusively to the world of experience is called subjective. Thus, ideas and feelings are subjective. The facts with which physics and chemistry deal are not exclusively subjective; they have objective, external characteristics. Indeed, physics and chemistry are interested in facts only in so far as they are objective. For these natural sciences the subjective ideas of the individual physicist or chemist are merely the means to an end, which end is the intelligent comprehension of the objective world. The same antithesis which is expressed by the terms " subjective " and " objective " is expressed by the terms " psychical facts " and " physical facts." The former are the directly known conscious processes; the latter are the facts of the external world as known through the senses and as studied in the objective sciences. These remarks on the various terms which are used in defining the sphere of psychology serve to indicate, in a sufficiently unambiguous way, the direction in which our studies must turn.

CHAPTER II

THE BODILY CONDITIONS OF BEHAVIOR AND EXPERIENCE

The introspective approach. There are two lines of procedure which may be adopted in the study of mental processes. On the one hand, we can begin with the description of some personal experience and from this central fact move outward until we arrive at a full explanation of all the causes and conditions of this experience. Thus, when I try to remember the name of a person whom I met some time ago, I find that I can recall the vague general fact that it was a short name, beginning with the letter " E," but it requires time and effort to fill in the rest. The questions which immediately arise are such as these : Where is the storehouse in which these memories were locked up? Why did one part of the name drop away and another part persist? What kind of effort is necessary to bring out the missing part? Evidently it will be necessary, before these questions can be answered, to go outside of immediate consciousness.

Indirect method of approach to psychological facts. The second line of procedure is the reverse of that just described. We can approach personal experience from without, reviewing briefly the conditions which make such experience possible and gradually coming to the particular facts which at this moment fill the observer's mind. This mode of taking up the study has the disadvantage of leaving the student with the impression that psychology is very remote from his inner experiences. On the other hand, it has the advantage of supplying him from the first with a body of facts which he is not able to contribute out of his direct observation of himself. Some patience will be required in coming thus indirectly to the study of mental processes, and the student will need to keep in thought, with very little aid from the text, the goal toward which the preliminary study is leading.

The indirect method is the one with which we shall begin. We shall take up, first, the facts of animal behavior and nervous organization and shall thus lay the foundations for an explanation of the facts of personal experience. Later we shall review the facts of consciousness itself in the light of this preliminary indirect study.

Characteristics of unicellular animals. Our method carries us back to the most primitive forms of animal life. Here we find minute microscopic beings whose whole body consists of a single cell. This cell is made up of a mass of living tissue known as protoplasm. Such a unicellular animal is capable of moving about by contracting its tissue; it is capable of reproducing itself by cell division; it is capable of digesting food and throwing out waste matter; and, finally, it is irritable when acted upon by external forces. When the student examines life reduced to the low terms which are exhibited in a unicellular animal, he realizes more fully than he is likely to realize when examining higher forms how thoroughly interdependent are all the phases of an animal's life. Consider how impossible life would be without the new supply of energy which comes through digestion; how limited in scope life would be without movement to bring the animal to new sources of food and carry it out of danger, or without cell division to increase the number of members in the species; and how utterly out of contact with the rest of the world the individual would be without irritability. The fact that all these functions appear in the simplest unicellular forms shows how fundamental they are.

Simplest types of behavior. The only facts on which we can base a judgment with regard to the inner processes in such an animal are the facts of behavior. These appear to be very simple. The animal has three forms of movement. It swims forward and takes in food. If it encounters a stimulus which is unfavorable, such as heat or acid, it darts backward and swings around in a direction which takes its mouth opening away from the stimulus. Fig. 2 shows a

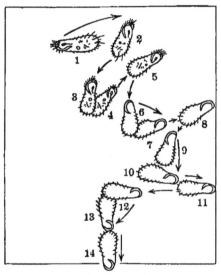

series of movements as executed by such an animal. The figure represents one end of a microscope slide which is heated at the upper edge. A unicellular organism, Oxytricha, in the position 1 is reached by the heat coming from the upper part of the slide. The animal reacts by turning to the right (position 2). This intensifies the excitation caused by the heat, and the animal backs to position 3. It then turns (position 4) and swims forward (position 5), again encountering the heat.

FIG. 2. Movements of a unicellular animal. (After Jennings)

It then darts back (position 6), turns (position 7), and swims forward until it comes against the wall of the trough (position 8). It then reacts as before, by backing (positions 8–9), and turning to the right (positions 9–10). This type of reaction continues as long as its movements carry it either against the wall or into the heated region. When it finally gets away, as it must in time if it continues its reactions, it swims forward, taking food as it did before disturbed. Thus we see that there are in the lowest animals very limited possibilities of behavior.

Consciousness no more complex than behavior. This meager repertoire of behavior betokens a relatively undifferentiated inner life. Yet even this animal is influenced by the impressions made upon it by the outer world. We may think of the heat as setting up a commotion among the molecules which make up the body, and this inner commotion results in a recoil. We distinguish between the irritability of the animal and its power of movement, but in reality these two functions are one. The animal recoils because it is internally aroused by the heat. Once the extraordinary condition is removed, the animal begins to exhibit its more peaceful form of behavior, namely, that of swimming forward, this evidently being the natural expression of its calmer inner condition.

It is hardly possible for us to imagine, in terms of our own consciousness, what must be the inner experience of such an animal, if, indeed, we have any right to think of it as having experience. Certainly a unicellular animal can have discriminations only of the grossest sort. When all is well and the animal is swimming forward and taking food, the inner state must be one of well-being. When the shock of a strong stimulus comes, there must be a kind of vague inner excitement. The two inner states probably differ just in the degree in which the forms of behavior differ.

Behavior more limited than sensitivity. If we study such animals with respect to irritability, we find that they respond to various forms of external energy. Thus, if light falls on the water, some species will collect in the darkness, others in the light, in such numbers as to indicate clearly in either case that they are affected by the light. Again, pressure due to contact with external objects, as shown above, and also vibrations of the water are effective in producing more or less intense movements. Acids or other strange chemical substances in the water will produce reactions similar to those called out by heat. In all these cases the animal exhibits only a few fixed forms of reaction. Our inference is that the inner processes aroused by all the different forms of energy are alike. The further inference is that the animal discriminates between that which calls for forward movement and that which calls for withdrawal, but is not able to make any finer discriminations.

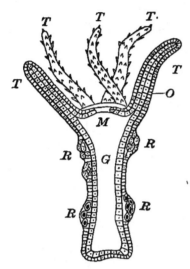

FIG. 3. The hydra

The figure shows a section through the body and exhibits the two cellular layers with a neutral layer between. The general body cavity G is lined by cells which are devoted entirely to the special function of digestion (the mouth opening is at M). R, R, R, R are the reproduction cells. The outer wall of the body is made up of muscle cells and specialized sensitive cells. T, T, T are the tentacles. (Adapted from Haller)

The study of unicellular organisms leaves us, then, with four important general facts on which to base our study. Irritability is a fundamental function of even the lowest forms of protoplasm; it is at first very little differentiated; it is the function which guides the animal in its responses to its environment; and, finally, the description of behavior is a very direct means of arriving at an understanding of the inner processes of irritability.

Specialization of cell structures and functions in higher animals. Turning now from the unicellular animal to a form somewhat higher in the scale, we find that structurally the more highly developed animals are characterized by the fact that their bodies, instead of consisting of a single cell, consist of an aggregation of cells; this we express by the statement that they are multicellular organisms. Fig. 3 represents a section of a simple multicellular animal which lives in fresh water and is known as a hydra. The animal is sack-shaped, with a mouth opening and tentacles at its upper end. The figure shows the walls of the sack-shaped body much magnified. The inner lining of this wall is made up of a layer of cells which are specialized to perform the function of digestion. The outer wall is specialized in certain of its cells for the reception and transmission of stimulations, and in other cells for the performance of movements. The processes of reproduction are provided for at special points in the body wall as indicated at R, R, R, R, in Fig. 3. Between the inner and outer layers there is an intermediate layer of tissue, in which cells sometimes appear from one of the primary layers. The intermediate layer is not sufficiently developed to constitute a separate series of organs. The multiplication of cells and specialization of functions here exhibited have advantages familiar to anyone who has observed the analogous fact of division of labor in social organizations. The cells of the body which are set apart for special purposes do not lose the general characteristics which belong to all living protoplasmic cells. For example, all the cells of the body absorb the necessary nutrition to support their individual lives, but the cells outside of the digestive layer do not take their nutrition from the external world; they derive it from the digestive cells which alone perform the special function of digesting foreign particles. So also with the function of irritability. This is not lost by the specialized contractile cells and digestive cells; it is merely reduced in these cells to a very low point and is very highly developed in the specialized sensitive or irritable cells, so that the movement cells or muscle cells and all other parts of the body come ultimately to receive their impressions from the outer world, not directly, but through the neural or sensory cells. The neural cells or nerve cells are specialized cells which take over the function of irritability. They are placed in the outer body wall, where they are in the most favorable position to be acted upon by external forces or stimuli, as forms of energy which affect the nervous system are technically called. They develop a more complex chemical structure than the other cells of the body, so that they are more easily set in action by external forces. They are, accordingly, highly important, but by no means independent factors in the organic economy. They are developed, not for some remote and separate life of mere irritability or sensitivity, but as essential parts of the developing organism, acting as paths through which external forces enter the body and cause inner states which will adapt the animal in its activities to the world in which it lives.

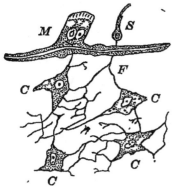

FIG. 4. Much-enlarged section of a muscle cell and a sensory cell of a hydra, together with the connecting cells which lie between them

M, muscle cell; S, sensory cell; C, intermediate cells; F, fiber connecting the sensory cells with the central cells. (Adapted from Haller)

Even in the simple organism under consideration, the process of specialization has advanced so far that there begin to appear various classes of neural or irritable cells, each serving a special function. Certain of these cells serve the direct function of receiving impressions from the outer world, and are known as sensory cells, while others serve the function of transmitting the impulse to the muscle cells. Fig. 4 shows a much-enlarged section of the outer body wall of a hydra. M is a muscle cell, heavy and elongated to make more effective the contractile function. S is a sensory cell which receives impressions. C, C, C, C are intermediate transmitting cells, and F, together with the other fibers shown, carry the impression through C from S to M.

Specialized nervous processes. The process which goes on in the neural cells may be described as follows : Some form of external energy acts upon the cells. The external energy, as noted above, is called a stimulus. This sets up a chemical process in the cell which is known as a process of excitation or a stimulation. The process of excitation liberates energy which was stored up in the cell. This liberated energy is transmitted to other cells in the body, either to the secondary transmitting neural cells, *C, C,* or to the active contractile cells such as *M.* This current of nervous energy has been compared to an electric current. It is, however, much slower than an electric current, its rate of transmission being in the higher animals about one hundred meters per second or less. We do not know its exact character, but probably it is more like the succession of combustions which takes place along the line of a fuse of gunpowder. Our ignorance of the exact nature of the nervous current need not delay the discussion, however, for we shall find that the importance of nervous currents for our further study depends upon their paths of transmission rather than on their chemical nature. The path of transmission will be determined primarily by the direction and connections of the fibers which unite the cell in which a given excitation originated with other parts of the body; secondarily, the path of transmission will depend on the fatigued or unfatigued condition of the cells and on the other currents of energy which are flowing through the system at the same time. All these complex possibilities may be summed up in the statement that in its transmission through the neural organs every nervous excitation is directed and is combined with other impulses, and is ultimately determined in its effects by its path of transmission to the muscles or glands and by its relation to other impulses. Furthermore, as soon as it is recognized that nervous impulses consist in currents of energy which have been liberated by the stimulus, it will be recognized that every nervous current must produce some effect before it is dissipated; for a current of energy must do some work — it cannot disappear. The effects produced by nervous impulses are of two kinds. First, the energy may be absorbed in the course of its transmission, in which case it will produce changes in the condition of the nervous tissue, thus contributing to the modification of the structure of that tissue. Second, it may be carried to the natural outlet of all nervous excitations, namely, the active organs of the body, where it will produce some form of behavior. If it contributes to changes in structure, these changes in structure will ultimately influence new incoming impulses which are on the way to the active organs. We may therefore say that, directly or indirectly, all incoming nervous impulses are transmitted to the active organs of the body after being more or less completely redirected or partially used to produce structural changes in the nervous organs.

Nervous processes of three distinct types. The range of nervous processes possible in the simple structures of a hydra is extremely limited; for this very reason the fundamental characteristics of nervous processes are all the more apparent. We can distinguish clearly the first step which is the reception of the external stimulus. This first step is commonly described as a sensory nervous process. The cell on which the stimulus acts is a receiving cell. The intermediate cells placed between the receiving cell and the muscle are called transmitting cells or central cells. The fibers passing from the central cells to the muscle or gland are motor fibers. It will be seen that the sensory, central, and motor processes cannot be sharply distinguished from each other; they are all phases of a single continuous process, the end of which is always some active process in the muscles; but for purposes of scientific explanation it is necessary to distinguish them as three distinct types.

Behavior varied and much more complex. If we contrast the hydra with the unicellular organism studied in earlier paragraphs, we are at once impressed by the fact that the hydra has a greater variety of forms of behavior. To be sure, all these forms of behavior belong under two fundamental types, namely, that of moving forward to capture food and that of withdrawing from danger. But each of these fundamental forms of action has been developed so 'that it is more elaborate and varied than it was in the unicellular animal. Thus the tentacles move in such a way as to sweep food into the mouth, and they contract in the presence of unfavorable stimuli, even when the body as a whole is not in full action. The body moves sideways, now in one direction, now in another. In short, the more complex animal is characterized by an increasing variety of action.

Not only so, but an action often consists of a series of related movements, making a complex chain of acts, all directed toward a single end. The body, for example, comes in contact with a piece of food. The animal swings around, the tentacles seize the particle, sweep it into the mouth, and the inner digestive canal closes in on it and begins its ingestion. Such a chain of coöperating acts shows that a high level of evolution of behavior has been reached where single elements of behavior are united into complex coördinations.

From this point on we shall dwell chiefly on the structural growth of the nervous system, but the statements made regarding the behavior of hydra should be thought of as repeated and even as amplified to correspond to each progressive complication of nervous structures.

Progressive evolution in both structure and behavior. When we turn from the hydra to the higher forms of life, we find that the multiplication and specialization of cells go on to the highest degree, producing in the animals at the upper end of the scale a variety of forms of sensitivity and of behavior which culminate in such capacities as those exhibited in man.

Centralized nervous system. We must confine our survey to a few of the major facts in this process of evolution. As we ascend the scale, there is a grouping of the central cells into complex organs and, second, a differentiation of the receptive or sensory cells resulting in the production of special organs for the reception of a great variety of stimuli such as light, sound, tastes, odors, and other forms of energy. These two types of development may advantageously be considered in succession. For the remainder of this chapter, the differentiation of the sense organs will be passed over and the evolution of the central organs will be briefly sketched.

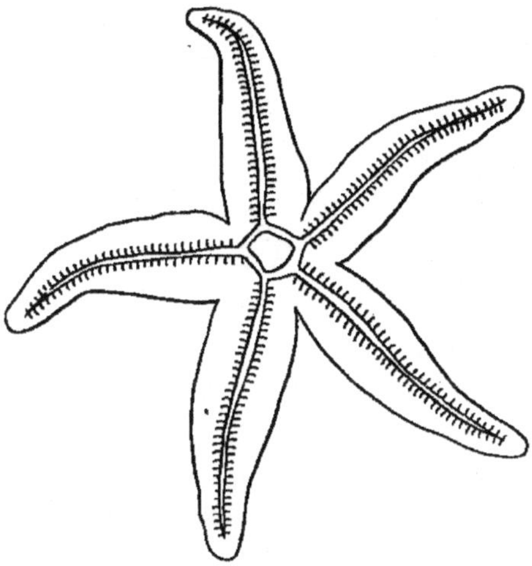

The nerve cells of the hydra are scattered diffusely throughout the body wall; there is no special part of the body in which the central cells are massed. The higher animals all have a more or less highly centralized nervous system. A simple type of centralization is seen in the starfish. Fig. 5 shows the general outline of this animal's body and the distribution of the central nervous cells. Each double line represents a group of cells. It will be

FIG. 5. Outline of a starfish, and nervous system of the same

Each arm of the starfish is supplied with a series of nerve cells indicated by the lines passing through the various arms. From these nerve cells, fibers extend to the surface and receive sensory impulses and send out motor impulses. (After Loeb)

seen that there is for each arm a central group of cells, to which sensory excitations come from the surface of the body and from which motor impulses go out to the muscles. There is also a central ring which binds together the different arms and centralizes in a · still higher degree the whole animal. This ring is in the neighborhood of the mouth opening, and its function is undoubtedly that of controlling the whole animal in taking food.

Another type of centralization appears in any one of the segmented animals, such as an insect. Fig. 6 shows such a centralized nervous system. Each segment has its group of central cells, and all the segmental centers are related by connecting fibers to one another and to the highly developed group of cells in the first segments, which are near the mouth opening.

Coördinating center of the body. The development of a complex central nervous system is of the highest importance in animal life. As we have seen, the body cells of the higher animals are specialized. There must be some central controlling group of cells or the body would not be able to carry on its manifold functions in a unified and harmonious fashion. The central nervous system is the controlling and unifying organ. The arms of the starfish are made to serve the mouth because the mouth ring of nerve cells is the dominating organ of the body. In the beetle all the organs of locomotion are made to serve the head, which is both the entrance to the alimentary canal and the seat of the important special

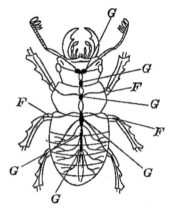

FIG. 6. A stag beetle, showing the outline of the body and the distribution of the nerve cells and fibers

Each segment of the body has a ganglion of cells G, G, G, from which fibers F, F, F are distributed to the surface of the body for the reception of stimulations and the distribution of motor impulses. The ganglion in the front section of the body is double and of greater importance than those in the posterior segments

organs of sense, namely, the eyes and the feelers. The central nervous system reproduces in outline the whole body and is a connecting tract through which stimulations are carried from one organ to the other.

It is hardly necessary to reiterate the statement made above that this evolution of nervous structures is paralleled by an evolution in behavior. The number of acts of which an insect is capable, the complexity of its methods of locomotion, of protection, and of reproduction, — all attest the intimacy of the relation between nervous structure and behavior.

Complex paths within the nervous system. Not only so, but the central group of nerve cells begins to have certain internal paths which take on the largest significance for the animal's life. The energy which comes in at the sense organ of a beetle sets up through the central nervous system a most complex chain of acts. Think, for example, of such an insect aroused by the smell of food. It first flies to the spot, guided by the increasing intensity of the odor ; it lights on the food and then seizes it. In such a series of acts the nervous system has acted in the most complicated way to control and keep in action the various muscles of the body in the interests of the whole organism which is dependent for its life on its ability to find food and absorb it.

Such considerations lead us to think of the nervous system itself as a complex organ made up of dominant centers and secondary centers with paths running between them. Our later study will fully justify such a conception.

When the nervous system reaches this stage of organization, many of its inner paths and centers are determined by the animal's inheritance. Just as a starfish inherits arms and a mouth from its race, and a beetle inherits legs and wings, so each animal inherits certain paths through its central nervous system. These inherited paths play a large part in controlling the life of the individual animal. The insect takes a certain type of food because its inherited sensory cells respond in a certain definite way to certain odors. Other special activities, such as depositing eggs and special modes of flight designed to carry the animal away from enemies, are due also to the organized tracts which run through the nervous system. Indeed, it appears in the study of insects and animals at the lower levels of evolution that practically all their modes of behavior are determined through inheritance.

Experience comparable to the lower forms of human experience. If we try to guess what are the experiences of such an animal, we must not draw on our own experiences of meditation and deliberation. Deliberate casting about in thought for a course of action is far from characteristic of an insect. The analogy which we should borrow from human experience is the analogy of a fully organized habit or, better, the analogy of one of our own inherited modes of action, such as that exhibited in the winking of the eye or jerking the head aside when an object moves rapidly toward the face, threatening to strike it. Conscious experience is made up in such cases, not of clearly defined knowledge of the thing which gives rise to the experience, but rather of a vague excitement, followed by unrest when the instinctive winking or dodging does not adequately meet the requirements of the situation, and by satisfaction when the activity proves sufficient.

Differentiation of vertebrate central nervous system. Passing by long steps up the scale of life, we may next consider the nervous system of one of the lower vertebrates. Here we find that the centralized organization has gone beyond that seen in the insects, but it is yet relatively simple. Fig. 7 shows the general form of the frog's nervous system looked at from above. In all of the vertebrates the nervous system is incased in the bones of the vertebral column and skull, so that the view here presented shows the appearance of the nervous organs after the bones and muscles and skin which cover these organs in the normal animal have been removed. The frog's nervous system may be roughly divided into two main sections. The first part lying behind the cerebellum consists of the long cylindrical spinal cord with the medulla, which is essentially an enlargement at the upper end of the cord. The cord and medulla are directly connected with the surface of the body by means of a great number of fibers. The incoming sensory impulses from the skin are received through certain of these fibers, and motor impulses are distributed to the muscles through others. There are many cells in the cord and medulla, their chief function being to form, links of connection between the incoming sensory fibers and the outgoing motor fibers. If the cord and medulla are separated from the higher centers by a cut just below the cerebellum, the animal continues to live and is capable of certain simple responses to sensory stimuli, the only departure from the normal being that activities called out by stimuli show a machine-like regularity. Thus, if a drop of acid is applied to the skin of the frog's trunk, the nearest leg brushes off the excited spot. The acid sets up a sensory process; this travels up to the cord and there passes through certain central cells and is sent back along motor fibers to the muscles. The whole process is like that described a few pages back as taking place in the hydra. There is no evidence that a frog having its spinal cord severed from the higher

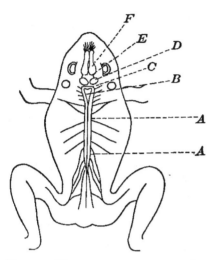

FIG. 7. The nervous system of a frog as it would appear if the skin and muscles and protecting bone were removed

A, spinal cord with some of the nerve fibers which extend from this organ to the surface of the body (in the posterior region a plexus of fibers extends to each of the posterior extremities; in the anterior region, a plexus extends to each of the anterior extremities); *B*, medulla; *C*, cerebellum; *D*, optic lobes, which are connected with the eyes by optic fibers that pass underneath the brain; *E*, optic thalami; *F*, cerebral hemisphere. The anterior portions of the hemispheres constitute what are known as the olfactory lobes. These lobes are directly connected by means of the fibers shown in the figure with the olfactory region. Many of the nerve fibers which extend from the medulla to the surface of the body are omitted in this drawing

centers has any ability to carry on the higher processes of discriminating reaction which involve intelligence.

If the frog is normal,— that is, if the connection between the spinal cord and the higher centers is intact,— the impulses received by the cord, in addition to circulating through the lower centers, are carried up to the higher centers. Here they are influenced by the action of higher centers.

Two types of higher centers: first, higher sensory centers; second, indirect centers. The centers above the cord and medulla, which constitute the higher group of structures in the frog's central nervous system, are of two kinds. First, there are certain sensory centers, namely, the large optic lobes and the olfactory lobes. These connect respectively with the eyes and nose of the frog and receive sensory impulses from these higher senses. The large size and forward position of these two centers indicate the importance of the functions which they perform in the animal's life. Especially, the large size of the optic lobes is directly related to the fact that the frog uses its sense of sight in capturing the insects on which it subsists. Second, there are, as will be seen from an examination of the figure, certain parts of the upper brain which have no direct connection with the surface of the body. Thus there are large masses of tissue in the cerebrum and in the optic thalami which lie between the olfactory and optic centers. These are higher centers, where the processes which are received in the sensory centers may flow together and fuse into higher and more complex forms of nervous activity.

The meaning of these higher centers will be understood if we use an analogy. In a large business concern there are minor clerks and managers who attend to all the immediate details. These lower officers are in contact with the outer world. Far removed from such direct contact, in a quiet, central office is a central manager, to whom the minor officers report when they need to bring other workers in the establishment into coöperation or when they have problems requiring greater deliberation and broader views than they can command.

The indirect nervous centers are fusion centers or association centers, to which all the lower centers refer their activities when these activities need a higher coördination. There is thus developed within the nervous system a higher level, which is of superior importance.

Large indirect centers characteristic of highest animals. If we follow the evolution of the nervous system from the frog up to man, the most impressive fact is that these indirect centers are the ones which show marked enlargement. A study of Fig. 8 will bring out the facts. *A*, in the upper left-hand corner of this plate, shows the brain of a codfish. At the right is the cord, enlarging under the cerebellum into the medulla. The cerebellum is much more fully developed than in the case of the frog. This is one of the indirect centers referred to in the opening sentence of this paragraph. The midbrain, which is the optical center, is very large, and at the extreme left the olfactory region can be seen. The cerebrum consists in this case solely of the corpus striatum, an organ which in the higher brains is subordinated to the cortex of the cerebrum.

B, in the plate, needs no special discussion. The increase in relative importance of the cerebrum is unmistakable. In *C* the preponderance of the indirect centers is even more evident. The surface of the cerebellum is folded so as to make more room at the surface of this organ for the nerve cells.

Finally, *D* shows the final type of brain which is characteristic of the highest animals. The cerebrum literally covers all the forward organs. It is folded or convoluted on its surface for the same reason as the cerebellum. The cord, medulla, and other lower organs are present and,

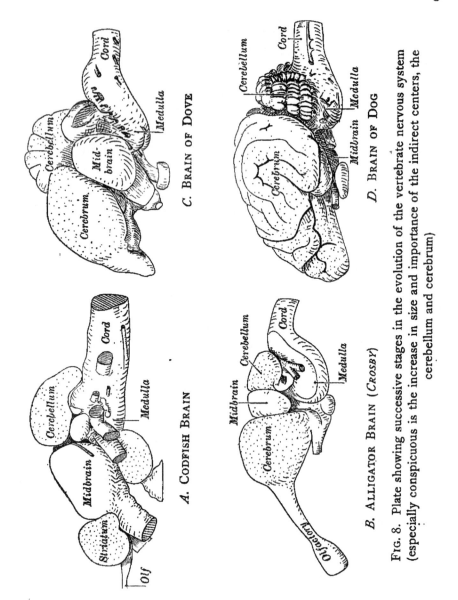

FIG. 8. Plate showing successive stages in the evolution of the vertebrate nervous system (especially conspicuous is the increase in size and importance of the indirect centers, the cerebellum and cerebrum)

C. Brain of Dove

D. Brain of Dog

A. Codfish Brain

B. Alligator Brain (Crosby)

considering the size of the animal's body, are organs of about the same importance as in the frog or codfish. The cerebrum and, to a less extent, the cerebellum are the organs which attract attention. The higher functions of the dog both in behavior and in the realm of intelligence must be related to the enormous development of his cerebrum. It is in the indirect centers of the cerebrum that those nervous processes take place which condition intelligence and the corresponding types of behavior. In the lower animals a sensory impulse passes very directly through a relatively small amount of central tissue to the organs of action. In these lower animals, also, most of the paths of transmission are inherited. In the higher forms, on the other hand, there is a vast amount of tissue, and the sensory impulse may be greatly modified by traveling along a complicated route before it is discharged into the muscles. In the course of this long journey it may be united with many sensory impulses from other sources, so that the final action is the resultant of many coöperating impulses.

Traces of past impressions also present. Not only so, but this complex tissue becomes a storehouse for a great variety of changes in structure which result from the reception of sensory impressions and the sending out of motor impulses. The phrase "tablets of memory" begins to take on a very vivid meaning to the student of brain anatomy. Here in the central masses of tissue to which the rest of the nervous system reports are the real seats of organized personal life, the records of which are deposited in the course of experience.

Meaning of evolution of complex organisms. The profound significance of this increasing inner complexity of the nervous system can be understood only when we recognize that increased inner complexity has always been the outcome of animal evolution in every organ and every function.

Let us study, for example, the evolution of those organs of the body that produce the temperature which is characteristic of the higher, so-called warm-blooded, animals. The simple organism is without the power of generating a constant inner temperature and is therefore utterly dependent for its body temperature on the environment. As a result, such an animal cannot carry on vigorous life in the cold. The complex organism, on the other hand, has purchased self-sufficiency in matters of temperature by the evolution of a complex set of temperature-producing organs. The range of such an organism's life is consequently enormously increased.

Another striking example of increasing self-sufficiency is furnished by studies of the reproductive processes. In the simple forms of life the offspring is exposed very early to the mercies of the environment. The parent organism has no adequate means of protecting the young. Gradually the parent grows more complex and in the same degree better able to protect the offspring. There is an increase in the food supply deposited with the egg and an increase in protective devices. The goal of this line of evolution is reached when the parent becomes sufficiently complex in structure to provide for the elaborate development of the offspring within the parent organism. The whole process of evolution is here seen to lead in the direction of self-sufficiency on the part of the organism. Instead of depending on the chances of environmental conditions, the organism builds up an environment of its own within which its reproductive processes may be brought to a high degree of completion before exposing the product to the external world.

Every organ of the complex animal bears witness to the truth that inner self-sufficiency is the end toward which organic evolution has been progressing. There are organs for the storing of energy, so that the individual shall be relatively free from the necessity of securing immediate nutrition. There are organs for the secretions of chemical reagents which shall convert the raw material used as food into proper ingredients for the building up of body tissues. Organisms have always exhibited in their higher forms organs of mobility, which make them free to move at their own initiative.

In all these cases the obvious significance of increasing complexity is increasing autonomy of the individual. The process of evolution has resulted in a more stable set of inner conditions, which make it possible for the vital processes to go on without interruption or hazard from fluctuations in the outer world.

Inner organization essential to highest forms of personal behavior. The meaning of a complex nervous system thus becomes clear. Nature is evolving an organism in which inner processes are to be of prime importance. Impressions must be received from the outer world, but the important question now is, What will be done with these impressions in the inner nervous system, where the impression is distributed and combined with other impressions and with traces of past impressions?

We are thus brought to the point where we realize the meaning of the sharp antithesis between inner personality and sensory impressions. Two men receive the same impression; to one it means much, to the other little. The reason for the difference is that in one case there is a highly organized central response, in the other there is no such response.

Our later chapters will have much to say about the inner organization of the nervous system. In the meantime, it should be kept in mind that behavior runs parallel with this highest evolution. Man is not only complex in his inner nervous life, but he is complex in his acts. When one thinks of the complexity of speech or of the forms of skill exhibited in the arts, one realizes that behavior and nervous organization go hand in hand at the highest levels of life as well as at the lower levels, which were studied in the opening paragraphs of this chapter.

Characteristics of behavior of higher animals. The purposes of our present discussion will be best served, therefore, by reviewing briefly some of the characteristics of the

behavior of the higher animals. First, the variety of movements is vastly increased. Up to a certain point in animal
evolution the number of organs of movement, of limbs and
oral muscles for example, increases to meet the increasing
needs of the animal; but ultimately a point is reached where
development of movement goes forward without any corresponding development of new limbs or muscles. This later
stage is characterized by the development of nervous structures which make it possible to use the given muscles in a
greater variety of combinations. Thus a skilled artisan depends for his perfected movements, not on the development
of new arm muscles or finger muscles, but on the development of finer coördinations of those muscles which all human
beings possess.

A second striking fact of behavior which parallels the
development of complex nervous centers is that slight stimuli may set up the most elaborate processes. The value of
the stimulus in such a case is determined not by the intensity or quality which it has in itself but by the complex
organization which it arouses to action. Conversely, a strong
stimulus may be absorbed in the elaborate organization and
produce no immediate effect. These statements can be illustrated by the behavior of a frog under the two kinds of
conditions discussed above, namely, when the animal has
been deprived of its higher centers and when its nervous
system is intact. If a stimulus is applied under the former
and simpler conditions, a response will follow immediately
with mechanical regularity. This response will be of a very
simple and direct type, usually consisting in a movement of
one of the legs up to the point of irritation. In a second
case we may apply the same stimulus to a frog in which the
cord and medulla are connected with the higher centers.
The reaction in this case will be of an entirely different
character. It will usually not come immediately, and its
form will depend on a great variety of complex conditions.

Thus, the frog may jump away, it may croak, or there may be a complete absence of apparent reaction. If such results as these appear in so simple an animal as a frog, the complexity of possible organization in a human being can be imagined.

Third, as perhaps the most important result of the development of indirect nervous centers, is the fact that the impressions and activities which appear in the course of individual life are stored up and enter very largely into the determination of nervous organization. As pointed out above, the lower direct centers are in the main determined in structure by heredity; the higher centers, on the other hand, are found to be undeveloped at birth, so that the stimuli which act upon the individual find at the beginning of life a mass of undeveloped tracts through which they may be transmitted. It has long been recognized that the infancy of all the higher animals, especially human infancy, is very much longer than the infancy of the lower forms. The reason for this appears as soon as we recognize that the higher centers of the nervous system are not mapped out by heredity and require time to mature.

SUMMARY

The statements which have been made throughout the chapter may be summarized in a table. This table shows the steady growth in the complexity of animal structure and animal behavior and opens the way for an understanding of the place of consciousness in the economy of life.

	LOWEST FORMS	HYDRA	INTERMEDIATE FORMS	HIGHEST FORMS
Body	Unicellular	Very simple multicellular	Increasingly complex	Most complex
Nervous System	None	Specialized cells diffused through wall of body	Organized and centralized	Characterized by the great development of indirect centers

	Lowest Forms	Hydra	Intermediate Forms	Highest Forms
Organs of Sense	None	Very little, if indeed at all, differentiated	Increasingly differentiated	Further differentiated, reaching complete differentiation (see later chapter)
Behavior	Simplest	Simple	Grows more and more complex	Most complex
	a, limited in variety	*a*, increasing in variety as compared with unicellular forms	*a*, shows variety of instinctive acts	*a*, specialized movements of great variety
	b, made up of single acts	*b*, made up of simple series	*b*, made up of combinations of factors	*b*, long coördinated trains
	c, very little modified by experience	*c*, very little modified by experience	*c*, somewhat modified by experience	*c*, guided chiefly by experience
	d, follows very directly on stimulus	*d*, direct, as in unicellular forms	*d*, for the most part direct, but in higher forms includes indirect or memory factors	*d*, chiefly indirect, as shown in man in such activity as speech
Type of Experience	Something like vague feelings	Vague feelings	Possibly vague recognition of those objects which call for instinctive reactions, but chiefly affective ; that is, made up of feeling	Instinctive recognitions and feelings present, but overlaid by intelligent consideration

CHAPTER III

THE HUMAN NERVOUS SYSTEM

External plan like that of all vertebrates. The structural plan of the human nervous system is the same as that of all vertebrates. Fig. 9 shows the outlines of the whole system. Through the vertebral column runs the cord. This enlarges at the upper end into the medulla. These two organs are, in proportion to the size of the body, about the same in all vertebrates. Above the medulla can be seen only the cerebellum and the cerebrum. The parts corresponding to the optic lobes and other minor centers of the upper brain are wholly covered by the enormous cerebrum. The significance of this development of the cerebrum and cerebellum has been indicated in the foregoing chapter.

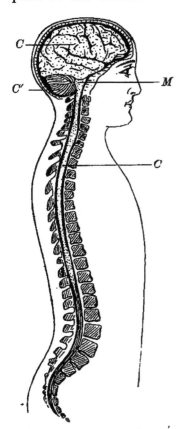

FIG. 9. General form and position of central nervous organs

General plan of the minute nervous structure as related to consciousness. The inner structure of this nervous system is of importance to the student of conscious processes. It is, to be sure, impossible to trace with the microscope the inner structures which are set in action when any given mental process takes place. For example, when one sees the letters of a printed page, there must be parts of the nervous system which are aroused, but we cannot trace the exact paths along which travels the nervous energy. We can trace the general plan of inner organization. We can see the broad avenues, but must infer most of the details. The problem presented to the student of psychology is not unlike the problem of planning a journey with a map. One sees where there is a passage and where one cannot go. Sometimes the map is not complete. But in many cases the map gives a general view of the journey and some idea of its probable details.

The nerve cell and its parts. The study of inner organization must begin with a description of the elements out of which the nervous system is made. The elements are cells of a highly specialized structure. These cells are called neurones. Each one is made up of a nucleus, a cell body of protoplasmic tissue surrounding the nucleus, and a series of processes extending from the cell body. The processes are of two kinds; namely, dendrites, or branching arms, which usually conduct impulses toward the cell body, and a single long nerve fiber which carries the impulse outward from the

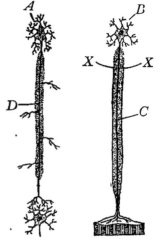

FIG. 10. Two nerve cells

Two nerve cells, *A* and *B*, are here represented with their axones *C* and *D*. *C* extends from the cell to a muscle; shortly after leaving the cell the axone is surrounded by a heavy protecting sheath, as indicated in the figure, and known as the medullary sheath. At *XX* there appears an outer sheath, known as the Sheath of Schwann. The medullary sheath ends at the point where the fiber divides into a fine network and passes into the muscle. The axone *D* communicates with another cell. (After Testute)

cell body. Fig. 10 shows two neurones with all their characteristic parts. It will be noted that the long fiber is made up of several parts. There is a sheath around most of the long fibers of the nervous system. This is not an essential part of the nervous structure, but an external protecting structure.

The neurones are organized into chains. An impulse acting on one cell is transmitted to other connected neurones until, finally, the impulse reaches a cell connected with a muscle fiber. The contact between neurones in the higher nervous systems is indirect, as shown in Fig. 11; that is, the fiber from one cell does not pass directly into another cell, but breaks up into a fine network of fibrils and interlaces with the dendrites from other cells. The connections of a single cell may be very numerous by virtue of the branching of the dendrites and because of the indirect relations between neurones. The point of relation between two neurones is known as a synapse. At the synapses, impulses are redistributed in the greatest possible variety of directions.

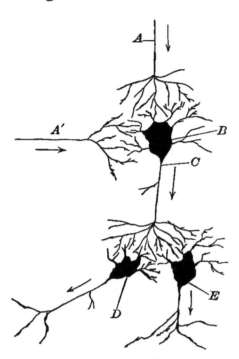

FIG. 11. A number of different types of connection between nerve fibers and cells

A and *A'* represent incoming sensory fibers which bring stimulations from different directions to the cell *B*. All of the stimulations acting upon *B* are transmitted along the fiber *C*, and at the end of this fiber may affect various cells, such as *D* and *E*. From the cells *D* and *E* the stimulations may pass in different directions, as indicated by the arrows. The stimulations from *A* and *A'* fuse in the cell *B*. The stimulation from the cell *B* is subdivided and redistributed from *D* and *E*. All connections are indirect or synaptic

Complexity of structure related to forms of action. An examination of neurones in various animals and at different stages of individual development shows clearly that the number of branches of the cell is an important factor in determining the complexity of the nervous organization into which the neurones may enter. Fig. 12 shows the increasing complexity of neurones as we ascend the scale of animal life, and also the increasing complexity of neurones of a single human being as the nervous structures mature. The lesson to be learned from these two series of figures is clear. The complexity of a cell and the number of systems of connections into which the cell may enter increase in direct proportion to each other.

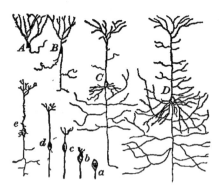

FIG. 12. The development in complexity of nerve cells in the course of animal evolution and in the course of the development of a single individual

A is the nerve cell of a frog; *B*, a lizard; *C*, a rat; *D*, man. The possibility of developing definite paths between various neurones increases in proportion to the increase in the number and complexity of the dendrites from the cells. *a* is a neuroblast without dendrites, from the earlier embryonic development of a human brain. *b* shows the beginnings of dendrites at the upper end of the cell. In *c*, in *d*, and in *e* the dendrites increase. The form of the mature cell can be seen by referring to *D* in the upper series. (After Cajal)

Synapses as paths of organization. Whether they are units in one of the lower centers of the nervous system or in a higher center, the cells are always connected through synapses and always transmit impulses indirectly, thus combining them and distributing and redistributing them. The nervous system has been compared to a telephone switchboard. The senses send in excitations and the central cells send these to the various muscles of the body. On the way to the muscles one set of sensory excitations unites with another set from some second organ of sense. The combinations and distributions are somewhat like those of the switchboard, only infinitely more complex. How complex they are, one can imagine from the statement that the total number of cells in the human nervous system has been estimated as somewhat more than 12,000,000,000.

Paths in spinal cord. Let us follow a sensory impulse through the lower paths of connection in the spinal cord. Fig. 13 shows a magnified section across the cord. The left side of the figure shows the appearance of the section as seen under the microscope, while the right side is diagrammatic and allows one to trace some of the paths through the tissue. The figure shows that the cord is bilateral; that is, made up of two similar parts, one for each side of the body. The nervous system throughout is

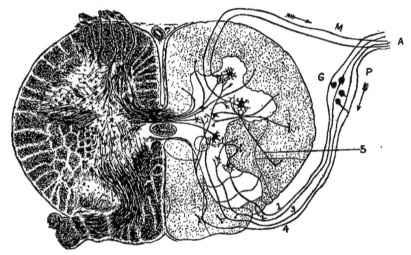

FIG. 13. Transverse section across the spinal cord

bilateral, just as are the nostrils and eyes and arms. In the middle of the cord is a mass of cells. They have a gray color and are called, collectively, gray matter. Around the mass of cells are bundles of fibers which, because of their glistening white color, are clearly distinguishable from the cells. Some fibers are seen running into the cord and out of it at the level of the section; some are running back and forth within the cord; the majority appear as mere spots because they run in a direction perpendicular to the plane of this section and are cut squarely across in making the section.

On the right side of the figure at A is seen a nerve trunk, or cable-like bundle made up of many nerve fibers. This bundle of fibers breaks up into two roots; the root P is a sensory root along which sensory impulses enter the cord; the root M is a motor root along which impulses leave the cord on their way to the muscles. At G is a group of cells outside the cord, constituting an independent ganglion. These are the cells which send their fibers to the skin and receive the impression of touch. If one has the patience to trace the fibers 1, 2, 3, and 4, one will find typical paths across the cord. This diagram alone is not adequate, however, for many of the fibers must be shown in a flat section of this kind as abruptly broken off. They pass in reality out of the level of this section. Fig. 14 is therefore added to give an idea of the way in which the various levels of the cord are related to each other and to the cerebrum. B represents a section of the spinal cord; A, a portion of the cerebral cortex. D_1 represents a region of the skin in which the sensory ending of a tactual fiber from the cell D is distributed. A pressure stimulation acting upon D_1 will excite the nerve cell and send a stimulation inward, as indicated by the arrows. This stimulation will pass upward and downward to various levels of the cord, as indicated by the branching of the incoming fiber at e. Certain portions of this incoming stimulation will be distributed through the spinal cord at different levels, as indicated by the small collateral branches passing horizontally out of the branches of the sensory fiber (see also Fig. 13). At f the incoming fiber communicates with a nerve cell which, in turn, connects with the cerebrum. This diagram is much too simple, more than one cell being necessary for the transmission of this stimulation to the higher centers. When the stimulus reaches g in the cerebral cortex, it acts upon the large cell there shown, and is transformed into a motor impulse. It then passes downward along the fiber *a*, which gives off horizontal collaterals at different levels of the cord. Through one of these collaterals or through the termination of the centrifugal fiber, as indicated at *b*, the stimulus is transmitted to a motor cell in the spinal cord, and from this cell is carried outward to the muscles indicated at *C*.

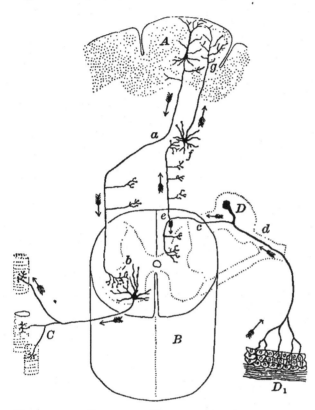

FIG. 14. A diagram to illustrate the course of the sensory stimulation when it passes upward from the level of the spinal cord at which it is received. (After Cajal)

Reflex tracts. When a sensory stimulation passes through the cord and comes out in an immediate reaction, the process is called a reflex. Thus, when one touches a hot iron and jerks back the hand, such a process is exhibited. The nerve cells in the cord are in this fashion in control of many of the simplest forms of behavior, such as the organic processes involved in digestion, and the simpler protective movements, such as the withdrawing of the hand above referred to. The nerve cells of the cord are larger than in other parts of the system, hence do not fatigue as readily; they watch over the body when the cells in the higher centers are asleep.

Transmission to higher centers. In addition to serving as a seat for the reflex centers, the cord is a communicating cable, as was shown in Fig. 14, carrying up to the brain messages from the surface of the body and carrying back messages to the muscles.

All nervous organs in part independent centers. The higher nervous centers above the cord are more elaborate organs, but they are in essential structure the same as the cord. Below the cerebrum every organ of the nervous system may be said to consist, like the cord, of a combination of relatively independent cell centers and transmitting tracts. In the cerebrum the whole surface of the organ is made up of independent cell centers.

FIG. 15. A diagrammatic section through a part of one of the folds in the cerebellum

A fiber, *a*, entering from some other part of the central nervous system, distributes its impulse to the small cells *c* and to the larger cell *b*. From *b*, the stimulus is carried outward along the descending fiber. *d* also shows the termination of an incoming fiber. The organs here figured serve to redistribute impulses from other parts of the nervous system. (After Cajal)

Cerebellum. In the cerebellum the central function predominates. This can be shown by examining a section of this organ. Fig. 15 shows one of the lamellæ, or folds of the cerebellum, much enlarged. It will be seen from this section that the cells lie, not in the center of the organ as in the spinal cord, but at the outer surface. Fibers enter the cerebellum in bundles and terminate in a fine network of fibrils about the cells which are situated on the surface. The surface, which is technically known as the cortex, is increased very greatly in extent by the folding, which can be seen in any figure representing this organ. The result of the folding is that provision is made for an enormous number of cells in a relatively small cubical space. Through the action of the cells in the cerebellar cortex, an impulse which comes into the cerebéllum as a single impulse from one of the higher centers, as, for example, from the cerebrum, may be subdivided into a great number of currents so as to arouse,

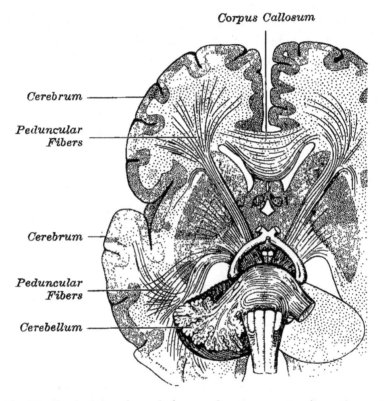

Corpus Callosum

Cerebrum

Peduncular Fibers

Cerebrum

Peduncular Fibers

Cerebellum

FIG. 16. The brain seen from below and cut open to show the paths of fibers from the cortex of the cerebrum to the lower organs

In the lower part of the figure near the middle is the medulla. One side of the cerebellum is shown on the left. Sections of the cerebral cortex constitute the chief part of the figure, especially at the left above and below. From the cortex peduncular fibers pass downward. Near the top of the figure the heavy band of fibers constituting the corpus callosum crosses from one hemisphere to the other. (After Edinger)

when distributed to the active organs, a whole system of muscles. Indeed, there is evidence that the cells of the cerebellum contribute in the way indicated to muscular coördinations in all parts of the body.

Cerebrum and its systems of fibers. From the cord and cerebellum and the other minor centers' of the nervous system we turn to the cerebrum. Our study of the evolution of the nervous system showed the dominating importance of this organ in all of the higher animals. The cerebrum is a complex organ to which sensory impulses come from all parts of the body and from which motor impulses are sent out to all the voluntary muscles. It is not directly

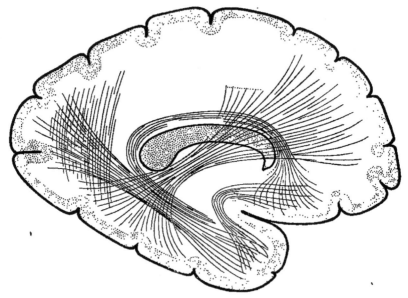

FIG. 17. Sketch showing some of the association fibers connecting various parts of the cortex of the cerebrum with one another. (After Edinger)

connected with the surface of the body, but is indirectly the organ in control of all parts of the body. It is a central clearing house for the organism. It is the part of the body most intimately related to consciousness.

In structure the cerebrum consists of an external folded or convoluted layer of cells known as the cortex. This cortex is from one eighth to one twelfth of an inch in thickness and shows many variations in structure in its different parts. To these variations in the structure of the cortex further reference will be made later. The central mass of the cerebrum is composed of fibers which provide for the connection of each point of the cerebral cortex with every other part of the nervous system. The general structure of the cerebrum may, perhaps, be comprehended most easily by referring to the systems of cerebral fibers. There are three types or systems of fibers.

First, there are great bundles of fibers connecting the cerebrum with the lower centers and constituting the paths along which motor impulses descend. These constitute the peduncular tract. Some of these fibers were shown in the diagram illustrating the paths in the spinal cord (Fig. 14); the whole system is shown in Fig. 16.

FIG. 18. A transverse section across the two hemispheres in a plane passing vertically through the cheek bones parallel to a line connecting the two ears

This section shows the fibers which establish communication between the two hemispheres. When the fibers in this figure are supplemented by those· represented in the two preceding figures, it will be seen that every point on the cortex of the cerebrum is in communication with all other parts of the nervous system. (After Edinger)

Second, there are fibers, as shown in Fig. 17, which connect the different points of the cortex of one hemisphere with other points in the same hemisphere. These fibers are technically known as association fibers. The third bundle of fibers extends from one hemisphere of the cerebrum to the other hemisphere. The fibers of this group are known as the commissural fibers, and go to make up the corpus callosum, or bridge of fibers, conspicuous in any median section of the cerebrum and shown in Fig. 18. This bridge was also shown in Fig. 16.

Structure of cerebrum as indicating way in which impulses are organized. No clearer evidence of the function of the cerebrum can be found than that which is given in the structure of its systems of fibers. An impulse which reaches the cells of the cerebral cortex through the sensory, or incoming, fibers of the peduncular tract is brought to the cortex for the purposes of redistribution and combination with other impulses. The elaborate system of interconnecting tracts provides for infinite recombinations of nervous

 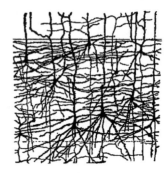

FIG. 19. Two sections representing portions of the cerebral cortex from two areas of the human brain

On the left there are shown the sixth and seventh layers of the visual center. The horizontal distribution of the dendrites of the large pyramidal cells is characteristic of this region. On the right is a part of the motor center, showing giant pyramidal cells which in size and distribution of dendrites differ from those in other centers. (After Cajal)

impulses. We shall refer in all of our later discussions to the organization of nervous processes which goes on in the cerebrum. The term "organization," so used, refers to the fact that a nervous impulse, when it reaches the cerebrum, is united with other impulses and is carried along complex series of paths, until finally it is discharged into the motor channels which pass outward to the muscles. No impulse which reaches the cerebrum can escape combination with other impulses; the purpose of the whole structure is to provide channels for the most complete interrelating of all the higher nervous processes.

Cerebral cortex complex. The cortex of the cerebrum has a structure of such complexity that it has been impossible, until very recently, to define with anything like certainty its various parts. Fig. 19 represents two typically different areas. An examination of these diagrams shows that the cells are of different types and the mode of interlacing of their dendrites is different. Fig. 20 shows a diagrammatic representation of some of the different elements which are characteristic of the cerebrum. By means of this figure the cells and fibers which in reality are interlaced can be distinguished from each other.

Localization of functions. Though we are ignorant of the meaning of many of the details of cortical structure, we are well informed as to the functions of many areas of the cortex. The cortex may be divided into three kinds of areas or centers ; these are sensory areas, motor areas, and association areas. The sensory areas are those which have the most direct relations to the various organs of sense ; the motor areas are those which stand in most direct relations to the active organs. There is no part of the cerebrum which has simple and immediate relations to the surface of the body, so that the terms " sensory " and " motor " are merely relative terms, the sensory centers being those points at which the stimulations from the organs of sense are first received in the cerebrum, the motor areas

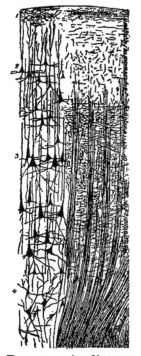

FIG. 20. A diagrammatic section showing the structure of the cortex of the cerebrum

On the left-hand side of the figure the cells alone are shown. On the right-hand side of the figure the fiber systems alone are indicated. The figure does not represent adequately the complexity of the structure. Many small cells are not here represented. A general impression, however, can be gained from the figure of the complexity of the cortex. (After Edinger)

being those points from which the stimulations pass out of the cerebrum on their way to the muscles. The association areas, as the name indicates, are areas of a still more indirect character, in which sensory impulses, after being received in the sensory areas, are recombined and redistributed. In a very proper sense of the term, all cerebral areas are associative areas, for they all serve the function of indirect combination and distribution of nervous impulses. Those which are specifically designated as associative have claim to the specific name because they perform a function of even higher combination than do the others. Figs. 21 and 22 show the centers of these types which appear on the surfaces of the human cerebrum.

Stimulation the first method of discovering cerebral localization. It may be interesting to digress for a moment from the structure of the cortical centers for a discussion of the methods by which these centers have been located. A great number of experiments have been tried on the higher animals. Certain of the areas have been artificially stimulated, and when muscles in different parts of the body have responded promptly and regularly to these stimulations, the connection between the areas stimulated and the muscles thrown into action has been recorded. Evidently, artificial stimulations of this kind would be of little value in locating sensory or association areas, for there are no clearly marked muscular effects when the stimulus is applied to areas other than those directly related to the muscles. For example, the stimulation of the visual center would show only the motor effects of such stimulation and would not give any clear indication of the sensory character of the area.

Extirpation and comparison of pathological cases. A second type of experiment which has been productive of results depends upon extirpation of the tissues. Certain areas of the cerebral cortex of animals are cut or burned out, and the loss in function resulting from this removal of the nervous tissue is carefully studied. This method can be used in locating both sensory and motor centers. There are cases of disease of the human nervous system analogous to these cases of

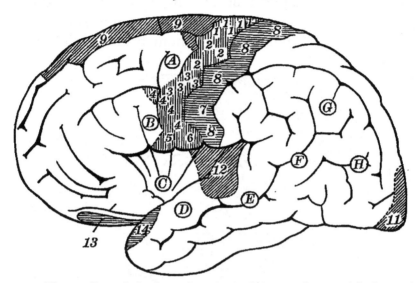

FIG. 21. The outline of the lateral surface of the cerebrum with the typical convolutions, as given by Flechsig

The shaded portions indicating the sensory and motor centers, and the small circles indicating certain well-defined association areas, are given according to Tschermak in Nagel's " Handbuch der Physiologie des Menchen." Vertical lines in the shaded areas indicate motor areas; horizontal lines indicate sensory areas; oblique lines indicate sensory-motor areas. *1, 1, 1, 1, 1* are the motor areas for the toes and foot; *2, 2, 2* are the motor areas for the shoulder, elbow, and wrist; *3, 3, 3, 3* are the areas for the fingers and thumbs; *4, 4, 4, 4* are the motor areas for the eye and other parts of the face; *5* is the center for the vocal cords; *6*, for the tongue; *7* is the sensory area for the head; *8, 8, 8, 8* are the sensory areas for the regions to which motor stimulations are distributed by the areas *1–6*; *9, 9* are the sensory-motor areas of the trunk; *11*, visual area and occipital area for the eye movements; *12*, auditory area and temporal center for visual fixation; *13*, olfactory bulb; *14*, probably olfactory area. The area where vertical and horizontal lines cross between the motor areas 1–6 and the sensory areas 7, 8 is probably connected with the muscle sense. *A*, motor writing center; *B*, Broca's motor speech center; *C*, probably memory-motor speech center; *D*, sensory music center; *E*, Wernicke's sensory speech center; *F*, memory-sensory speech center; *G*, memory reading center; *H*, sensory reading center. All of these lettered areas are associational centers

extirpation in animals, and careful study of the loss of human functions shows that the human cortex is subdivided in much the same way as that of the higher mammals.

Embryological methods. There are other methods of investigating cerebral areas which deal with the internal structures. One of the most productive of these methods depends upon the fact that the different areas of the cerebrum do not develop at exactly the same period in the embryological or infant life of a human being. The human

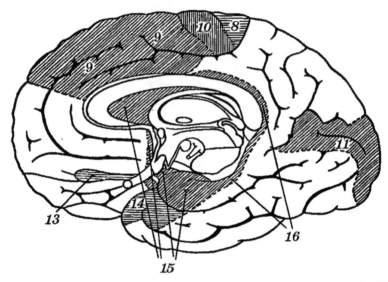

FIG. 22. The median surface of the human cerebrum showing, as in Fig. 21, the various areas

8, sensory area for the lower extremities; *9, 9*, sensory-motor areas for the trunk; *10*, motor area of the lower extremities; *11*, visual area and occipital motor area for visual fixation; *13*, olfactory bulb; *14*, probably olfactory area; *15, 15, 15, 15*, olfactory areas; *16, 16*, probably gustatory areas. (For reference to authorities for this figure, see Fig. 21)

embryo exhibits in its early stages a development of the nervous system about the central fold or fissure, known as the fissure of Rolando. This area of earliest development is in the region marked in Fig. 21 as the motor area and the area of tactual sensitivity. Later, the nervous system matures in the remaining sensory centers in such sequence that it is possible, by the study of the microscopic anatomy, to secure a fairly complete chronological account of the development of the different regions. The association areas are the latest to develop. Indeed, in the association areas the development can be traced for a period after birth, and indirect evidence seems to make it clear that the development goes forward well on into mature life.

Association areas. The visual area in the occipital region, as indicated in Figs. 21 and 22, is the area through which impulses resulting from retinal stimulation are first introduced into the cerebrum. A similar area for the reception of auditory impulses appears, as indicated in Fig. 21, just below the Sylvian fissure. Without entering further into a discussion of the various centers, it will be enough to call attention to the relation between the visual and auditory areas and the association area lying between them. The association area in question, known as the parietal association area, has developed in the course of the evolution of the cerebrum between the visual and the auditory centers as the area in which the stimulations from these two centers may be brought together and combined. There are many evidences that the combinations of visual and auditory impulses do, as a matter of fact, go on in the parietal association center. For example, there is in this parietal region one area which is of great importance in the function of speech. If this association area involved in speech is disturbed, the individual may remain quite capable of receiving visual impressions through his eyes and of receiving auditory impressions through his ears. He may even be capable of articulation, which is a motor function, but he will lack the ability to interpret the impressions which he receives when he hears or sees words or to give expression to a coherent series of ideas. The area in question has therefore been designated as the ideational area. It is ideational rather than sensory, because it is the seat of a series of functions more elaborate than those which are involved in the mere reception of impressions. It is the center for the combination of visual or auditory impressions. More than this, the association area is a center which becomes more and more highly organized in its inner structures through use, so that its influence on any present impulses is, doubtless, such that we are justified in saying that it adds to these impulses the effects of past experience. In an important sense it associates present impressions with past impressions, as well as combines present impressions from different senses. It thus serves in a large way the function of a reorganizing center for visual and auditory impressions.

Significance of the central position of the general motor area. Another important fact, which will be observed immediately on the inspection of Figs. 21 and 22, is that the general motor area occupies a relatively central position in the cerebrum. Around the motor area are a group of association areas where impulses are united on their way to motor discharge. The area of touch and of general sensibility seems to offer an exception to the general rule of distribution of sensory and association centers around the motor area. This sensory area is not separated from the motor area by an association area, as are the other sensory centers. We see in this relation of the cerebral centers for touch and movement the structural fact which corresponds to the functional fact that the skin and other tissues which give rise to tactual sensations would naturally, as the earliest organs, stand in so intimate a relation to the muscles that the later and more highly developed organs of sense could not be expected to duplicate this relation. As the primitive tactual sensory surfaces came to be supplemented by newer and more highly specialized organs of sense, the nervous centers for the newer senses were forced to take up more remote and complex relations to the motor area, while the original senses did not lose the intimate relation which they bore from the first. The development of the higher senses furnished also opportunity for greater variety in the combination of sensory impulses ; consequently the associative functions and the areas corresponding to them increased with the development of variety in the sensory functions. The association centers, which are the structural areas given up to the function of working over sensory impulses, naturally developed between the centers which performed functions of reception, or the sensory functions, and those which performed the functions of motor discharge. The topography of the cerebral centers thus reflects directly the gradual evolution of more and more elaborate systems of nervous organizations.

Speech centers. Another group of facts which will serve to make clear the character of the association areas is to be found by examining that portion of the cerebrum which is known as the speech area. This region of the brain was first recognized by the anthropologist Broca as intimately related to the functions of speech. He found that disease in this area resulted in impairment of the patient's ability to use or understand language. Later studies of aphasia, as the pathological loss of speech is called, have increased our knowledge of this area, especially since it has become possible through the examination of a large number of cases to distinguish a variety of forms of partial aphasia. Thus, a person may be able to understand words which he hears, but be quite unable to understand words which he sees on a printed page. This form of so-called visual aphasia is paralleled by forms of auditory aphasia, in which the subject is able to read, but cannot understand words which he hears spoken. These two forms of partial aphasia indicate that the connection between the speech center and either the auditory or visual center may be interrupted without destroying the connection between the speech center and the other sensory area. If the disease of the speech center is strictly localized so as to interrupt only its connection with the visual center, the other functions may remain intact, while the visual forms of recognition of language are interrupted. Conversely, if the connections with the auditory centers alone are interrupted, visual recognition may continue.

Turning now to the various forms of motor aphasia, or forms affecting the power of expression as distinguished from the forms of sensory aphasia mentioned, we find that an individual may lose the power of articulation without losing the ability to write, or he may lose the ability to write without losing the ability to articulate. In either one of these forms of motor aphasia, the subject may be comparatively free from sensory deficiencies. The lack of ability to articulate, when all of the other phases of the function of speech are present, shows that the connection with the visual and auditory centers may be complete, as well as the connection with the motor area for the hand movement involved in writing, while the motor connection with the center which sends impulses to the muscles of the vocal cords may be temporarily or permanently interrupted.

Broca's convolution an association center. Broca's convolution thus turns out to be an association area in which a great variety of lines of connection converge. It is not a part of the nervous system which acts independently in the control of a separate faculty of speech; it gains its significance in the individual's life as a center for the organization of stimulations received in other parts of the cortex and transmitted through the cells and fibers of this area on the way to the motor area.

Phrenology not in accord with clearly known facts. It may be well to call attention at this point to the fundamental distinction between the teachings of phrenology and the discoveries of modern brain physiology. Phrenology maintained that different parts of the brain are given over to different faculties. For example, phrenology believed in a certain area for the recognition of form, another area for the recognition of number, an area for the function of parental love, and one

for the general trait of combativeness. There is no justification for a theory of localization based upon a subdivision of
consciousness into such mythological faculties. The cortex
can be subdivided into areas concerned first with sensory
impulses, second with motor impulses, and third with organization. Conscious processes must be considered as having
their physiological conditions, not in separate points assigned
to imaginary faculties, but rather in the organized activity
of sensory, motor, and association areas. For example, the
recognition of form naturally includes certain sensory functions and certain associative processes. The general neural
basis for such sensory and associative processes we know,
as has been shown in the foregoing paragraphs. To be sure,
we do not know at the present time all the details of the
cerebral map, but the broader outlines are too clearly defined
to leave any room for mistaken notions with regard to the
kind of functions which are provided for in the different
areas of the cerebrum.

Frontal association area. One area of the cerebrum which
has been the subject of much speculative discussion is the
frontal area, or that portion. of the cerebrum which lies in
front of the motor area. In certain cases large portions of
this area have been destroyed without apparent interference
with the individual's normal functions. There is a famous
case known as the American Crowbar Case, in which a
common laborer, through an accident in blasting, had a very
large portion of this frontal lobe removed by a crowbar passing through the roof of his mouth and out through the top
of his skull. The individual in question continued to live
with no serious interruption of his regular nervous or physical functions. Such cases as this may possibly indicate
that the association areas are not fully developed in some
individuals. In general, it is doubtless true that association
areas, more than other parts of the nervous system, are left
open for development through individual experience. If this

conception is accepted, it is not surprising that an individual might be deprived, as in the case cited, of the possibility of further development, or even of some of his higher forms of association without the loss being obvious to himself or to those who observe him. Recent experiments, which have been tried in the extirpation of the small frontal area in cats and monkeys, show clearly that the frontal area is the part of the nervous system involved in newly acquired habits. The fact that man, who alone of all the animals has a large frontal lobe, is the learning animal *par excellence* further confirms the general view derived from these experiments.

General principles of nervous action. It remains to call attention to a few of the general facts which are known with regard to action within the nervous organs.

Active organs as termini of all nervous impulses. Nerve impulses under normal conditions always travel forward in the single direction from the sensory centers toward the motor centers. There is no reversing of a nervous current. If it were otherwise, a central nervous process might travel down a sensory fiber and arouse the sense organ. We should see colors and hear sounds whenever the central system was excited. Under normal conditions this does not happen. The sensory impulses come only from the sense organs and always move, even though the path be complex, in the direction of the motor centers.

Principle of facilitation. When currents pass through the nervous tissue they leave behind paths or tracts which facilitate the later transmission of like impulses over like paths. Indeed, it seems that in many cases this facilitation of transmission goes far enough to reduce the length of the path. Where the first transmission was over a long complex path, later transmissions reach the same end by a more direct route.

Principle of association of centers of high tension. When two centers in the cerebrum are in simultaneous action, there is a tendency for a path or connection to be set up between the two. The active centers may be thought of as points of high tension and the currents which they send out tend to flow together.

Diffusion as opposed to organization. Impulses can travel through the tissue not merely along the paths which are defined by the branches of the cells but also from cell body to cell body. This is especially true in the early stages of the life of an individual when tracts are not fully developed, and it is true at all stages of individual development for very strong stimulations. The result of such indefinite transmission is a diffuse condition of excitement. Such diffusion is often the first stage of organization. After a period of diffusion, paths are worked out to carry by definite channels impulses which at first were spread vaguely through the nervous tissue.

Principle of progressive organization. Under the foregoing principles the nervous system is continually becoming more and more highly organized. The effect of experience is to be found not merely in the fact that certain paths are recorded in the nerve cells, but also in the fact that in their totality these parts develop into increasingly complex series of interconnections. This is the essential fact which must be kept in mind if we would understand the progress of the individual from infancy to mature mental life. Each day's experience builds up new systems of tracts in the nervous tissues and thus leads to higher and higher levels of behavior and experience.

If we keep this formula in mind, we shall be able to understand the higher levels of consciousness. Such higher levels are always due to the interrelating of lower forms of experience. Ideas are made up of related present impressions and the results of past impressions. Thoughts are made up of interrelated ideas. The formula in every case is one of more and more complex interrelations.

CHAPTER IV

CLASSIFICATION OF CONSCIOUS PROCESSES

Classification derived from study of nervous organs. The study of consciousness has often been taken up without the preliminary discussion of the nervous system through which the foregoing chapters have carried us. It would be entirely legitimate, as remarked in an earlier chapter, to begin the study of mental processes by looking inward on one's own experiences and describing the various facts which introspection there discovers. The array of facts which would thus come to light would, however, be confusing in their variety and complexity. It is much simpler to approach the facts of mental life with the type of classification suggested by the knowledge that sensory processes enter the central organs and are there redistributed and organized on the way to the motor organs. With this classification to guide us, the facts of experience fall into order and lend themselves to orderly scientific treatment.

Classification from observation superficial. An analogy will help to make clear the difficulty of classifying facts on the basis of unguided observations. If an ordinary man were asked to classify the organs of the body, he would begin by pointing out the arms and legs as important subdivisions. Then he would point out the trunk and head, and so on. The student of physiology realizes that these gross external subdivisions are, indeed, important, but they furnish for science an inadequate basis of study as contrasted with such fundamental distinctions as those between muscles and bones, between organs of respiration and organs of circulation, and so on. The moment we divide up the body on these last-mentioned lines of functional differentiation we find that our science is following productive trains of description and explanation.

In much the same way popular distinctions of the different phases of experience must be revised before they can be used by science. A striking illustration of this is to be seen in the fact that in popular thought pleasure and pain are usually treated as facts of the same order, though contrasted in quality. A moment's consideration will make it clear that pain ordinarily arises from some definite point in the body. It is a type of experience which we classify in science along with those experiences which come from the stimulations of the skin or the inner surfaces of the body and are technically known as sensations. Pleasure, on the other hand, has a totally different kind of origin. It is not a phase of sensation ; it does not come from particular points of stimulation. It must be treated as a type of experience which grows out of general organic excitations of a much more central character than those which are involved in the production of pain. Again, such a term as " attention," which has a large practical use in ordinary life, is one of the most confusing terms when it is carried over into scientific study. If one recognizes, as he must in psychology, that attention is capable of a great variety of different degrees, he will find it possible to extend this term over every possible experience. There are forms of intense and vivid consciousness for which some term, such as "vividness" or "attention," is undoubtedly required in science. There are other forms of consciousness which are relatively vague and indistinct, yet when dealing with these cases we cannot fail to recognize the necessity of using the word "attention" or some such phrase as "low degree of attention," if we have adopted the word into our scientific vocabulary. These illustrations make clear the problem which confronts psychology when the attempt is made to secure an analysis which is at once satisfactory for purposes of scientific treatment and explanation and in keeping with ordinary introspective observations.

Historical threefold classification. In the history of psychology many efforts have been made to develop an appropriate scientific classification of mental processes. One of the classifications which was for a long time generally accepted is that which grouped all forms of experience under the three general heads of knowledge, feeling, and volition. There can be no doubt that such a threefold classification describes certain fundamental differences in conscious experience. The man who is engaged in thinking out some problem of science is certainly not at that moment absorbed in an intense feeling or emotion. On the other hand, the man who is thoroughly angry over some situation which has arisen is by no means in a condition to consider logically and judiciously the facts which appeal to his thoughtful neighbor who is free from emotional excitement. It is somewhat more difficult to justify the classification of volition as different from knowledge and feeling, for no serious thought is possible without some voluntary effort, and no emotion ever arises without inducing some form of action. Yet, even though volition is intimately interwoven in all forms of knowledge and feeling, there are certain cases of decision which are not to be regarded as typical processes of knowing, or processes of feeling; hence the term "volition" is needed for a full description of mental activities.

Historical twofold classification. Another somewhat different type of classification has been used by certain writers; according to this, only two different types of experience are distinguished; namely, knowledge on the one hand, and active processes on the other. This twofold classification offers less difficulty to explanatory science than the threefold classification, because it is more general. In bringing together a great variety of facts under the active processes so called, we are freed from the necessity of making any sharp distinction between the feelings, which are undoubtedly active aspects of consciousness, and decisions, which from any point of view must be regarded as active.

Without ignoring in our later discussions the historic distinctions between knowledge, feeling, and volition, it will be possible to draw from our study of the nervous system a more productive classification.

Classification according to nervous processes. The most fundamental fact discovered with regard to nervous structures was that they couple the sense organs with the organs of behavior. Consciousness arises during the translation of a sensory impression into a motor response. Every conscious process will, first of all, have certain aspects which are due to the sensory impression and, second, certain other aspects which are related to the motor response.

Third, every nervous process in its passage from the sense organ to the point of discharge encounters certain other nervous processes and is fused with them. Consciousness is in an important sense the result of fusions of many impressions. Whoever would understand the facts of experience must ask how they are built up out of the combination of many elements. We must study, therefore, the fusions which condition conscious phenomena.

Fourth, every sense impression on its way to the motor discharge is modified in character by past processes in the nervous system. The past is brought over into the present by the structural changes which are recorded in the nervous system and influence every new impression in its passage through this system.

Fifth, the most impressive lesson which was drawn from the study of the evolution of ánimal forms was that in the highest nervous systems great areas are set aside for a type of indirect recombinations which are of such importance that they must be distinguished from the fusions referred to under *third*, above. The recombinations due to the action of the association areas are of a higher order and are to be distinguished as indirect or abstract processes.

Example of scientific analysis and classification. The classification of facts here outlined will, perhaps, be better understood if an example is used. Let one look at a printed word. The experience which results may seem to the unthinking observer to be a single simple process of recognition. A moment's consideration will bring out endless complexities. In the first place, the experience breaks up into impression and interpretation. There is a part of the word-consciousness which comes from the page, a part which comes from past experience. The part of the experience which comes from the page proves on closer examination to be complex. There are black and white impressions in sharp contrast with each other which fuse into the complex image of letters and unite into a single image of a word. There are motor tendencies which often are vivid,— one tends to say the word, or there is an incipient impulse to obey its dictates as one realizes in one's own experience when the word " down " is contrasted with the word " up." Finally, the meaning calls up elaborate thought-processes which carry one far beyond the present word and arouse associations of indefinite complexity.

This example serves to show how even superficial study of a single experience demonstrates the necessity of some plan of classification under which the various aspects of a mental process may be described and explained. Furthermore, the example is a fortunate one with which to demonstrate the importance of those indirect elements of experience not derived from sensation. The impression is the least important part of the word-consciousness. Our scheme of classification is important not merely as a means of securing a complete description but also as clue to the scientific explanation of mental processes. The student of psychology must constantly keep in mind the necessity of standing outside himself and getting a true perspective of his mental processes. One is likely to overemphasize the impression which comes from without and to overlook one's own contribution; it is accordingly the business of scientific psychology to restore the balance and give a true emphasis to that which comes out of past experience and that which is due to the central and motor processes which attach to the impression.

Relation of classification to introspection. The classification of psychological problems is therefore frankly borrowed from the clue furnished by the study of the nervous system rather than left to the accidents of introspection. Introspection will not be ignored, but the facts derived by looking into experience will be ordered according to the formula derived from objective studies. Perhaps a more fortunate method of expression will be to say that the classification having been determined through a study of nervous structures, introspection will be used to reveal the classes of facts which the study of the nervous system teaches are important.

Sensations. First we shall seek facts of sensation. Impressions come to us from the outer world through each of the senses. Red, green, a shrill sound, a musical tone, an odor, a taste, a pressure against the skin are typical cases of this class. There is no difficulty in justifying an examination of sensations.

Reactions and attitudes. Then there are reactions to sensations. In some cases these reactions are very direct; this is true where the whole process is simple. Most experiences have grown very complex and the reaction to the impression comes only after an interval during which the sensation has been coupled with many other factors of experience. It is sometimes extraordinarily difficult to determine how reactions are related to impressions. The psychologist finds it better in such cases to postpone the full discussion of reaction until after he studies the complex of facts added to sensory impressions. A complete postponement of the study of reactions would, however, make difficult the explanation of those simple processes in which the reaction follows directly on the impression. The reactions will therefore be taken up first in an introductory way in chapters immediately following the treatment of sensations, and later the topic will be amplified by a study of the more remote and complex forms of organized reaction.

The conscious fact which parallels a reaction deserves a name. The word "attitude" serves very well this purpose. We say in common parlance that we feel an attitude of interest or disgust. Our study will show us that all attitudes of mind are aspects of consciousness related to reactions. We have attitudes of belief and incredulity, attitudes of sympathy and aloofness. All these are as distinct from sensations as facts of consciousness can be from each other. We shall attempt a classification of some of the more fundamental attitudes.

Fusion and perception. The term "fusion" suggests certain simple combinations of sensory facts such as the recognition of an orange as the source of a certain color, a certain odor, a taste, and a sensation of roughness to the touch. In experience all these qualities fuse. They are located together in front of us or at the side. They make up our experience of an object. We speak of the experience as a sense percept.

Memory. The term "memory" includes a great many factors of which we make use, but which we seldom unravel from the complex of present experience. One meets a friend, and past experience, unnoticed as a separate aspect of mental life, determines one's whole recognition. One reads into the present all the pleasant associations of earlier days. On other occasions one labors to call up some forgotten or half-forgotten fact. The effort to recall makes one actually aware of the distinction between the present and the past. Here is an opportunity in treating of memory to draw productive distinctions between many different kinds of memory.

The process of ideation. There are ideas and combinations of ideas which constitute the highest forms of mental activity. The idea which one has when he thinks of honesty is something more than sensation or attitude or memory; it is the understanding of a whole series of relations. We speak of this as an abstract idea, meaning by that term that we have cut loose from impressions and are in a world of our own making. The processes of abstraction exhibit the creative power of a highly developed individual as no other mental process can. The animals do not have, so far as we can judge, abstract ideas. They have sensations, attitudes, percepts, and memories, but, their powers of organization stop short of abstract ideas.

How one forms an abstraction is extremely difficult to observe through mere introspection. A mind absorbed in studying geometry cannot observe itself at work. That is why abstract geometrical ideas are difficult to explain. Obviously, however, the system of psychology which omitted these would be altogether deficient.

Higher forms of action. After dealing with the processes of ideation we may very properly come back to a reëxamination of behavior. Those forms of behavior which are characteristic of mature intelligence are commonly grouped together under the caption " voluntary choice." The discussion of voluntary choice will not duplicate the treatment of reactions and attitudes as indicated on page 66.

Relation to historic classification. The foregoing classification is to be followed in the following chapters. For the sake of keeping it in some relation with the historic classifications, it may be said that the term " knowledge " is in a measure synonymous with sensation, perception, memory, and ideation. Feeling and volition are, roughly speaking, synonymous with attitudes, while the higher forms of behavior classified under voluntary choice are quite synonymous with the higher phases of volition. The effort should not be made, however, to push this reconciliation of the two classifications too far. There is a large element of effort and hence of volition in every fusion and every formation of an abstraction. There is a large element of feeling in most perceptions. The adoption of a classification of psychological facts based on studies of nervous processes is a frank abandonment of the historic threefold classification.

Practical applications. Following the study of the various classes of psychological facts will be certain studies of a practical type which may be termed applications of psychology. A part of these applications will be formulated with a view to helping the student to see his own mental processes from a psychological point of view. A part will deal with some of the larger social problems, with a view to showing that community life is capable of proper organization only through a complete understanding of the nature of human consciousness.

SUMMARY

The following summary of the foregoing discussion will serve as a guide to the subsequent chapters:

I. Sensations
   This will require a description of the sense organs and their action and a description of those aspects of consciousness which come as impressions from the outer world.
II. Attitudes
   This will require an explanation of the relation of consciousness to bodily activity and a classification of forms of conscious experiences which arise as a result of the individual's reactions to impressions.

III. Fusions of Sensations

As sensations become motives or sources of reactions they are united into complexes. These complexes are called percepts and are always present where an individual distinguishes objects in the world about him.

IV. Memories

Past experiences are retained in structural changes in the nervous system and either in explicitly distinguishable form or in less obvious character enter into present experience. Psychology must include under this head many facts which escape introspection. Here as elsewhere throughout the discussion the largest regard must be had for the fact that the explanatory principles of psychology depend on a clear understanding of motor processes.

V. Ideas and Ideational Forms of Thought

These include all the higher forms of organized experience. They are conditioned by the higher complexes which are developed in the cerebral association areas.

VI. Voluntary choice is the phrase employed to mark off the highest forms of behavior from the lower forms. The concept of personality enters into this discussion.

VII. Applications to individual experience and to social organizations.

CHAPTER V

SENSATIONS

Sensations not copies of external forces. For the ordinary man there is no problem for psychology presented by a sensation. A sensation is for his thinking an inner reflection or copy of an external fact. He dismisses as curious speculation any statement which would tend to impair his confidence in the directness of the relation between sensations and external or objective facts. Yet, as was pointed out in an earlier chapter, the progress of science has forced upon us a distinction between objective colors and sounds, on the one hand, and subjective or experienced sensations of color and sound, on the other hand. For example, color as we see it in our individual experiences is not a form of vibration, while color as the physicist finds that he must describe it in order to explain its physical nature is a form of wave motion easily convertible into other wave motions, such as those of heat, which in turn give us sensations of a sort quite different from colors.

Laws of sensation as one of the first problems in psychology. The moment we admit a distinction between subjective color and external light vibrations, certain important scientific questions immediately suggest themselves. Thus, we are led to inquire what are the laws of subjective color as distinguished from the physical laws of objective light? For example, in passing from one color in the subjective series to the next color, as from red through orange and yellow to green, we find ourselves taking a series of steps and reaching qualitative differences so marked that we speak of the sensations as opposite or as sharply contrasted. This marked difference in qualities is related to animal interests of a practical sort. Red fruits and green are to be distinguished; the color of the foliage and of the blossom are to be discriminated. In physics, the transition from the red vibration to the green is one continuous series of changes in rate of vibration. All the vibrations are qualitatively alike; there is no contrast. So far as light vibrations are concerned, they are utterly heedless of animal interests.

Another example of the difference between the subjective series and the physical series is to be found in the fact that sensations arise only from the middle of certain physical series. Thus the physicist knows that there are rays of light made up of vibrations slower than those which give us sensations of red, and that other rays are more rapid in vibration than those which give sensations of violet. The range of sensations of sound, in like fashion, is short, contrasted with the series of sound vibrations known to the physicist.

Relation of sensations to sensory nervous processes. The relation between sensations in consciousness and physiological processes in the organs of sense is much closer than is the relation between sensations and the physical facts above discussed. Thus, to take a striking illustration, it is because we have an organ of sense which is affected by light and no special organ affected by weak currents of electricity that men overlooked for so long a period both the prevalence of forms of electrical energy and the close relation between light and electricity. Such an illustration calls attention to the fact that experience differs in certain of its aspects from the physical world, because experience is related to the physical world only indirectly, through the organs of sense.

Other examples are abundant. When the ear is aroused by the complex sound coming from a drum and a trumpet, there are sensations corresponding to each element of the complex because the sensory cells receive the vibrations from one instrument at one point and the vibrations from the other at another point. The two elements of sound do not obliterate each other or cause a blur in consciousness. They do not give rise to a single sensation, even though the sound wave which strikes the ear is a single complex air vibration. The further details of this matter will come out in later sections of this chapter.

Sensations as elements. Our first problem, then, is to study sensations as related to the facts of physics and to the facts of physiology of the sense organs. Later, we shall study sensations in their relation to one another and to the higher forms of experience. It will then be pointed out that sensations as they appear in consciousness are always elements of complex forms of knowledge. There is no such experience as an isolated sensation of red or of green or of sound. All sensations are referred to some point in space; they are associated with certain interpretations and otherwise brought into the stream of personal experiences. But in all these later combinations, sensations retain their qualitative independence to an extent which justifies us in recognizing them for the purposes of science as elements, or separate and distinct aspects of consciousness. The problems of fusion of sensations with each other and the laws of these fusions may therefore properly be postponed; for the present, we turn to a discussion of sensations as elements of consciousness related to certain facts of physics and to the processes in the organs of sense which lie between the physical world and consciousness.

Psycho-physics as a division of psychology. The field of study which we here enter has sometimes been called psycho-physics. This name originated as the name of one branch of the study of sensations to which our introductory examples have not referred. Psycho-physics in its earlier days studied especially the facts of intensity of sensation. If a physical sound becomes stronger, it does not follow that the related sensations will become stronger in a corresponding degree. The facts of intensity will be referred to briefly in our later discussions.

In taking up the problems of psycho-physics, we shall begin with one of the most highly developed and highly differentiated groups of sensory processes; namely, those of vision. We might have taken first the simpler sensations, such as those of touch, but the facts regarding color are so much more complex and significant that it will be advantageous to encounter at once all the major principles involved in such a study.

A. Visual Sensations

Meaning of term "quality." Visual sensations, like all sensations, can be described only to a person who has experienced them. Red and blue and yellow and black are names of visual sensations. If the reader has had experiences corresponding to these words, he will recognize that each of the experiences referred to is a unique fact in his mental life. Red may be like orange or yellow; it may be soft and pleasing, or glaring and unpleasant; but its essence is its redness, and this essence, which is called the quality of the sensation, can be illustrated but cannot be defined in terms of any other experience.

Chromatic (or color) series and achromatic (or gray) series. If we consider all possible visual sensations, we notice at once that there are two general groups, — those which belong in the series of colors and those which belong in the black-gray-white series. The latter series is in some respects the simpler. Beginning with the darkest black, one may arrange various shades of gray in an unbroken series up to the brightest white. The color series is more complex. It is made up of sensation qualities which, to be sure, shade into each other through intermediate colors ; but the members of the series have a marked individuality which leads us to designate them by a variety of entirely different names rather than by a common term, such as is used in referring to the gray series. Thus, red and yellow are different qualities, though they shade into each other through orange ; when we pass from one to the other, the transition is so marked that we are compelled to describe red and yellow as different qualities.

Fundamental color names. The question of how many fundamental visual qualities there are, is one that has often been discussed. Popular language has clearly marked out at least four color qualities besides the blacks, grays, and whites. These four colors are red, yellow, green, and blue. The names of these colors are, as their form clearly indicates, older than such derived names as orange, indigo, violet, or any of the compound names, such as green-blue and yellow-green. The loose use of the four older color names makes it clear, however, that there is no particular red or green which can be selected as having exclusive right to the name. In making up a system of color terminology for such works of reference as a dictionary, this fact comes out very clearly. The best that can be done is to take the average of a large number of usages and exhibit a sample of the color chosen. Color names, therefore, while suggesting something of the popular discrimination of colors, supply no final evidence as to the number of primary sensation qualities.

The various scientific studies on this subject of the number of color qualities may be divided into three groups. One group regards red, green, and blue as the only primary colors, all others being looked upon as derived forms. A second group adds yellow, while a third group considers that there are an indefinitely large number, certainly more than four. The solution of the question, since it does not depend merely upon introspective observation, waits upon the complete formulation of certain facts discussed later.

The color spectrum and circle. More important than the determination of the exact number of primary color qualities is the presentation of a complete description of the series of color experiences. The most complete single series of colors known to physics is produced by passing ·a pencil of white light through a prism. The different colors which compose this ray of white light will be refracted to different positions, and the whole will be spread out into a colored band with red at one end and violet at the other. Between these lie orange, yellow, green, blue, in the order given. This whole series of colors produced from white light is called the spectrum. Mixed

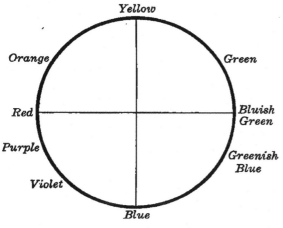

FIG. 23. Color circle

The center of the circle represents white. All colors placed at opposite ends of diameters of the circle are complementary colors

colors are not present in the spectrum, notably purple, which consists of a mixture of red and blue. When purple is introduced, the series of colors seems to return upon itself. For this reason, the colors of the spectrum plus purple may conveniently be represented by a closed figure, either a triangle or a circle. The color circle is given in Fig. 23. Four, or better nine, color names are used to indicate some of the chief qualities of the series, the exact number of such qualities being left somewhat indefinite, for reasons indicated above. Between the colors explicitly named in this circle there are transitional forms of sensations.

Saturation, brightness, and mixtures. There are also transitional forms of sensation from this color series to the gray series. Thus, from any color there is a series of sensations in which the color quality gradually fades into a colorless gray of the same intensity as the original color. Such a series is called a saturation series. The full color is said to be a saturated quality; the more the quality approaches gray, the less saturation it is said to have. Each color is also capable of variations in brightness. A red of

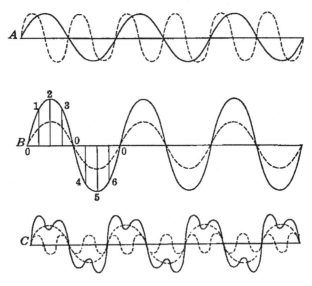

FIG. 24. Wave forms

great light intensity is said to have a high degree of brightness. A color of small light intensity is said to have a low degree of brightness. The relation of brightness to saturation is such that when a color becomes very bright or very dim its characteristic quality tends to disappear. Finally, color qualities may be compounded so as to produce a great variety of intermediate qualities, such as orange-yellow and blue-green, which are sometimes thought of as intermediate qualities, sometimes as equally primary with the others.

External light. Turning now from the series of visual sensations, let us review very briefly the characteristics of external physical light. The physicist recognizes physical light as a form of vibration in the luminiferous ether. These ether vibrations have three characteristics; namely, rate of vibration, amplitude of vibration, and complexity of vibration. For purposes of exposition we may compare light waves to simple water waves, which are represented in outline in Fig. 24. In waves of this type a single particle of water oscillates up and down in straight lines, while the wave as a whole travels in the horizontal direction.

The rapidity with which each particle oscillates is called the rate of vibration. The rate determines the length of the waves from crest to crest, so that we may refer to waves as having different lengths : rapid vibrations corresponding to short wave lengths, and the slow vibrations corresponding to greater wave lengths. The amplitude of a wave is determined by the extent of the oscillations of each particle. The complexity of a wave depends on the mode of the movement of the particles ; a complex movement results from the action of a number of wave impulses acting on the same particle at the same time.

The wave forms represented in *A*, Fig. 24, have like amplitude — that is, like range of movement above and below the horizontal line — but differences in rate, one wave being twice as rapid as the other. The waves in *B* are alike in rate but different in amplitude. The lines 1, 2, 3, 4, 5, 6 show the paths of six single particles which participate in the larger wave motion. When a particle is in its original position, it lies at some point along the horizontal line, as at *O*. At successive periods it moves to the height 1, 2, or 3 or to the low level 4, 5, or 6. *C* represents a complex wave form. The two regular waves, indicated in dotted lines, acting upon the particles together, result in the complex form of vibration represented in the full-drawn line.

Comparison of physical and mental series. In the following table a comparison is exhibited between the physical facts and the corresponding facts of sensory experience :

PHYSICAL FACTS	FACTS OF SENSORY EXPERIENCE
Simple light vibrations of medium amplitude	Color sensations
These simple vibrations appear in every possible rate, thus forming a single continuous series of variations in rate	The sensations differ in certain well-marked stages, forming a series of distinct color qualities, limited in number
These rates vary from less than 435 million million vibrations per second	No color experience (sometimes experience of warmth)
(435 million million vibrations per second)	Red
through all possible rates	Successive qualities (yellow, green, blue)
to 769 million million vibrations per second	Violet
and beyond	No color experience
Compound vibrations	Either whites, grays, less saturated colors, or purples
The compound sometimes consists of vibrations of about 435 to 500 million million per second, combined with those of about 660–769 million million per second	Purple
In some cases widely different rates are combined, sometimes in special pairs, sometimes in more complex groups	White or gray
In some cases various rates other than those above mentioned are combined	Various grays and unsaturated colors
Amplitude variations	Changes in intensity and saturation
Increase in amplitude to the highest	Increase in intensity and decrease in saturation toward white
Decrease in amplitude to the lowest	Decrease in intensity and in saturation toward black

Relation between the physical and the psychical facts dependent in part on the organs of sense. The differences between the physical series and the sensation series are so striking that much scientific investigation has been devoted to the effort to bridge over the differences, as far as possible, by setting between the two groups of processes described in the above table a third group of processes; namely, the physiological processes in the eye and central nervous system. Not infrequently it has been impossible, with the means of scientific investigation in our possession, to discover by direct observation all the physiological links between certain physical facts and certain facts of experience. In such cases, theories have been developed by science to fill the gap. These theories go beyond direct observation in their statements, but do so with definite regard to such facts as can be observed. We turn, therefore, to a consideration of some of the physiological facts and theories, taking up, as a necessary introduction to the physiological facts, a study of the structure of the eye.

Evolution of organ of vision. The human eye is a very complex and highly sensitive organ. It will be well for us in attempting to understand the eye, to go back to an earlier point in the evolutionary series and begin our study with more primitive visual organs. The line of evolution between the simplest eyes and the human eye is not direct, for the human eye is in its sensitive parts a division of the brain brought to the surface of the body. The eyes of invertebrates show, however, how sensitivity to light first became a specialized function of animal tissue.

Even in the lowest forms of plant and animal life there is a certain sensitiveness to light. A flower is affected by light, in some cases enough to produce movement on its stem, in all cases in its inner growth conditions. So also the unicellular animal forms are stimulated by light to vigorous action. In the simpler multicellular animals, in addition to the differentiation between neural cells and muscular cells which was described in an earlier chapter, there is a further differentiation among the neural cells. In the jellyfish, for example, it is found that at certain points on the surface of the body the cells of the nervous system are grouped into small spots of pigmented cells (see Fig. 25, A). The pigment is not a part of the nervous system, but it serves to absorb the light which falls upon this part of the animal's body more than do the unpigmented regions. The result is that the influence of the light is enhanced by the presence of the pigment, and the growth of larger and more sensitive sensory cells in the immediate neighborhood of these spots brings about a condition which is favorable to the reception of light. We may, for convenience, refer to the pigment, since it is not true nervous tissue, as an accessory organ. We shall find in the study of later developments of the eye that the accessory parts of the eye are quite as important as the nervous organs themselves, the evolution of the two groups of structures going on in parallel lines.

Higher forms of visual organs are represented in Fig. 25, B and C. Thus we find a larger group of cells sensitive to light stimulations. The pigment is present as in the most primitive eyes, and the whole organ is placed in a depression in the surface of the body. This depression serves to protect the delicate cells more effectively than they could be protected on the general body surface, as in the case of the jellyfish. This protection of the cells undoubtedly works to the advantage of the cells, furnishing them the conditions necessary for becoming more sensitive, while at the same time the wall of the depression furnishes them the space in which they become more numerous. In later stages of development, as indicated in Fig. 25, D and E, the depression in the body wall is filled with a protecting fluid. This fluid is of a thick, gelatinous consistency, and in the most primitive forms translucent, not transparent. The light stimulation

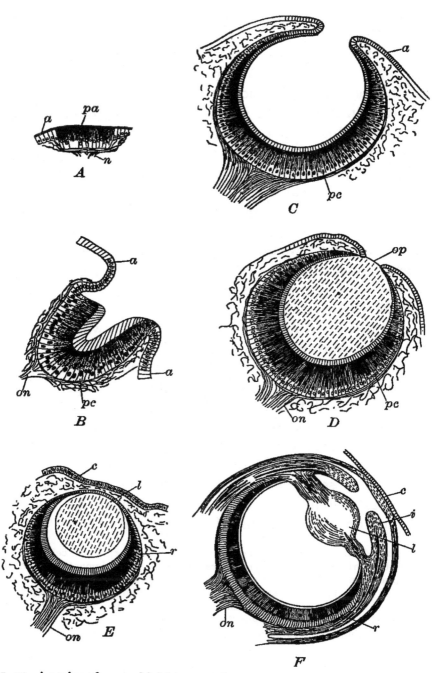

FIG. 25. A series of eyes which have reached various levels of development*

which acts upon the sensory cells of such an eye as this will obviously not be very intense or definite. Something has been sacrificed to protection in the fluid, which obstructs the light. This disadvantage is, however, more than offset by the fact that the fluid furnishes favorable conditions for increase in the number and sensitiveness of the cells. Such an eye as this cannot distinguish more than vague changes in illumination. An opaque object passing before the animal might, by its shadow, be recognized as something standing between the animal and the light, but the form or distance of the object certainly could not be recognized except through the intensity of the shadow and the period of its duration. A bright object would give a somewhat more definite impression, but nothing comparable to the impression received by the eyes of the higher animals.

Later stages of development of the eye are represented in the figure. In Fig. 25, *D*, *E*, and *F*, it will be seen that the outer covering of the eyes begins to develop a lens. In the earliest forms, this lens is spherical in shape. Such a shape is mechanically simple, but optically very imperfect. The image which it throws on the sensory surface is distorted, and the different rays of light are focused at different points, causing the hazy colored fringes technically known as chromatic aberrations.

Organ of sense as selective organ. Such an evolutionary series as that just described could be made the basis of a chapter on the relations of the animal's inner life and

* Fig. 25, *A*, shows a simple pigment spot. The ordinary epithelial cells which constitute the surface of the body are represented at *a*. The pigment particles represented at *pa* make this portion of the surface of the body more susceptible to the action of light. Fig. 25, *B*, shows a somewhat more highly developed organ. The surface of the body is here depressed so as to protect the sensory cells. These specialized cells are notably larger than the epithelial cells at *aa*. This is the eye of Patelia. Fig. 25, *C*, represents the eye of Nautilus. The central cavity is filled with water. Fig. 25, *D*, is a camera eye with a large lens filling its cavity; *op* represents the lens. Fig. 25, *E*, is the camera eye of Murex with the cornea, *c*, covering the lens. Fig. 25, *F*, is the complete eye of cuttlefish with the lens, *l*; cornea, *c*; iris, *i*, and other portions as before. (From Conn's " Method of Evolution ")

development to the outer world of nature. Evidently it is greatly to the animal's advantage to be sensitive to changes in light and thus also to gain indirectly impressions from all objects which reflect or absorb light. The inner life processes are very dependent on these impressions; therefore, a part of the organism is set aside to keep watch and guide the organism. The organism is thus enabled to select from the world in which it lives those impressions which have to do with its own existence. Furthermore, as we shall find when we come to study other organs of sense, other parts of the body surface are specialized to keep the animal in contact with aspects of the outer world other than light. The organs of sense are accordingly to be defined as specialized avenues through which forces of the external world that are important to the animal's life affect the organism.

The human eye — its muscles. We pass over the varying forms of visual organs exhibited in the animal world and take up briefly the human eye. The human eye is an independent organ separated from the body wall and placed in a protecting bony cavity or eye socket. Before taking up the internal structure of the eyeball it may be well to refer to the external muscles which hold it in place and move it about independently of the head. These are important accessory organs and increase the range of vision greatly by making it possible to move the eyes easily without moving the head. The human eye is supplied with six such muscles. By means of these muscles the eye is capable of rotation, with the nicest adjustments in any direction whatsoever. In ordinary life the behavior of one eye is closely related to the behavior of the other eye, so that the muscles coöperate in producing certain joint movements, or binocular movements as they are called.

Many of the facts of human vision are closely related to the fact that the eyes are themselves very active organs. Looking at an object involves a great deal of muscular adjustment. Looking to the left involves a different type of muscular adjustment from that involved in looking straight ahead. These facts should be borne in mind as important for much of our later study.

The outer wall and the lens. A sectional view showing the internal structure of the eyeball is given in Fig. 26. It will be noted immediately that this organ is in many

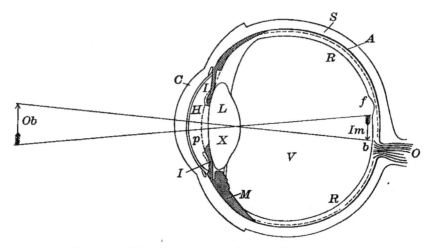

FIG. 26. Diagrammatic section of the human eye

O, optic nerve; *S*, sclerotic; *C*, cornea; *A*, choroid coat; *I*, iris; *R*, retina; *V*, vitreous humor; *H*, aqueous humor; *L*, crystalline lens; *X*, optic center of the lens; *b*, blind spot; *f*, fovea centralis; *p*, pupil; *M*, ciliary muscles, which control the curvature of the lens; *Ob*, object outside of eye; *Im*, image on the retina. (After Wundt)

respects more highly developed than any of the eyes represented in Fig. 25. By the development of an independent outer wall of cartilage the eyeball has been made a free portion of the body, as noted in the last paragraph. In the second place, it will be observed that the lens, which we saw in some of the lower forms as a spherical organ, has been elaborated in the course of animal evolution, so that it now has the very much more advantageous form of a double convex lens, indicated in the figure at *L*. This lens has certain other complexities in structure which tend to free it from optical defects. It is not homogeneous throughout; furthermore, by means of the iris,' or adjustable diaphragm, which is placed in front of it, only the center, which is the most efficient portion of the lens, is utilized in ordinary vision. By means of certain muscles which form a circle around the lens and control a transparent capsule which surrounds it, the lens can be modified in form so that it is made more or less convex according as light which is to be focused upon the sensory surface comes from a source near at hand or far away. The details of this adjustment of the lens need not be discussd here; it is enough to call attention to the fact that when the eye is to look at an object far away, the lens is relatively less convex than when the eye is looking at an object near at hand. The adjustment is carried out reflexly. There are limits beyond which it is impossible for the lens to adjust itself; the near limit for the normal eye is about eight inches from the eye, the remote limit for the normal eye is at an infinite distance. Individual imperfections in adjustment appear. For example, the lens in old age becomes somewhat less elastic than in early life and, because of this lack of elasticity, it is incapable of taking on a high degree of convexity. Other abnormalities appear, in that the far limit of certain eyes is at a relatively short distance in front of the eye; a person whose limit of remote vision is thus nearer than a point infinitely far away is described as near-sighted. Most of the defects in the functioning of the lens can be relieved more or less completely by the use of an artificial lens outside of the eye. The function of the artificial lens is exactly that of the lens in the eye, and the possibility of correcting defects in the lens of the eye by various combinations of glass lenses is limited only by the possibilities of physical optics. This makes it perfectly clear that the lens is not to be treated as a part of the nervous system but rather as an accessory organ developed for the purpose of applying the stimulus to the organ of sense in such a way as to produce a clearly defined image on the retina.

Transparent media. In the human eye all of the media through which the light must pass are highly transparent. A certain portion of the outside coat of the eye — namely, that portion which lies directly in front of the lens — is transparent. Between this transparent wall, or so-called cornea, and the lens of the eye there is a chamber filled with transparent fluid known as the aqueous humor. The lens itself is of a very high degree of transparency. Back of the lens is a mass of gelatinous matter known as the vitreous humor, which fills the whole eyeball and maintains the proper spherical form of the eyeball. These transparent media are products of evolution and show an important advance over the translucent gelatinous substances which we find in the more primitive eye.

Choroid coat. The pigment layer which was seen in the most primitive eyes is present in the human eye in the so-called choroid coat. It covers the whole inner surface of the eyeball. It serves the same purpose as does the black lining of a camera; that is, it prevents the rays of light which have acted upon the sensory surface from being reflected back so as to interfere with other entering rays. It is richly supplied with blood vessels, which provide for the nutrition of the sensory cells.

The retina. We have, up to this point, referred only to the accessory organs of the eye. We turn now to the examination of the retinal surface, which is the true sensory organ. It is made up of a series of layers of cells distributed over the inner surface of the eyeball and placed between the choroid coat and the vitreous humor. The retinal layer is represented in section in Fig. 27. The rods and cones, which constitute the inner layer lying next to the choroid coat, are undoubtedly the organs which are most immediately affected by the rays of light. The rods and cones are highly developed cells which are specialized for the reception of light stimulations. They may be thought of as small vessels containing chemical substances which are especially susceptible to changes under the action of light. The chemical activity set up in the rods and cones by the light which enters the eye liberates energy, which is transmitted through the successive layers of cells represented in the figure until, finally, it reaches the large nerve cells of the retina, indicated at the level VIII in the figure. The energy which originally entered the eye in the form of vibration in the luminiferous ether is thus transformed into chemical action in nerve cells, and the chemical action in the nerve cells is transmitted to the fibers which pass out of the eyeball and communicate with the central nervous system.

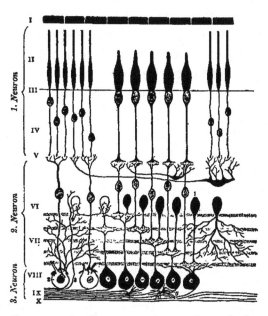

FIG. 27. A diagrammatic section of the retina

I is the pigment epithelium, *II* is the layer of rods and cones. The rods are the small, slender organs. In the retina the rods and cones are, throughout the larger part of the organ, mixed together; in the fovea only cones appear. *III*, *IV*, *V*, *VI*, *VII* show various intermediate structures between the rods and cones and the nerve cells which are situated at *VIII*. From the nerve cells at *VIII* the optic fibers pass out, as indicated at *IX*, toward the blind spot, where they leave the eyeball. *X* represents the limiting membrane of the retina. A ray of light entering the eye passes through the retina in the direction from *X* to *II*. The light does not produce any effect upon the cells or fibers until it reaches the layer of rods and cones. (After Greeff)

Rods and cones and their functions. The rods and cones undoubtedly represent different types of receiving organs. The central part of the retina, which is more important for clear vision than other portions, is made up of cones exclusively. Passing from this limited central region of clear vision, known as the *fovea centralis*, toward the outer areas, or periphery, of the retina, the rods become more and more numerous. The functional differences which correspond to these structural facts can be easily observed. Let a colored light of moderate size and intensity be brought into the outer part of an observer's field of vision. This light will cast its image on the periphery of the retina where the rods predominate, and the observer will not experience a color sensation but rather a sensation of colorless light. If, now, the colored light is gradually made to approach the center of clear vision where the cones predominate, its color quality will become more and more obvious, until, finally, at the center of clear vision it will be clearly seen. We may state this result in general form by saying that the center of clear vision is also the center of color vision, while the areas at the extreme periphery of the retina are totally color blind. The areas intermediate between the extreme periphery of the retina and the center of clear vision are partially color blind ; that is, they respond to a limited number of colors. This limitation of ability to respond to colors is offset in the rods by a distinct advantage on the side of susceptibility to slight changes in colorless light. An observer very frequently has the experience early in the evening of seeing a faint star in the outer edge of the field of vision, and finds the moment he turns to look directly at the star that it is impossible to see it. The periphery of the retina was sufficiently sensitive to the slight illumination to make possible a sensation from the faint star, whereas the center of the retina was incapable of responding to this slight illumination. The significance of this differentiation of the retina in the development of the animal kingdom is evident. The periphery of the retina and the extreme edges of the field of vision do not have the same significance for the animal as the center. It is more advantageous that the animal should be able to concentrate its highest forms of nervous activity upon a limited area. On the other hand, it is important that the outer regions of the retina should be sensitive in such a way as to give immediate warning of any changes in illumination, for changes in illumination mean movement, possibly the approach of danger, and this should be recognized sufficiently to warn the observer. If, then, it is desirable to give the object stricter attention, the eye can be turned so as to bring the image upon the center of clear vision.

Color blindness. The differentiation between the different parts of the retina, which has just been described as characteristic of the normal retina, does not always appear. There are certain persons whose eyes are not fully responsive to colors; these persons have at the center of the retina a condition similar, at least so far as color processes are concerned, to that which appears toward the periphery of the normal retina. This inability to respond to different color stimulations may in some cases be complete, so that the individual sees the world as a normal individual sees an engraving; that is, as if it were made up only of differences in light and shade without the qualitative differences which we describe as color differences. A much larger number of individuals have a partial deficiency, analogous to that which appears in the intermediate zones of the normal retina. The various forms of partial color blindness are extremely difficult to define with precision, for the simple reason that the color sensations of the partially color-blind individual constitute his world of color sensations. He usually has no means of comparing his experiences with those of the normal individual. His efforts to describe his own experiences to a normal individual are complicated by the necessity of using terms devised for the normal individual rather than for his own peculiar experiences. Fortunately for science, there have been a few cases in which the same person has been able to observe directly both the normal color sensations and the partially color-blind series. The defect in such individuals appears only in one eye, while the other eye is of the normal type. It has, furthermore, been possible by certain methods of comparing color mixtures to make an analysis of other cases of color blindness. The net result of these investigations has been to show that the color series of a partially color-blind individual is of a simpler type than that of the normal individual with a fully developed retina. One very common form of partial color blindness, known as "red-green blindness," has been thoroughly investigated. The following table shows the comparison between the normal color system and the two types of red-green blindness, which have been worked out:

NORMAL	TYPE I	TYPE II
Red	The red end of the spectrum short; what is seen is gray, or unsaturated yellow	Yellow
Orange	Unsaturated yellow	Unsaturated yellow
Yellow	Unsaturated yellow	Unsaturated yellow
Green	Yellow	Gray, or unsaturated yellow
Blue	Blue	Blue
Violet	Violet	Violet

Such facts as are shown in this table and in the cases of total color blindness emphasize the intimacy of the relation between retinal development and the development of experience. They make it clear that the number of sensation qualities which an observer can distinguish depends not on the number of physical processes in the outer world but on the number of physiological processes which are aroused in the nervous system by the various kinds of physical energy.

Color-mixing. Another group of facts closely related to those discussed above are the facts of color-mixing. If a given point on the retina is stimulated at the same time by two or more rays of differently colored light, the chemical process set up cannot be the process which is appropriate to either color acting alone. Experience shows that the process is a compromise between the processes which would have resulted if each ray had acted alone. Thus, if at the same moment a ray of red light and a ray of yellow light fall upon a single cone, the result is that the observer sees orange, which corresponds in quality to the color lying in the spectral series intermediate between red and yellow. If instead of merely using red and yellow we use red, yellow, and blue at the same time, we find, by observing the resultant sensation, that a compromise between the three chemical tendencies in the cone is very different from any one of the processes taken alone. Indeed, in such a case the retina is not capable of giving a compromise color process, but falls back into the process which the study of color blindness shows to be the most primitive form of chemical activity; namely, the chemical process corresponding to gray, which we found as the only process in the eye of the totally color-blind person and in the periphery of the normal retina. When all the colors of the spectrum fall at one time on a cone, as in full daylight, the result is a sensation of pure brightness or white.

If a red ray is mixed with a blue ray, a unique compromise process results, which is not directly related to any of the simple colors of nature; namely, the process which gives rise to a purple sensation. Purple is a color quality which can be explained only in terms of the retinal process. Red and blue, which are the physical facts conditioning the experience of purple, are at the extreme ends of the physical spectral series, yet they cause in the retina a single process which gives the sensation quality purple. This goes to show that the retinal processes for red and blue are closely related in character, in spite of the great difference in the respective rates of vibration in the physical processes which excite these retinal processes. The color circle, which was described in an earlier paragraph, is therefore not to be explained as a physical circle but as a circle of retinal processes and corresponding experiences. Indeed, it may be said in general that the laws of color-mixing are primarily laws of retinal behavior rather than laws of the physical world. The fact that all the colors of the spectrum when mixed together produce gray is, as has been pointed out a number of times, a physiological fact and a fact of experience rather than a fact of physical vibrations.

The principles of color mixtures were worked out first by physicists and have furnished a basis for most of the theories of color vision. Briefly stated, the general principles of color-mixing are as follows : When two colors near each other in the spectral series enter the eye at the same time, there results a sensation and a retinal process which is intermediate to those demanded by the two colors when they act alone upon the retina. This intermediate process is not the same as that which would result from stimulation of the retina by the intermediate pure color, for the sensation is not as fully saturated as it would be if it had resulted from the action of a pure color. As the distance between the two colors of the mixture is gradually increased, the chromatic quality of the resultant grows less and less marked, until finally the sensation is of the simplest possible type ; namely, the sensation gray. This shows that the retina is forced by certain mixtures of very different colors to return to the simple undifferentiated form of activity which characterized it before the differentiation into chromatic qualities began. Two colors which are opposed to each other in such a way that they give when mixed no color whatsoever, but merely the sensation gray, are known as complementary colors.

If the distance in the color circle between two colors which enter into a mixture is greater than that required for the complementary effect, the resulting color will be some shade of purple. If purple is introduced in the color circle, there is no shade of color which does not have its complement. The color circle shown in Fig. 23 may be made, therefore, the basis for discussion of complementary pairs, provided the arrangements of the colors opposite each other are made with this end in view. If more than two colors are mixed, the total result will be the sum of the partial effects and can be foreseen by considering the partial processes as if they occurred successively.

Pigment-mixing subject to physical law. It may be well to call explicit attention to the fact that the statements here made regarding color mixtures do not apply to mixtures of pigments. The mixture of pigments is a physical fact, not a physiological process. The action of pigment on light is to absorb certain rays and reflect others. Mixtures of pigments affect light in a complex way, and hence produce results which cannot be explained by merely inspecting the separate pigments.

A single case of pigment-mixing may be taken as an example. Thus, if yellow and blue pigments are mixed, they produce an impression of green. This result is due to the fact that the yellow pigment absorbs a good deal of light and reflects only those colors which are near it in the spectral series. Blue does the same. The only color which survives the joint absorptions of yellow and blue pigment particles is green, for green is reflected in a measure by both yellow pigment particles and by blue. The fact that green results in this case calls for an explanation absolutely different from that which applies to the gray which results from the mixture of yellow and blue light.

After-images. The consideration of certain other facts is necessary to complete the discussion of visual sensations.

If light acts upon a retinal element for a given period, the effect will continue for a time after the external light ceases to act. The observer will notice what is known as an after-image of the light at which he has been looking. Everyone has doubtless observed the vivid after-images which result from looking at the sun or other very bright objects. Most of the after-images which we receive from ordinary objects are so faint that they are overlooked, unless special effort is made to notice them and to retain them. In general, the experience which continues after the withdrawal of the external light resembles only for a very brief interval the sensation originally produced by the external light. So long as the original impression and after-image are of the same quality, the observer is said to have a positive after-image. An example of such a positive after-image can easily be secured by rapidly rotating a burning stick in a circle, when the observer will see an uninterrupted circle of light, because the stimulus returns to each of the points of the retina before the original process has had time to change. Very soon after the external stimulus is withdrawn, experience undergoes a radical change. The general principle of this change may be described by saying that every black changes to white, every white to black, and every color to its complement. Since these changes are known from the conditions to be due to physiological processes rather than to external light, we describe the conditions for these after-images in the following terms: The retina tends to set up as soon as possible a process opposite to that which was produced by the original stimulus. This chemical process, opposite in character to that produced by the external stimulus, is due to the tendency of the physiological organism to restore the chemical substances which have been used up in the first process of stimulation. The experience of the observer follows, during this process of recuperation, the retinal activity rather than the external physical fact. Thus, after looking for a time at a brilliant red light, the observer sees very soon after the light is withdrawn a colored area of like spatial form and extent as the original but of a quality exactly complementary to the red; namely, blue-green. In like fashion, the negative after-image of a blue surface is yellow. If the stimulating surface is black and white or gray rather than colored, the negative after-image will be of such a character that what was bright in the original image will appear dark in the after-image, and, conversely, what was dark in the original image will appear white in the after-image.

Contrasts. After-effects in the retina very frequently operate to modify the retinal processes produced by subsequent light stimulations. For example, let an observer who has been looking steadily at a bright red light for a time and has a strong tendency toward a green after-image look at a blue surface; the blue surface will not be seen in its normal color, but will be seen as a mixture of blue and green, the green being contributed in this case by the after-image process in the retina. The mixtures between after-effects and color stimulations here under discussion give rise to many forms of color contrast. In view of the continual movement of the eye from point to point in the field of vision, the observer is always carrying more or less marked after-effects from a given part of the field of vision to the neighboring parts. If, for example, a red and a green field are placed in close juxtaposition, and the eye after looking at the red surface tends to move in such a way as to bring a portion of the retina which has been stimulated by the red into a position such that it will be stimulated by the green light, the green sensation received from the summation of the external stimulation and the after-image will be more intense than a green sensation received without the preliminary stimulation from a red. The result is that green seems to be more saturated when it lies near red. In general, every color is emphasized by being brought into close relation with its complementary, and grays tend to take on colors complementary to surrounding fields. This effect appears even when no eye movements can be detected. There is probably a diffusion of contrast effects through the retina even when the eye fixates steadily a single point.

The tendency of grays to take on colors may be well illustrated by shadows. If a field which is illuminated by a yellow light is interrupted by a shadow which is, in reality, gray, this gray shadow will take on a bluish tinge by contrast with the yellow field. This fact has long been observed by those who reproduce the colors of nature in painting, and the shadows in painting will usually be found to be, not reproductions of the physical facts, but rather reproductions of the impression made upon the observer.

Theories of color vision. It remains to add a few remarks concerning the less certain conclusions regarding the relation between light sensations and external ether vibrations. The effort has frequently been made to describe the physiological processes in a single comprehensive formula or theory, which shall include all the facts. No attempt will here be made to review all of those theories. It will be enough to present one of the simplest and most suggestive, and leave it to the student to criticize and reconstruct it in the light of the facts discussed above and reviewed in the tables given below.

Mrs. Franklin's genetic theory of processes in the retina. The theory which was formulated by Mrs. Franklin is as follows : The primitive retina of the lower animals and the periphery of the human retina have only one . chemical process with which to respond to all light stimuli. This single chemical process, when set up through the action of light, arouses in the central nervous system a process which is the condition of a gray sensation. This is the original undifferentiated type of retinal activity. As the evolution of the retina goes forward, this original chemical process, which may be called the gray process, is so subdivided that colors produce certain partial phases of the original chemical activity. The partial chemical activities produce each a specialized form of nervous process and a specialized form of sensory experience. The breaking up of the gray process into special color processes begins with a development, first, of the partial processes which correspond on the one hand to blue, and on the other hand to orange or yellow, sensations. This first differentiation corresponds to the wide difference between the extreme ends of the spectral series. The original gray process does not disappear with the rise of the blue and yellow processes, but remains as the neutral and more general form of response. At this stage the yellow and blue processes are each called out by a great variety of stimulations. Thus, the yellow process is aroused by red light, orange light, and green light, as well as by yellow light. As the development goes on, the yellow chemical process is subdivided into more highly specialized processes, corresponding to red and green. The result of this successive differentiation of process is that the highly organized retina may, when stimulated by the appropriate form of light vibration, respond with specialized chemical processes to red, green, yellow, or blue. If yellow and blue, which were the first forms of light to arouse differentiated processes, act at the same time upon the retina, the partial processes which are differentiated out of the gray cannot both be in action at once without being swallowed up in the original fundamental process of gray. If red and green act together upon the retina, the yellow process appears as the more fundamental form of chemical process. The facts of color blindness can be explained by stating that the differentiation of chemical processes is not complete in the color-blind eye. Negative and complementary after-images are due to the physiological instability of the partial chemical substances left in the retina after a process in which a colored light has partially disintegrated the retinal substance. Contrast has been included by earlier discussions under the same head as after-images, though by a spread of stimulation effects contrasts appear where there are no immediate after-images.

The student will see at once that many of these statements are hypothetical. They serve, however, to gather together the facts, and they give a genetic account of primitive as well as of present retinal conditions. The theory or hypothesis should be clearly distinguished from the facts, and yet it is evident that the facts justify us in attempting to explain the relation between physical processes and conscious processes by something which goes on in the retina. In order to keep the facts clearly in the foreground, it may be well to return to a general summary of the different groups of facts discussed in this section.

SUMMARY TABLES

TABLE A. COLOR BLINDNESS

Physical Facts	Physiological Processes	Sensations
I. Full series of simple vibrations	Highly developed retina with, however, a limited number of modes of response to external light	A differentiated group of sensation qualities including all colors
II. Full series of simple vibrations	Partially developed retina with a number of possibilities of response to external stimulation which is more limited than in the normal retina	Partial color blindness
III. Full series of simple vibrations	Retina so little developed as to have only one mode of response	Total color blindness

TABLE *B*. COLOR MIXTURES

PHYSICAL FACTS	PHYSIOLOGICAL PROCESSES	SENSATIONS
I. Series of simple vibrations	Highly developed retina with a limited number of distinct modes of response	Limited number of sensation qualities, constituting a series of distinct qualities
II. Two simple waves, closely related in number of vibrations, entering the eye together, thus making a compound wave	Retinal response which compromises between the two responses which would have resulted had the two vibrations acted separately	Single color sensation somewhat less saturated than in the simple series
III. Two simple waves, very different in number of vibrations, entering the eye together, thus making a compound wave	Retinal response which tends to take the simplest and most general form of retinal behavior	A color very little saturated, or a single purple or gray
IV. Large numbers of waves entering the eye together, thus making a most complex wave	Simple response of the rudimentary type	Gray

TABLE *C*. AFTER-IMAGES AND CONTRASTS

PHYSICAL FACT	PHYSIOLOGICAL PROCESS	SENSATION
I. Strong light vibration followed by the withdrawal of physical light	Response followed by a continued action of the retina and a final reversal of the retinal process to restore the tissue to its normal condition	Color sensation continuing after external light and then changing into complementary color quality

B. Auditory Sensations

The task of defining sound sensations and of describing their conditions will be a comparatively simple one on the basis of the elaborate study already made of visual sensations.

Physical sound. The physical stimulus which causes the nervous processes, which, in turn, condition auditory sensations, consists of longitudinal air vibrations. When a vibrating body strikes the air particles about it as it vibrates backward and forward, the air particles are alternately driven together and rebound from one another. Successive waves of condensation and rarefaction result, and these waves are carried forward in all directions until they strike some receiving surface, such as the ear. These air vibrations can be defined in the same terms of rate, amplitude, and complexity as were used for the light vibrations in the preceding section (p. 77), although it should be noted that the form of vibrations is different in the two cases.

Pitch, or tonal quality. With regard to the relation between sensation and external sound vibration, it is to be said, first, that when the objective waves are regular, they give rise to experiences of tone; when the vibrations are irregular, the resulting sensation is one of noise. The rates of the regular vibrations which are recognized as tones are directly related to differences of pitch. Middle C on the piano scale has a rate of vibration of two hundred and fifty-six double vibrations per second. Toward the bass end of the scale the vibrations decrease in rapidity, while toward the treble they increase. The lowest rate which is ordinarily heard by the normal ear is about thirty-two vibrations per second, although rates of sixteen, or even ten, per second have been described by some observers as audible. At the upper end of the scale one can hear vibrations of thirty thousand to forty thousand per second. Sounds produced by insects are of this order.

Intensity, or loudness. Intensity of tone varies according as the amplitude of vibration of the single air particles is great or small.

Complexity of a regular type the source of differences in timbre. Ordinary sensations of tone are produced by complex waves. If two or more forms of vibration are transmitted to a given particle of air at the same moment, the particle will move in a path which is the resultant of all of the different paths through which it would have moved had the various impulses of vibration acted upon it successively. When one compares a given tone from the piano with the tone of the same pitch from a violin, he will recognize that the characteristics of the tones are different, though they are of the same pitch. The violin string vibrates not only as a whole but also in certain sections, and the piano wire vibrates as a whole and at the same time in sections. The rates of vibration of the string and wire as wholes may be exactly the same. The sections in the two cases and the rates of their vibration will nearly always be different. The result is that any particle of air set in motion by either piano wire or violin string will have its main path determined by the vibration of the whole wire or string, while the minor details of vibration will be determined by the vibrations of the sections of the wire or string. The phase of tonal quality thus determined by the complex of minor vibrations is known as timbre. The main, or fundamental, tone is modified by the minor higher tones, or overtones as they are called. Tones of the same pitch derived from various instruments have various timbres, just in so far as they have different overtones.

Noise due to irregular vibrations. The experience of noise is dependent upon a form of vibration which is so complex as to be highly irregular. A vague regularity appears in most noises. We speak, accordingly, of certain noises as low and rumbling, and of others as high and shrill, but for the most part the tendency toward regularity of vibrations gives way in noises to a confusion of irregular oscillations in the air particles.

Evolution of the ear. Turning from the physical stimulus to the auditory organ, we find here, as in the case of the eye, that by a long process of evolution there has been produced a sensory organ which has a variety of accessory parts and a delicate sensory surface, which latter transforms the air vibrations into nervous processes. The most primitive ear, such as is found in the cœlenterates, consists in a sack-shaped opening in the side of the body. This sack-shaped depression, or vesicle, contains hard calcareous particles, and is lined by sensitive cells which are similar in their general appearance to the cells in the primitive eye. The whole organ can be easily explained by comparing it to a child's ordinary rattle-box. If the animal is shaken, or if any sound vibrations strike against the wall of the vesicle, the calcareous particles, or otoliths as they are called, are set in motion and tend to strike against the sensitive cells. The result is that the cells will be stimulated by each movement of the animal's body or by the vibrations which enter the vesicle. As the ear develops through the animal series there appear a number of accessory organs which serve to facilitate the reception of vibrations, and there comes to be a division between the two original functions of the ear; namely, that of sensory response to the movements of the body as a whole, and that of response to vibrations from the water or air.

The human ear, pinna, and meatus. After this brief reference to the primitive ear we may turn immediately to a description of the human ear. The outer cartilaginous organ, known as the pinna, has in man very little function. It serves in a rudimentary way to concentrate the sound waves and direct them toward the inner ear. The long funnel-shaped pinna of a horse's ear serves a function which has been lost in the process of evolution. By moving its ear the horse collects sounds from different directions, and thus becomes very acutely sensitive to sound and at the same time recognizes the direction from which the sound comes. But the horse loses fine qualitative shades of sound

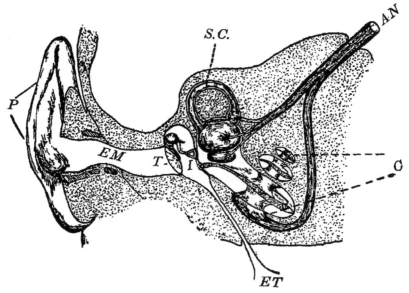

FIG. 28. Diagrammatic section showing the structure of the ear

P, external pinna; *EM*, external meatus; *T*, tympanic membrane; *I*, internal meatus, or tympanic cavity. Extending from the tympanic membrane to the inner ear there are three bones constituting the chain of ossicles: malleus, incus, and stapes. *ET*, Eustachian tube, passing from the internal meatus to the cavity of the throat; *SC*, one of the three semicircular canals; *AN*, the auditory nerve, which divides into four parts as indicated in the figure, one branch connecting with the semicircular canals, two with the parts of the vestibule, and the fourth with the core of the cochlea, *C*. The canals of the cochlea are indicated in general outline; for details see Fig. 30. The vestibule is the general region lying between the canals and the cochlea. (Modified from Czermak)

because the funnel modifies in some measure the form of the air vibrations. The human ear has so evolved that it interferes little with quality. This shows that the sense of hearing in man is not a locating sense but a sense devoted to the finest discriminations in quality. The evolution of the ear is undoubtedly related to the evolution of speech.

The cylindrical canal which connects the surface of the body with the inner cavities of the ear is known as the external meatus. This canal is liberally supplied with protective bristles, and with secretory glands which tend to protect the ear from all foreign particles, and it is curved in shape so that nothing but very small, slender objects can penetrate to the inner parts of the ear.

Nature has a relatively easy problem of protection of delicate organs in the case of the ear because air vibrations can be conducted along a narrow passage. In the case of the eye, the organ must lie exposed on the surface of the body. Nature has put a ring of bony structures around the eye, but the protection of the ear is much more complete.

The tympanic membrane. The inner end of the external meatus is closed by means of a circular membrane, known as the tympanic membrane. This tympanic membrane is a composite membrane made up of circular and radial fibers. It is slightly depressed in the middle so as to be somewhat funnel-shaped and is loaded by being connected on its inner surface with a small bone, known because of its shape as the malleus, or hammer. The malleus is controlled by a small muscle, known as the tensor tympani. When this muscle is contracted it draws the malleus inward, and with the malleus the tympanic membrane, thus increasing the tension of the membrane and emphasizing its funnel-shaped form. The adjustments of the tympanic membrane, as well as its shape, are of importance in giving the ear the largest possible range of ability to receive sound vibrations. No artificially constructed diaphragm, such as those employed in the phonograph or telephone, is capable of as wide a range of response to tones as is the adjustable, complex diaphragm in the ear.

Air chamber on inner side of the tympanic membrane. In the functioning of the tympanic membrane a difficult mechanical problem arises, because the air pressure in the external world is constantly undergoing changes. With every change in the barometric pressure there would be an interference with the action of the tympanic membrane, if the spaces behind this membrane were air-tight. Nature has, accordingly, provided on the inner side of the tympanic membrane an air chamber communicating with the atmosphere so that any change in atmospheric pressure will result in an equal change in the pressure on both sides of the tympanic membrane. This air chamber on the inner side of the tympanic membrane is known as the internal meatus, or tympanic cavity. It consists of an irregular cavity in the bone, which is in communication with the throat by means of a small canal, known as the Eustachian tube. The wall of the Eustachian tube is flexible, so that it collapses except when a current of air is forced through it by a change in pressure, either in the internal meatus or in the external atmosphere. For this reason, the ordinary voice vibrations which arise in the throat are not communicated directly to the internal meatus.

Chain of ossicles. Since there is an air chamber on the inner side of the tympanic membrane, there must be some means of carrying the sound vibrations received on the tympanic membrane across this cavity to the inner ear. The means for transmitting the vibrations received by the tympanic membrane consist of a chain of three small bones, known as the chain of ossicles. The first of these ossicles has been mentioned; it is the malleus, or hammer, which is attached by its long arm to the middle of the tympanic membrane. The head of the malleus articulates with the surface of the second bone, which is known as the incus because of its anvil-shaped appearance. One of the branches of the incus articulates in turn with the third bone, known as the stapes, or stirrup. Any vibration received by the tympanic membrane is thus communicated to the stirrup. The stirrup fits into an oval opening, known as the fenestra ovalis, which leads into the inner ear. The stapes is connected with the walls of this fenestra ovalis by means of a membrane, so that it constitutes a tight-fitting piston which can move backward and forward in the fenestra ovalis. Beyond the oval window the inner ear is filled in all of its parts with lymphatic fluid. Sound vibrations, which are originally vibrations of air particles, are thus transformed by the mechanism described into vibrations in the lymphatic fluid which fills the inner ear.

The inner ear. The inner ear is divided into three principal parts : vestibule, semicircular canals, and cochlea. The vestibule is an irregular ovoid cavity about one fifth of an inch in diameter, which opens on the one side into the snail-shell-shaped cavity, known as the cochlea, and on the other into a system of slender canals, known as the semicircular canals. The vestibule itself is divided into two parts, known as the saccule and utricle.

The semicircular canals. The semicircular canals are not organs of hearing. They are organs which have taken up in the process of evolution that function of the primitive ear which was concerned with response to the grosser movements of the animal's whole body. There are three of these canals, and they lie in such positions that each one occupies a different plane in space. Any change in the position of the head, or of the body as a whole, will cause a redistribution of the pressure within the system of canals, and this change in pressure affects the nerve cells which are distributed in the wall of the enlarged portion, or ampulla, of each canal. The whole system of canals serves as an organ of equilibration. The sensory stimulations which come from this organ do not give rise in developed human beings to clearly differentiated sensations. The result is that the ordinary observer does not know that he has a special sense organ of equilibration. The stimulations are for the most part taken up by the lower centers of the nervous system,

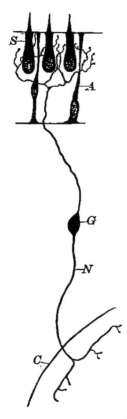

FIG. 29. Diagrammatic section of the sensory cells in the vestibule

The receiving cells are situated on the surface, as represented by *S*. These receiving cells are surrounded by supporting cells, as indicated at *A*. The nerve fiber is distributed among the receiving cells. The true sensory cell at *G* is in the ganglion, rather than directly at the surface. This sensory cell sends its second fiber inward to the central nervous system, represented by *C*. (After Herrick)

where they are distributed to the muscles which keep the body erect; they probably never reach the higher regions except in company with a great mass of other excitations, such as touch sensations from the soles of the feet and muscle sensations from the neck and trunk. When they become excessively intense they give rise to the experience of dizziness. In some cases the indirect effects of their action come into consciousness. When the reflex muscular adjustment carried out by the lower centers is unusual, as when one descends suddenly in an elevator, the muscular reactions, rather than the primary sensory stimulation, give rise to a clearly recognizable experience. The observer feels an unusual tension in his abdominal muscles or muscles of some other part of the body.

The cochlea and sensory areas in the vestibule. Turning from the semicircular canals to the other canal leading out of the vestibule, namely the cochlea, we find here the organs which are concerned in the reception of tonal stimulations. It is not clearly known whether noise stimulations are received in the cochlea or not. The probabilities are that noise stimulations affect certain cells constituting sensory areas in the wall of the vestibule. At all events, it is true that there are cells situated in the wall of the vestibule which seem to be suited to the reception of simple stimuli (see Fig. 29). The vestibule is the direct descendant of the primitive vesicle. This fact would seem to argue in favor of the view that noise stimulations, which are undifferentiated and probably earlier than tonal stimulations, affect these cells in the vestibule. Whatever may be true of noise, it is certain that the tonal excitations are received through the complicated structures which have been developed, and appear in the cochlea. The cochlea is a highly developed organ, richly supplied with cells and fibers for the reception of a great number of different stimulations. It consists of a double spiral canal, which winds around two and a half times. The winding of this canal is merely an anatomical device for compressing the whole organ into as small a space as possible. The canal, which is cylindrical in form, is divided into three parts, — the scala vestibuli, the scala tympani, and the ductus cochlearis. This division can best be seen by making a section across the cylindrical passage. Fig. 30

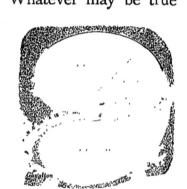

FIG. 30. The structure in the cochlea as seen when a transverse section is made across the canal

The parts are clearly marked in the figure. Special attention should be given to the basilar membrane and the organ of Corti situated upon it. The nerve fibers are distributed among the cells of the organ of Corti from the ganglion in a manner similar to that represented for the vestibular cells in Fig. 29. (After Herrick)

shows such a section with the division. The scala tympani is partially separated from the rest of the cochlea by a bony shelf which extends for some distance into the canal. The division is completed by an important membrane. This membrane, known as the basilar membrane, is made up of a series of fibers which differ in length as the membrane passes from the lower to the upper extremity of the canal. At its lower extremity the fibers are short, and at the upper end of the canal they are about twelve times as long. Helmholtz, the great German physicist, called attention to the striking similarity between the structure of the basilar membrane and the system of strings of a musical instrument capable of giving a variety of different tones. He also advanced the hypothesis that the fibers of the membrane are so related to external tones that a given fiber is set in vibration by each particular rate of vibration. It is a well-known principle of physical science that any fiber or rod will vibrate sympathetically with a tone which has the same rate as it would assume itself, if it were set in vibration by some other cause. This principle is known as the principle of sympathetic resonance. The basilar membrane is so situated that the vibrations which enter the inner ear through the fenestra ovalis reach it by passing up the scala vestibuli and the ductus cochlearis. The scala tympani is a canal which carries back the vibrations after they have acted on the basilar membrane. It is connected at the upper end of the cochlea with the scala vestibuli and serves to conduct away the vibrations rather than allow them to be reflected back into the vestibule; for its lower end does not open into the vestibule, but communicates through an opening, known as the fenestra rotunda, with the internal meatus. The basilar membrane thus stands in the direct path of the vibrations, and it is, probably, the organ which takes up the vibrations through sympathetic resonance and makes them effective in exciting the sensory cells.

Sensory cells in the cochlea. A system of receiving cells, analogous to the rods and cones in the eye, is placed directly on the basilar membrane. At any given point they form an arch extending across the membrane, and, therefore, are capable of taking up any vibration which sets the fibers of the membrane in motion. The arch of cells is shown in Fig. 30 and is known, from the physiologist who first described it, as the organ of Corti. Among the cells that constitute the organ of Corti there are distributed nerve fibers which come from auditory ganglion or true sensory nerve cells situated in a cavity in the bony core of the cochlea. Whenever the cells of Corti are set in vibration, they excite the fibers. The external air wave is thus transformed in the organ of Corti into a nervous process.

Contrast between auditory and visual processes. It is to be noted that the transformation is of a distinctly different type from that which takes place in the eye. In the eye the physical stimulus produces a chemical activity in the rods and cones. In the case of the ear the stimulus continues in the form of vibrations until it produces its final effect upon the nerve cells. There is a less fundamental change in the character of the stimulus as we pass from the external world to the nervous process in the ear than there is in the corresponding transition in the eye. This fact shows itself most clearly when we come to deal with compound sound vibrations. It makes no difference how many tones are sounded before the tympanic membrane, the complex vibration will be faithfully transmitted by the chain of ossicles and the other accessory organs and will, at all points in its transmission, be a detailed reproduction of the total complex of sound impulses which gave rise to it. Furthermore, it is shown by an examination of sensory experience that there must be a separate sensory process for each component of the tonal complex. If an observer listens to a tonal complex, such as an orchestra, the sensory excitations do not fuse as do the chemical processes resulting from a number of colors which act upon the retina together. Each tone in the complex retains its independent value for experience. It was this fact, together with the form of the basilar membrane, which led Helmholtz to suggest his hypothesis. Whether that particular hypothesis is true or not, we may confidently assert that the different parts of the organ of Corti are specialized in some way or other, so that each rate of external vibration, whether it reaches the cochlea alone or as part of a complex of vibrations, excites a particular part of the sensory organ and so gives rise to a distinct sensory process. The ear is thus seen to be an analyzing sense capable of carrying to consciousness at one and the same moment a vast complex of sound. There is nothing in auditory sensation to correspond to white among the retinal sensations unless it be mere noise. But even here there is a fundamental difference, because the various elements of a noise can be heard separately, especially if some of the elements have a tonal character. For example, the ear has no difficulty in hearing at the same time the noise produced by a train and the sounds produced by the human voice.

Beats, difference tones. There are certain special cases of complex air vibration which should be mentioned in this discussion of sensations. If two closely related tones are sounded together, they will reënforce the vibration of the air particles which they affect so long as their phases are alike, but the moment their phases come into such a relation that one tends to set the air particle vibrating in a given direction and the other tends to set the same air particle vibrating in the opposite direction, they will partially counteract each other in such a way as to keep the air particle for a moment in a state of equilibrium. Fig. 31 represents, in the form of a water wave, two vibrations which at the outset coöperate in giving a larger wave. As one lags slightly behind the other, they come later to counteract each other in such a way that no vibration takes place, as shown at *M*. The result of such a combination of tones, which is a purely physical affair, is that the observer receives not only the two primary vibrations but also a series of rapid variations in intensity, which succession of intensities fuses into a new impression. The observer therefore hears, in addition to the two fundamental tones, an alternate rising and falling in the loudness of the sound, which fluctuation gives rise to experiences known as beats. If these beats are slow enough to be distinguishable, they will be recognized as quite distinct from the tones. If, on the other hand, they become too numerous to be separately apprehended, they may sometimes be heard as an additional tone, when they are designated as difference tones. For example, if two tones, *c* and *g*, are sounded together, these tones having vibrations at the rates of 256 and 384 vibrations per second, the result will be a complex in which both *c* and *g* will be distinctly heard ; but there will also be heard a third tone, the

FIG. 31. Diagram to represent the formation of beats

The two curves represented by the light line and the dotted line begin together, showing the same phase at the same time. The wave motion represented by the dotted line is somewhat more rapid than that represented by the full line ; consequently, the relation of the two waves changes so that in the region *M* the two are in opposite phases. The heavy line indicates the results of the combination of the two waves. *a, b, c, d, e, f, g, h* indicate the strong curve which results from the reënforcing influence of the two wave motions. *M* indicates the result of the counteracting influence of the two. (After Ebbinghaus)

number of vibrations of which equals the difference between the number of vibrations of *c* and *g*. That is, the difference tone in this case will be a tone of 128 vibrations per second.

Summation tones. Again, there are complexities in the tonal experience such that often tones are heard in a tonal complex which, in number of vibrations, are equal to the sum of the two fundamentals. Such tones are known as summation tones. They do not seem to be purely physical facts, explicable in terms of the physical effect upon the air particles, for they cannot, in all cases, be reënforced by physical resonators (the apparatus which is commonly used in the detection of single tones in tonal complexes). Summation

tones seem rather to be due to certain physiological processes, perhaps to interferences of the vibration processes
in the basilar membrane or to secondary vibrations in the
bony walls of the cochlea. In ordinary experiences difference tones and summation tones play no important part,
but the result of these tones upon harmonies and discords
in music is a matter of some importance and one which
has been made the subject of careful examination.

Harmony not a matter of sensation. By these discussions
of tonal sensations and their combinations we have been
led to the point where it would be appropriate to take up
the matter of harmony. Certain tones, when sounded together, give the observer an experience which is not merely
that of tones sounding together, but is also an experience
of the smooth fitting together of these tones, while other
combinations give the observer a distinct impression of jar
or discord. The effort has often been made to explain
harmony and discord as due to beats and like facts ; that is,
to certain simple processes in the organ of sense. We shall
dismiss the matter in a somewhat dogmatic fashion by saying that such explanations of harmony, by processes of a
purely sensory type, are not satisfactory. There is probably
a close relation between recognition of harmony and motor
processes, such as those of the vocal cords and those of the
inner organs which, as will be seen later, are aroused during
emotional experiences.

Absence of after-images in auditory sensations. Before
closing the discussion of tonal sensations it should be noted
that the nature of the auditory sensory process is such that
contrast and after-effects do not appear to any great extent
in tonal or noise sensations. The process in the nerve cells
terminates as soon as the external vibration ceases. This
characteristic of sound sensations explains why it is that
these sensations can be used in musical compositions. A
succession of colors, given in anything like the same

relation as a succession of tones in music, would produce a hazy blur of after-effects.

Tone deafness. Cases of tonal deafness, or inability to receive certain tones, have been described. A person capable of the usual tonal discriminations in many parts of the scale is quite unable to distinguish tones in a certain limited part of the scale or at one end of the scale. This deficiency is undoubtedly related to some lack of normal functioning in a given region of the basilar membrane, or organ of Corti. In old age a person may also show increasing deficiency in ability to hear very high tones.

SUMMARY

Without attempting to summarize all that has been said in the discussions of tonal sensations, it may be advantageous to prepare a table which may be used for the purposes of comparison with the earlier tables referring to visual sensations.

PHYSICAL VIBRATION	PHYSIOLOGICAL PROCESS	SENSATION
Series of air vibrations below 10 per second	No physiological excitation	No sensation
Continuous series of changes in rate of air vibration from 32 per second to 30,000 or 40,000 per second	A very large number of different processes in the basilar membrane and organ of Corti; the number being, however, less than the number of physical processes	Large number of sensations ranging in series from lowest to highest pitch
Same as above	More limited number of physiological processes because of incomplete development of the organ of Corti	Partial tone deafness
Complex vibrations	Separate physiological process for each component of the complex	Recognizable complex of tonal sensations
Complex vibrations	Interference of vibration in the physiological organs	Summation tones not paralleled by objective vibrations

C. Sensations of Taste and Smell

Taste and smell differentiations of a primitive chemical sense. Sensations of taste and smell may be considered together. Indeed, in the primitive forms of animal life, taste and smell constitute a single chemical sense. Of the two the sense of smell is distinctly later in its development, appearing as an important separate sense with the appearance of the air-breathing animals.

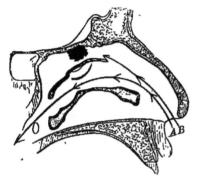

FIG. 32. The inner cavity of the nose

The arrow *A* indicates the path of the air in ordinary respiration; *B* indicates the path of the air when the animal sniffs. The olfactory region is indicated by the black area in the upper part of the cavity

Position of olfactory organ in the nasal cavity. It is unnecessary here for us to consider at any great length the nasal cavities in which the olfactory cells are situated. These cavities are not true accessories to the organ of sense, as were the cavities in the ear. The organ of sense is rather accessory to the general organ of respiration. The position of the sensory cells is such that they are not in the direct path of the great volume of air which is used in the process of respiration. Fig. 32 shows the area within the nasal cavity which is covered by olfactory cells. The arrow *A* in the figure indicates the path of the air current in ordinary respiration. It will be noted that in such ordinary respiration very little of the air is carried up into the upper part of the nasal cavity and thus brought into contact with the sensitive cells. If for any reason it is desirable that the sensitive cells should receive the full current of air which enters the nose, the animal must sniff the air forcibly into the nasal cavity, in which case it will follow the direction of the arrow *B* in the figure.

Structure and function of the olfactory surface. The olfactory surface itself is made up of two kinds of cells, as shown in Figs. 33 and 34. There are, first, certain supporting cells which line the nasal cavity ; and second, there are distributed among the supporting cells true sensory cells, from which fibers pass inward to the central nervous system. The nerve cells in this organ are immediately on the surface, in such a position that particles brought in through the air currents come into direct contact with the cell body proper. This direct exposure of the nerve cells to stimulation is undoubtedly related to the fact that these cells are very easily fatigued. It is a well-recognized fact that an odor which is very striking at first soon grows less and less impressive, even though the stimulus may continue in its original intensity. Furthermore, the olfactory cells do not seem to be very definitely specialized, and there are no selective organs between the external stimulus and the sensory organs which determine the effect of the stimulus on the nervous organs. There is, accordingly, no clearly defined limit to the number and variety of olfactory sensations. By way of contrast with the visual organ, for example, there is, in the case

FIG. 33. Section showing the different cells which compose the mucous lining of the nose in the olfactory region

By the staining process, the special sensory cells are clearly distinguished from the other cells as black. In one of these cells the nerve fiber will be seen passing directly out of the cell toward the central organ

of the olfactory sense, nothing which corresponds to the rods or cones and operates to reduce all external stimulations to a limited number of sensory processes. Consequently, the number of olfactory sensations is very large, and the effort to classify them is defeated by their variety.

Olfactory stimuli. With regard to the character of the external stimuli which affect the cells of the olfactory surface, our knowledge is somewhat limited. Minute particles probably detach themselves from external objects and are carried by the air currents during inspiration into the nasal cavity. These particles, or effluvia, produce a chemical effect upon the olfactory cells. In general, it seems to be true that those substances which are most frequently brought into contact with the olfactory surface produce the least effect, whereas new and unfamiliar substances produce a strong effect. The relation between the external effluvia and the olfactory processes is probably the outgrowth of the long evolutionary process, in which the sense has developed as its chief function the ability to warn animals of the presence of unfamiliar substances in the atmosphere. Noxious gases are, from the nature of the case, relatively uncommon, and the olfactory sense, in serving to warn us of their presence, not only shows its adaptation to the stimuli which are unusual but shows, also, the significance of the whole development as aimed at the preservation of the organism.

FIG. 34. Olfactory cells and supporting cells (much magnified)

The supporting cells are here shown to be larger than the true sensory cell and somewhat different in form

Smell a rudimentary sense in man. Animals make much larger use of the sense of smell than do human beings. They often take advantage of the presence of strange effluvia in the atmosphere and react positively to these odors, seeking the source of the odor, if it leads them, for example, to food. It is to be said in this connection that the human sense of smell can be much more highly cultivated than is commonly the case, if attention is directed to these sensations in early life. Such attention aids discrimination, but does not change the organ itself.

Taste qualities and taste organs specialized. Turning from smell to taste, we notice first that the qualities of taste sensation are more easily reduced to a classified list. The qualities most constantly recurring are bitter, sweet, sour, and saline. If we add to the list alkaline and metallic, which may be compounds, it is possible to classify all taste experiences as belonging under the one or the other of the six classes, or as compounds of these. This reduction of all tastes to a few qualities leads one to look for structures in the organ of taste which shall explain the reduction of the physical manifold to a small number of sensory qualities. The study of the organs of taste shows that they are specialized structures, probably of a selective character.

Organs of taste. The taste organs are distributed throughout the mouth and throat. They appear in greatest abundance on the papillæ of the tongue. Fig. 35 shows a magnified section through the side of one of the large papillæ. At certain points in the walls of the papilla

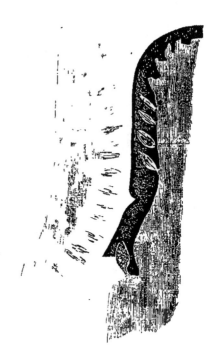

FIG. 35. The depression between the sides of two papillæ on the surface of the tongue

Liquids may pass down into this opening. On its sides are taste bulbs. Their number and distribution are indicated in the figure

there can be distinguished groups of cells clustered in bulb-shaped organs. These are known as the taste bulbs. Each bulb is made up of a number of cells grouped about its wall and constituting a minute pear-shaped organ (Fig. 36). Among these cells in the bulb are distributed tactual nerve fibers and special taste fibers (Fig. 37), which come from nerve cells located in the immediate vicinity of the medulla. The cells of the taste bulb are chemically affected by certain fluids which act upon them, and the chemical processes set up within the peripheral cells are transmitted first to the nerve fibers, and through these to the nerve cells, and, finally, from the receiving nerve cells to the central nervous system. Probably not all the cells in the taste bulbs act equally in receiving taste stimulations. Some of the cells in the bulbs seem to be specialized for the taste function, while others play the part of supporting cells. The peripheral organs are not true nerve cells, as were the receiving cells in the olfactory organs; they are intermediate between the sensory fibers and the outer world. Their function is, undoubtedly, selective. This accounts for the more definite and independent character of the taste quali-

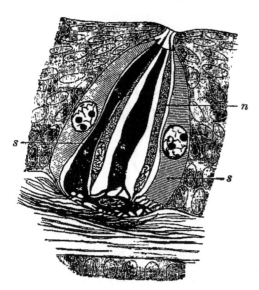

FIG. 36. A diagrammatic section of a single taste bulb showing the character of the different cells

The cells marked *n* are the special sensory cells. The cells marked *ss* are supporting cells. It will be noticed that the cells constituting the bulb are somewhat larger than those which form the general surrounding tissue

ties as compared with odors. The selective character of the taste cells is strikingly shown by the fact that not all taste bulbs receive with equal facility the various taste stimulations. Thus, the cells in the back part of the tongue are much more sensitive to stimulation from bitter substances. Cells in the front part of the tongue respond more readily to sweet solutions. On the sides of the tongue the areas are especially sensitive to sour and saline stimulations. To be sure, the localization is not absolute, especially for sour and saline, but it is very far in advance of anything found in the olfactory surface.

Gustatory stimuli. The substances which act upon these taste bulbs must be in liquid form. If one dries the tongue thoroughly, the substances which would otherwise produce taste impressions can be pressed against the tongue without producing any effect. For example, a piece of dry salt placed upon the dry surface of the tongue will not give rise to any taste sensation.

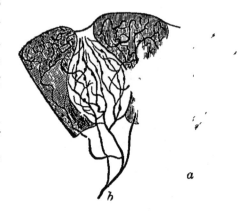

FIG. 37. A diagrammatic sketch showing two neighboring taste bulbs

The supporting cells have been removed in the two bulbs. The bulb on the right has four specialized gustatory cells. The network of fibers at the base of these cells shows the mode of distribution of the gustatory nerve fibers. In the bulb on the left and in the intermediate tissue between the bulbs, the terminations of the tactile nerve fiber are shown. The tongue is thus seen to be an organ of touch as well as of taste

D. SENSATIONS OF TOUCH

Organs of touch. The group of sensations popularly classified under the sense of touch might very properly have been considered at the beginning of this chapter, for touch is the human sense which is most closely allied in character and in the structure of its organs to the primitive senses of the lower animals. Indeed, the surface of the body is a relatively undifferentiated mass of protective and sensory cells, which are open to stimulations of all kinds and capable of responding in some degree to almost any form of external energy. The true nerve cells for the sense of touch are situated in the immediate neighborhood of the spinal cord. They are primitive bipolar cells,

as shown outside the cord in Figs. 13 and 14. The branch
which passes out of one of these bipolar cells toward the
surface of the body is the receiving sensory fiber. When it
reaches the skin, it breaks up into a fine network of fibrils.
These fibrils are distributed among the cells of the skin.
The nerve fiber which travels inward from the receiving cell
extends into the spinal cord. Such a fiber was described
in the discussion of the spinal cord. It will be recalled that
this central fiber branches so as to extend upward and
downward through a large section of the spinal cord, sending out at various levels collateral branches which transmit
the stimulation to the motor cells at the different levels of
the cord or transmit the stimulation to the higher nervous
centers.

Differentiation of the tactual fibers; temperature spots.
The sensory fibers which pass to various parts of the surface
of the body seem to be differentiated in their functions to
some extent in spite of the uniformity of their structure.
For, while it is probably true that there is no region on the
surface of the body which is not susceptible to stimulation
in some degree by all forms of external energy, provided
the energy is strong enough, yet it is certain that there are
regions capable of responding easily to slight changes in
pressure and temperature. Indeed, there are areas which
show special susceptibility to pressure, and others which are
especially sensitive to temperature. The specialized areas are
usually points or, at most, limited areas. The most striking
demonstration of this differentiation of the skin can be secured by taking a metallic point which has been reduced somewhat in temperature and passing this point slowly across the
skin. At intervals the point will be recognized as distinctly
cold, while on other parts of the skin it will be recognized
merely as an external pressure without temperature quality.
Those areas where the point is recognized as distinctly cold
have been designated cold spots.

Pressure spots. A second type of specialized points on the surface of the skin includes those points which are specially susceptible to stimulations of pressure. If one applies a fine hair to points on the skin, it will be found that there are certain points at which the pressure will be recognized, while there are other points from which no sensation will arise. Those points which respond to the slightest stimulation are called pressure spots. The number of pressure spots discovered in any special region will depend, of course, upon the intensity of the pressure exerted by the hair, so that the term "pressure spot" is a relative term and depends for its exact definition upon the intensity of the stimulus applied to the skin.

A part of this differentiation of sensory excitations is due to the structures which surround the tactual sensory fibers, but beyond this there is a demonstrated difference in the receiving fibers themselves.

Other " spots." Heat spots and pain spots can also be found. The heat spots are much more diffuse and difficult to locate than the cold spots, but they are analogous to the cold spots in their response to changes in temperature stimulation. Pain spots appear in certain parts of the body and may, perhaps, be defined as specially sensitive pressure spots. Whole areas of the body surface, as, for example, the cornea of the eye, are so sensitive that any stimulation which is recognized at all will be recognized with the quality of pain rather than that of simple pressure. There are certain reasons for treating pain as distinct from pressure. Thus, when a sensory nerve fiber has been injured and is gradually recovering its functions, pain sensibility and pressure sensibility are restored at different stages of the recovery.

Relativity of temperature sense; chemical and mechanical senses. One characteristic of the temperature spots is their change in sensitivity when stimulated for a period of time by any given temperature. For example, the hand which has grown cold from a long exposure to cold air will react to water of a moderate degree of temperature in such a way as to give rise to the sensation of warmth, while the same hand, after it has been exposed to warm air, will give sensations of cold from the same water. This relativity, as it is called, of the temperature sense is due to the fact that the nervous processes involved are chemical processes which, when once established, change the condition of the sensory organs so that the reception of later stimulations depends upon both the present stimulation and the condition induced by past stimulations. Similar facts have been noted in the discussion of color contrasts and olfactory fatigue. There is no marked relativity in the case of sensory processes of hearing or of pressure. There is a basis in these differences with regard to relativity for a distinction between the chemical senses on the one hand,

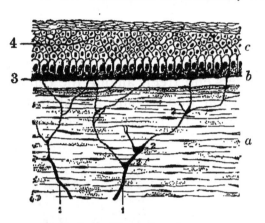

FIG. 38 A. Tactual end organs

A section of the cornea of the eye much magnified. The small cells in the upper part of the figure show that the tissue is made up of a number of small, compactly arranged cells. A nerve fiber is seen distributing its branches among these cells. This is a typical form of distribution of the tactual fiber, which ends freely in the surface of the body. (After Testute)

FIG. 38 B. A Pacinian corpuscle. (After Testute)

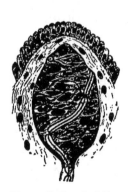

FIG. 38 C. A Missenian corpuscle. (After Testute)

including the temperature sense, the senses of smell, taste, and vision, and the mechanical senses on the other hand, including those which depend upon direct excitation of the nerve fibers; namely, pressure and hearing. The chemical senses show greater relativity and more striking after-effects than do the mechanical senses.

Organs of touch at the periphery. The peripheral endings of tactual fibers are in some cases surrounded by special structures; in other cases the fibers end freely among the cells of the skin. A number of typical end organs are shown in Figs. 38–41. Some evidence has been accumulated to show that the differentiated qualities of tactual sensation are related to these specialized structures. Thus, there are certain organs which appear in the conjunctiva where there is no sensitivity for pressure, but where there is sensitivity for cold. This leads to the inference that they are special organs for cold. Again, certain tactual cells seem to be especially numerous in regions sensitive to pain. Pain, however, is the only type of sensation from certain other regions where the fibers end freely

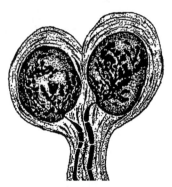

FIG. 39. Two Golgi-Mazzoni corpuscles of the type found by Ruffini in the cutaneous connective tissue of the tip of the human finger

among the epithelial cells. The evidence is, therefore, not conclusive that the end organs in the skin are specialized; they may be primarily protective organs.

Muscle sensations and organic sensations. Sensations from the inner organs of the body have sometimes been classified under the tactual sense; sometimes they have been regarded as constituting separate classes. All the inner organs of the body have sensory nerve fibers similar to the tactual fibers which end in the skin. Thus, the muscles, joints, linings of the organs of the thoracic, and especially of the abdominal, regions are all supplied with sensory nerves. In discussing the experiences received from the limbs, it is sometimes

convenient to distinguish under the name "muscle sensations" the experiences resulting from the excitation of the
sensory fibers ending in the muscles. In like manner,
sensations from the abdominal organs
are sometimes classified as organic
sensations. The motives for minute
analysis of these sensations from the
inner organs are not strong, because
these sensations are relatively undifferentiated. In the normal course
of life they come into experience
with a great mass of skin sensations,
and they never are intense except
when they are abnormal.

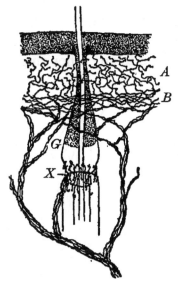

FIG. 40. Shows the com-
plex distribution of a tactual
nerve fiber in the immediate
vicinity of a hair

The freely ending nerve fibers
in region *A* directly under the
epidermis are to be compared
with the freely ending nerve
fibers shown in Fig. 38 A. These
fibers before their distribution
in the area *A* form a network in
the cutis in the area *B*. Around
the shaft of the hair are certain
glandular tissues marked *G* in
the figure. Branches from the
general nerve trunk are distributed, as indicated at *X*, about
the hair and its surrounding tissues. (After Retzius)

E. Sensation Intensities

Intensity a general characteristic.
While it has been necessary to discuss sensation qualities in terms of
the relation of these qualities to various organs of sense and various forms
of external energy, it is possible to
treat the matter of sensation intensities in a somewhat more general way.
The relation of changes in the intensity of objective sounds to changes
in the intensity of sound sensations
is of essentially the same type as the
relation between the intensity of pressure stimuli and pressure sensations.
Indeed, it is in this sphere of sensa-
tion intensities that the general methods of modern experimental investigation were first most fully developed. The
early experimental investigators had the largest confidence

that they would be able to develop general mathematical formulas which would define the relations between external stimuli and sensation intensity with a degree of comprehensiveness and precision comparable to that which is attained in the physical sciences. As a result, they performed the most laborious experiments and collected a mass of data which is not equaled in quantity by the data relating to any other single sphere of psychological phenomena.

Weber's Law. The general principle which was established by these investigators is commonly known as Weber's Law. This law states that the increase in sensation intensity does not follow directly the increase in the physical stimulus. While the physical stimulus is increasing either continuously or by additions of small increments, the sensation increases in recognizable intensity only after there has been a certain percentage of increase in the intensity of the external stimulus. To make the matter concrete, if a certain intensity of light is continuously increased or is increased step by step by small additional amounts of energy, there may

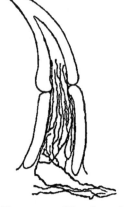

Fig. 41. Tooth of Gobinus showing distribution of nerve fiber throughout the canal of the tooth. (After Retzius)

result in subjective experience no appreciable increase whatsoever. Before a change in the intensity of the sensation can arise, the external light must be increased by about $\frac{1}{100}$ of its original intensity. Various investigators have found somewhat different fractions ranging from $\frac{1}{186}$ or $\frac{1}{167}$ to $\frac{1}{57}$, but in any case when the fraction is determined for a given intensity of light, say one hundred candlemeters, the same fraction holds, at least approximately, for all other medium intensities. The meaning of Weber's Law can be made clear by considering the following negative illustration. If we add to a single candle the small quantity of light necessary

to increase it by $\frac{1}{100}$, an observer will be able to recognize
the change. If, now, we add to a light of one thousand
candlepowers the same $\frac{1}{100}$ of a single candlepower, the
effect will be absolutely unappreciable ; that is, the sensation
in consciousness will not be modified at all. Ten candlepowers must be added to one thousand before an appreciable
change takes place in the observer's experience.

General statement of the law. The law holds in general
for all spheres of sensation intensity. The ratio of increase
in the different spheres of sensation differs. Thus, while
it is $\frac{1}{100}$ for light, it is given by Wundt as $\frac{8}{100}$ for pressure.
Other fractions are reported for other spheres of sensation.
In general, however, the relation is always of the same type.
It has been expressed briefly in the statement, if the sensation is to increase in an arithmetical ratio, the stimulus
must increase in a geometrical ratio. The range of applica-
bility of this general principle is limited in each case to
stimuli of moderate intensities.

Mechanical explanation of Weber's Law. After the law
has been established as a statement of an empirical fact, it
is by no means easy to determine its value for the explanation of mental life. It probably expresses a law of nervous
behavior which is a special case under the general mechanical
principle, that any increase in any form of physical activity
becomes more and more difficult as this activity reaches a
higher level of intensity. For example, it is extremely
difficult to add to the speed of a locomotive beyond a certain
point. If the locomotive is moving at the rate of fifteen
miles an hour, a moderate increase in the amount of energy
applied to the machinery will increase the speed by a mile
an hour. If, however, the engine is moving at the rate of
sixty miles an hour, the amount of energy which must be
expended to add one mile to its speed is very much greater
than the amount which was necessary to add this same in-
crement of speed when the engine was moving at the rate

of fifteen miles. This mechanical principle is applicable to the action of the nervous system. If the external stimulus acting upon the sense organs is producing a certain moderate degree of chemical activity, that chemical activity can be intensified by a small addition to the external stimulus. If, however, the stimulus acting upon the nerve cells is so strong that it demands nearly all of the energy that the cell is capable of giving out, then the small addition to the stimulus will produce no effect. Since this is a general principle of all nervous behavior, it is a principle which appears alike in all the different spheres of sensation.

Other views regarding Weber's Law. Other interpretations of Weber's Law have been given in the history of psychology. One such interpretation, given by Fechner, was of a most ambitious type and was intended by its author to express in exact mathematical terms the general relation between mind and matter. The significant fact which Fechner was emphasizing, that the relation between consciousness and the physical world is not direct, is abundantly established by considerations of a more general character than those which Fechner took up. We have seen in our earlier discussions of sensation qualities that there are many other phases of experience which do not parallel the physical facts with which they are related. The importance of Weber's Law as a demonstration of the indirectness of the relation in question is, therefore, relatively less now than it was in the time of Fechner, and his definite mathematical formulas are of no value. The whole study of sensation intensities was, indeed, more productive for general psychology in the experimental methods which it served to cultivate than in the contribution which it made to the content of psychology. The discussion of sensation intensities may, accordingly, be dismissed without further detail.

CHAPTER VI

EXPERIENCE AND BEHAVIOR

All consciousness complex and selective. A man comes into a room and sees a piece of paper on the table. He walks to the table, picks up the paper, and after looking at it throws it down again. If we try to give a psychological explanation of these acts, we find ourselves adopting some such formula as this. The act of going to the table and picking up the paper is due to curiosity and an inner desire. Curiosity and desire are aroused by the sensory impression which the paper made on the man's eye. After the first act of picking up the paper, a new series of visual impressions fell on the retina; these new impressions aroused a new series of inner processes and the act of throwing down the paper followed. Experience is thought of under this formula as a series of cycles, each beginning in a sensation and ending in an act.

The formula is much too simple. When we consider carefully the first statement "sees a piece of paper," we find at once that we are dealing not with a sense impression alone; we are dealing with a vigorous form of behavior. The act of looking at an object involves the turning of the two eyes in a very complicated way on the object and involves also the focusing of the lenses inside the eyes. Not only so, but looking at an object is a highly selective performance. The room into which the man came offered to his vision a hundred shades of color and a hundred varieties of brightness. Out of all these he fastened on one small patch. The walls of the room were quite as bright as the paper and very much more extensive; they offered sensations which in their quality and intensity would overwhelm the piece of paper if sense impressions alone determined the flow of mental life. The fact that the man looked at the paper rather than at the walls is the first and most essential fact which the psychologist must take into account if he would give an adequate explanation of the later act of picking up the paper.

The selective character of conscious processes related to sensory impressions. Our common descriptions emphasize the active character of the processes of recognition here under discussion. We say the man is interested in pieces of paper, while he has no special interest in walls. Or we say that the man is trained to give attention to what is on the table, but is indifferent to the walls of the room. Sometimes we go further and give the explanation of the man's interests and his attention by saying that he has cultivated certain associations or certain modes of thinking which determine the directions in which his mind turns.

Such statements make it clear that psychology cannot rest content with the explanation that each cycle of experience begins with a sensory impression. By the time the mind receives a sensory impression the selective process has gone a long way; the selective process which is involved in attending to a sense impression is itself a preliminary stage of no small importance.

It will not be amiss to recall at this point one of the important lessons drawn from our study of the evolution of the organs of sense. Our organs of sense are by their very structure selective organs. The eye cannot respond to rays of light below the red or beyond the violet. The ear does not record sounds of the slowest rates of vibration or those of the highest pitch. Evidently the organism has been determined in its evolution by causes which are more fundamental than those of mere sensation, for there has been no evolution of universal sense organs, but only evolution of organs capable of receiving certain impressions which the organism can use in promoting its own life.

Selective consciousness related to behavior. The key to this whole matter is found in a study of bodily activities. Every animal is a reacting being. All its functions relate to what it can do. For example, there is a certain range of objects which are of such size that they can be picked up by the human hand or moved by human fingers. It is an impressive fact of biology that the range of human vision corresponds to this range of action. We do not have microscopic eyes like the fly. Nor, on the other hand, do we have distance vision like the eagle's. With our present organs of behavior we could not react to the minute objects which the fly sees, nor could we use far-sighted eyes to advantage from our position near the ground, for even if we could see at great distances, we could not move fast enough to take advantage of our superior sight. The range of human vision has been determined by the range of possible human reactions. The impressions of the eye are of importance only when there is a corresponding power of action.

Common interests and their relation to behavior. That action is a determining consideration in mental life will be clearly seen when one begins to look at ordinary experience with a view to finding what is back of sensations. One who is not interested in doing something with trees will pass them a thousand times and never really see them. The maple tree has a shape wholly different from that of the elm. The barks of the two are quite different. The casual observer passes these trees day after day and his retina receives the appropriate sensory impressions with their varying characteristics, but the impressions go to waste. Let this observer be induced to try to draw the trees, and his experiences undergo a vast change. The impressions begin to be vivid; they have not undergone any modification in their character as sensory excitations, but they have taken on new importance in the psychological world. The psychological character of the impression can be described only by saying that the impression has been selected for attention or has been made vivid and distinct by virtue of the effort to use it.

Another example is found in the familiar experience of not hearing a clock tick so long as one is absorbed in reading. When the reading is over and there are no dominating ideas in the mind, the ticking begins to be heard. The fact is, of course, that the ear recorded the ticking in both cases. While one was reading, the nervous system was pouring its energy into the eyes which were looking along the printed lines. There was, furthermore, the general muscular reaction characteristic of purely visual attention, the tense breathless interest in the story on the printed page. The auditory impressions were absorbed into this stream of active processes and were lost. When the activity of reading is over and the body and the nervous system fall back into the miscellaneous activities characteristic of partial relaxation, there may be a turning of the head to listen and then the ticking may occupy the center of attention.

One might multiply examples indefinitely. On the street we pay little or no attention to the people whom we are passing. Our one purpose in most cases is to avoid collision, and our attention to sensory experience is just enough to serve this end. The skilled cabinetmaker sees in a piece of furniture elements which the untrained layman would not notice. The hunter observes what the stranger in the woods overlooks. Everywhere it is behavior that determines the emphasis on sensory impressions.

Study of evolution of organs of action as important as study of senses. The relation of bodily activity to mental processes will be more fully understood if we trace the evolution of the muscular system and its operations much as we

traced the evolution of the organs of sense. In an earlier
chapter the primitive muscle cells in the body wall of the
hydra were shown in Fig. 4, and the contrast in both form
and function between the muscle cells and the neural cells
was pointed out. The muscle cell is large and elongated.
It is large so that it can store up more energy than could
be stored in a small cell, and its elongated form favors contraction. Fig. 42 shows a single muscle cell of one of the
higher animals. A muscle is made up of a mass of such
cells. Every muscle is supplied with a nerve the ends of
which are distributed to the cells and produce contractions
of the muscle by discharging motor impulses into the cells.
The phenomena of contraction are illustrated in Fig. 43.
This process of contraction consists in an inner chemical
change which uses up a part of the energy stored up in the

cell body. The proc-
esses may be com-
pared to combustion.

FIG. 42. A highly developed muscle cell

When a piece of
wood burns, it gives off a part of the energy stored up in
its complex chemical substances. So it is with the muscles;
they give out energy and have left behind certain waste
products which may be described as the ash of combustion.

**Evolution from gross muscles to highly differentiated
muscles.** The highly specialized muscle cells of the type
shown in Fig. 42 have been evolved from the cells which
make up the surface of the body in such simple animals as
the hydra. Furthermore, the muscles of the higher animals
have in the course of evolution become differentiated into a
large number of highly specialized groups of muscle cells. A
single illustration will make clear the type of evolution which
has gone on in all parts of the body. The mouth of one of
the lower animals, such as a fish, is opened and closed by
very simple muscles. In the higher animal forms the differentiation of muscles goes much further. The opening and

shutting of the human mouth, for example, is not a single gross performance as in the fish. The muscles of the lips have been evolved and so highly differentiated that one side of the mouth can be moved, as it is in many forms of facial expression, quite independently of the gross opening and closing of the jaw, which is the only form of movement of which the fish is capable.

In like manner the hand exhibits a high differentiation of the muscles. When we study the ability of a human being to move one finger apart from the rest of the hand, we realize how far differentiation of the muscles has gone.

Behavior dependent on nervous control. The highly differentiated muscular system of the human body takes on a greater significance for the student of psychology when it is kept in mind that the muscles are always connected

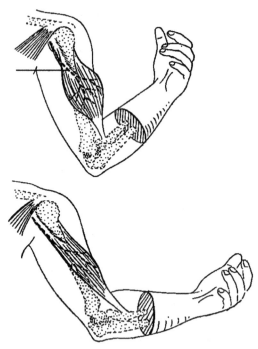

FIG. 43. The contracted and relaxed state of a muscle

The dotted lines within the muscle show the distribution of the nerve fiber

with the nervous system and are absolutely dependent on the nervous system for the impulses which cause their contraction. In the lowest animal forms the muscle cells had a general irritability, but in the process of evolution the muscle cells have been specialized to store up great quantities of energy. They do not in their later specialized stage receive impressions directly from the outer world. They contract only when they are excited by nervous impulses. The higher the animal, the more its muscles have become dependent on the nervous system. The result is that when the muscular system becomes highly differentiated there must be a parallel evolution of the nervous centers related to these muscles. There has been, accordingly, a steady evolution of the controlling nervous organs. When we study the human hand and its complex possibilities of adjustment or when we study the delicate movements of the human face, we must always have in mind the fact that there are corresponding differentiations of the nervous system.

Coördination as necessary counterpart of differentiation. There is another consequence of this differentiation of the motor organs which is of importance for our study. The highly differentiated muscles may, indeed, contract each by itself in the performance of some special function for which it was evolved, but for the most part the special muscles act in systems. The individual muscle becomes for the purpose of the moment not a separate organ, but a part of a system of coöperating muscles. For example, the single finger may move by itself, but in many of the activities of life the single finger contributes its strength to a grasping movement which enlists all the other fingers and the whole hand. In a grasping movement the finger is not a separate organ. Here, then, we have a complex situation ; the differentiated muscles which move the finger must sometimes act separately, sometimes as parts of a combination of many muscles. In the same way the nervous centers must be both specialized and capable of entering into combination.

Individual development in behavior. The history of individual development of muscular control shows how complicated is this matter of muscular action. There is a natural tendency on the part of the infant to contract certain of the muscles of the body in a primitive gross combination. Thus, the infant can close the hand on any small object like a pencil which is laid across the palm. The fingers all enter into this act, and the muscular·system of the hand and arm coöperate in a single performance. This primitive act is very like that exhibited by the animals lower in the scale than man. In the course of later life the child will have to acquire by practice the ability to move his individual fingers without including the others. Thus, if he learns to play on the piano, he must not move all the fingers together. In such a case he must learn to differentiate the fingers from each other.

Conversely, there arises even in infant life the necessity of developing a careful coöperation between the different parts of the body. The two hands must work together in grasping an object. The head and eyes must turn toward an object which the hand is to grasp. Later in life the fingers which have become skilled in striking the piano keys separately must coöperate in striking the chord.

In these examples the body is seen to be a highly evolved system of reacting organs constantly developing, on the one hand, in the direction of finer and more delicately adjusted movements and, on the other hand, in the direction of more complex combinations of these differentiated forms of behavior.

In terms of our description we may distinguish three stages of muscular activity, always recalling that there are corresponding stages in the development of processes in the nervous system. First, there are gross adjustments; second, differentiated forms of movement; and third, coördinated forms of action. The term "coördination" here introduced will recur frequently in later discussions. Its meaning will be clear from the foregoing discussions. A coördinated movement is one in which groups of differentiated muscles coöperate under the control of nerve centers, thus producing complex but completely unified acts.

Inherited coördinations or instincts. There is one important fact of heredity which must be included in the preliminary discussion of bodily movement before we are in a position to understand fully the relation of behavior to consciousness. The higher animals come into the world with many coördinated forms of behavior fully provided for in the inherited structure of their nervous systems. For example, a human infant is able at the beginning of life to use the lips and tongue in the complex act of sucking and he is able also to swallow through the coöperation of the muscles of the throat. Such an inherited complex of coördinated acts is called an instinct. The nervous centers in control of the lips and tongue are evidently coupled by lines of connection which the long experience of the race has laid down, and the infant is equipped from the first not only with differentiated muscles and controlling centers but with a fully developed organization in his nervous system which results in the coöperation of the differentiated centers.

Glands as active organs. To this discussion of the development of the muscles and their contraction should be added the comment that there is another group of active organs; namely, the glands. These secrete under the stimulus of the nervous system, and their behavior can for purposes of our discussion be regarded as like that of the muscles.

A constant tension of active organs as background of all behavior. In order to understand the relation of the behavior of the muscles and glands to consciousness, one general fact which is very commonly overlooked must be kept clearly in view. The active organs of the body are at all times during life in a state of tension. There are constantly pouring out of the nervous system streams of motor excitations. These are distributed to different parts of the body in currents of varying intensity, but there is always a stream of motor impulses going to the active organs.

One reason why this fact is not clearly recognized is that we ordinarily think of the nervous system as in action only when some part of the body is actually moving. Thus, if the hand moves from near the body to a distant point in order to pick up some object, we realize that the muscles of the arm are contracting. But if the individual sits rigidly in his seat, resisting the impulse to reach for the object, we overlook the fact that his muscles are on the stretch, often to an extent involving much greater effort than would be required to grasp the object.

Evidences without end could be adduced to show that the muscles are in constant action. The neck muscles are constantly in action holding up the head of a waking man. Let the neck muscles relax for a moment, as they do when the man begins to get drowsy, and gravity will pull the head forward, giving a striking exhibition of the work which the neck muscles are doing most of the time.

Again, consider what happens at all times by way of bracing the body for movements. The trunk muscles tighten when the hand begins to reach out because the trunk must balance the new weight which is taken up in the hand.

Not alone the trunk muscles but the whole inner mechanism of the body is drawn into action even by the most trivial movement. The blood circulation accommodates itself to every act. This means that the contraction of an arm muscle calls for more blood to the arm. The call affects the heartbeat and the contraction of the muscles in the arteries which control the pressure of the blood in all parts of the body. The adjustment of blood circulation affects respiration and digestion and the inner glandular action, until finally the whole body is involved in the effort to move the arm.

Meaning of sensory impressions dependent upon inner conditions. We are now in a position to understand the facts which were taken up in the early paragraphs of this chapter.

A sensory impression does not come into a nervous system that is in suspense waiting to be aroused to action. A sensory impression is not the first or primary step in a series of nervous processes. The sensory impression comes into an inner world full of action. The new impression may change the mode of action or it may be absorbed into the processes under way. Again, using another figure, we may say that the inner world is constantly weaving its material into a pattern. The new sensory impression is new raw material. It may be necessary to shut down the machinery and recast the pattern in order to deal with this new material. Ordinarily it is not necessary to shut down. Ordinarily the new raw material is perfectly familiar and with very little disturbance of the routine is absorbed into the existing pattern, and the machinery goes on as it was working.

Other analogies could be drawn on to help in describing the situation ; the best are always those which are closest to mental life itself. Thus a social group receives a newcomer. The arrival is not the beginning of the group's social activity. The arrival may make no striking impression on the conversation. On the other hand, the new arrival may turn all currents of thought and social life into new channels. The new social situation in any case will be the result of what was, plus the modifying influence of what now is.

Sensory processes and the equilibrium of action. So it is in the action of the nervous system. Before a particular sensory impression comes, the nervous system is in a state of general excitation. Continuous streams of incoming sensory impulses and streams of outgoing motor processes constitute a complex of nervous life. The character of this complex is determined primarily by those inner paths of combination which have been developed in the organism's history and in its past struggles with the world. Into this inner world with its stresses and strains comes a new sensory impulse. In the great majority of cases the new impulse does not work any radical effect. The central processes are under way and they go on as before, absorbing into their main current the little stream of new sensory energy. Every now and then the new impulse is so strong or it fits into the workings of the central nervous system with such a power to change the equilibrium of action that a radical change takes place. One is reading and hears his name called from the next room. The name arouses action because it is imperative in its command over one's action. The call need not be strong, but it is one of the keys to a vigorous form of behavior entirely opposed to reading. In such a case the action is abruptly changed in its direction of operation.

Importance of sensations dependent on organization. Even when one of the abrupt and impressive changes in central nervous action comes, it is not the sensory impulse as such which explains the change. The ability of the individual to react is here the chief consideration. An impression can never be strong unless the organization of the individual is prepared to receive it. Indeed, as pointed out earlier in the chapter, the whole evolution of the animal world indicates that the sense organs themselves evolve in the direction dictated by the demands for action.

Sensations unduly emphasized through introspection. The discussion of activity as taken up thus far in this chapter has made very few appeals to the reader's conscious analysis of his own experiences. The reason is that the view of consciousness here presented is not the one suggested by introspection. Introspection tends to bring into overemphatic relief new sensory impressions. It is not difficult to note what goes on in consciousness when a color is seen or a sound is heard, for the points in consciousness where a color or a sound becomes vivid are relatively easy to distinguish from the main current of mental life. Consciousness pauses for a moment and gives emphasis to the arrival of the newcomer. It is much more difficult to look at the main current of experience because a person is in the midst of the current, absorbed in its movement and thus without any contrasts by means of which to make himself vividly aware of that which fills his whole mind. Just as the social group which was referred to a few paragraphs back is not aware of its own atmosphere and of its own appearance but is clearly conscious of the new member, so personal consciousness must adopt new scientific methods of recognizing its own characteristics.

Attitudes. Perhaps the use of a special term will help in bringing out what is here being emphasized. There is in every mental act an aspect which comes from the individual's reactions on his impressions. We may call this aspect of experience an attitude. Thus there are attitudes of liking and disliking. If the attitude is vivid, one may readily analyze it out of the complex and say, " I like the color or the sound or the taste," or "I dislike the impression." If the attitude is not so vivid or so distinctive in character, it may be more difficult to separate it for purpose of study from the impression. A color may receive the attention of an observer, thus arousing a very definite and positive attitude called attention, but it is difficult to describe what one means by the word " attention." It is also difficult to disentangle attention from the color experience itself. Yet a moment's scientific consideration of the matter will make it quite evident that the conditions of attention are to be found in the individual's organization and active processes. No sensory impression carries in itself the qualities which command attention. Attention is a contribution of the inner world; it is an attitude of the individual.

Attitudes not related to sensations but to behavior. Our attitudes are as manifold as our modes of response to impressions and ideas. In the next chapter we shall select for treatment some of the chief attitudes of ordinary life. In the meantime, it is the purpose of this chapter to reiterate the fact that all attitudes are phases of behavior. The psychology of the individual must study modes of behavior quite as much as sensations. Indeed, if one is to be emphasized more than the other, it is the business of science to bring out the significance of behavior, since this is likely to be overlooked by the superficial observer.

SUMMARY

Relation of sensation to reaction. It may be well to summarize the conclusions reached up to this point by means of a diagram.

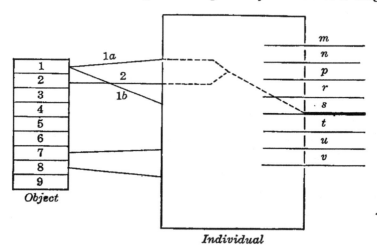

Individual

FIG. 44. Diagram showing relation of sensory impressions to reactions

Let the rectangle at the left of Fig. 44 represent some object n the physical world — a book or a piece of machinery. The object has many physical characteristics which are represented by the subdivisions 1 to 9. Some of these impress a human being; others lo not. For example, the machine may send out waves of electric energy for which we have no organ of sense; the book may send out ultraviolet rays of light which lie beyond the range of vision. Subdivision 7 represents the power of emitting electric energy; subdivision 8, the power of giving out ultraviolet rays. When energy from 7 and 8 reaches the surface of the human body there s no organ for the reception of the stimulation. Subdivision 1, on the other hand, represents the power to reflect red light, and subdivision 2 represents solidity or resistance to touch. These do impress the human body if they strike the right points, as indicated by the dotted lines continuing lines 1 *a* and 2. Line 1 *b* represents a ray of light which does not strike the eye, but strikes some part of the skin and produces no effect.

Let us follow the dotted lines which represent currents of sensory excitation entering the central nervous system from the eye and finger. It is not usual for the central nervous system to receive only two sensory impressions at any given moment, but for the sake of simplicity the others are omitted.

As soon as these sensory processes enter the central nervous system they begin to flow toward the muscles which constitute the second surface of the body represented by the right-hand boundary of the rectangle standing for the individual. In the muscular system there are certain contractions — *m, n, p, r, s, t, u,* and *v,* which are the results of motor impulses flowing out from the nervous system.

In the central nervous system the two incoming currents are brought together by the organized paths in this system. They then pass through the motor centers and are distributed in such a way as to reënforce *s*; that is, one of the muscular tensions which was present from the first.

We commonly say that the sensory impressions caused the reaction *s*. What really happened is that certain attributes of the object aroused the sensory impulses which in turn were fused by the individual's inner nervous organization in such a way that the reaction *s* of which the individual was all along capable was brought into emphatic play.

Consciousness does not reflect merely the entrance of sensory impressions into the nervous system; if it did, vision and touch from the same object would remain as unrelated facts in experience. Consciousness includes the incoming impressions, but emphasizes the fact that they are combined on the way to a common center of motor discharge. Consciousness is related to the central organization and thus to the reactions of the individual quite as much as to the incoming sensory impressions.

We find ourselves, accordingly, in harmony with the conclusion to which our general study of the nervous system led us. We found, it will be remembered, that the indirect centers of the cerebrum — that is, the organizing areas of the brain — are the parts of greatest importance to the student of conscious life. We now see that this means that the fusion of sensory impressions on the way to their discharge as motor processes is the physical fact most closely related to consciousness. Consciousness does not depend primarily on the character of sensory impressions or of muscular contractions, but is determined largely by the organizing processes which follow the reception of sense impressions and their discharge into motor channels.

CHAPTER VII

CERTAIN FUNDAMENTAL ATTITUDES

Reactions toward objects and reactions away from objects.
If we consider the simplest forms of animal behavior, we
find that they divide into two classes ; there are, on the one
side, activities in which the animal seeks those ends which
gratify, such as food, warmth, and contact with its own
kind ; and there are, on the other side, activities in which
the animal seeks to escape from harm. The simplest
animal forms show these two types of behavior, as has
been pointed out in an earlier chapter (Fig. 2, and p. 16).
The human infant shows the same fundamental forms of
behavior.

Pleasure and displeasure. There are in conscious life
fundamental attitudes corresponding to these two types of
behavior. We like what we seek, and our attitude toward
impressions arousing this type of reaction is described by
the common word " pleasure." What we try to avoid
arouses within us the opposite attitude, or one of displeasure. In popular language the antithesis commonly expressed is between pleasure and pain. Pain is, in reality,
a very intense form of tactual sensation which comes from
the injury of bodily tissues. Such sensations stir up the
most violent efforts on the part of the organism to throw
off the offending object ; hence the common failure to distinguish between the sensory part of the experience and the
attitude of displeasure.

Pleasure and displeasure appear in a great variety of
particular forms. Thus, when the body is taking in food,

there is a series of activities which are among the most gratifying that the individual can experience. The nervous system is prepared to respond positively to the stream of sensory stimulations which come to the organs of taste and smell from objects suited to the organism. The organism is coördinated in its internal behavior to receive the objects that gratify, and the nervous activity accompanying the whole process is of the most favorable type. Again, the comfort of sitting in a warm, bright room is different from that of taking food; but here, as in taking food, all the body's reactions are harmonious and favorable, and in a general way the attitude of the individual is of the same quality as that which appears in the act of taking food.

Displeasure exhibits in like manner different forms. The odor of some object may be disgusting because it throws the body into violent activities aimed at rejection. In the same general way, one tries to get away from a glaring light. In both cases the action is one of self-protection, and the mental attitude is one of displeasure.

There are negative conditions as well as positive which produce the typical attitudes of pleasure and displeasure. Thus the organism which is deprived of food or of warmth will make strenuous efforts to correct the deficiency, and the attitude which accompanies these efforts may be of the most intense displeasure. In like manner the relief which comes with the escape from impending danger may give the highest satisfaction.

Cultivated feelings. In general, it may be said that whatever impression promotes the normal reaction of the organism is accompanied by pleasure; whatever defeats normal behavior or arouses protective recoil is unpleasant.

The history of psychology is full of efforts to classify pleasures and displeasures and to show the exact relations of these phases of experience to sensations. The difficulty in reaching any final classification is that with the progress of individual development new types of pleasure and displeasure arise just in the degree in which one learns to seek or reject objects. Each human being starts with an instinctive tendency to seek certain ends and reject others. To these fundamental likes and dislikes he adds others connected with his mature experience. Thus each of us sets up certain property rights. One likes to have at hand, subject to his instant command, certain conveniences. If one cannot find his pen or his tennis racket, he is sometimes thrown into a state of distress hardly less violent than that exhibited by the infant who cannot find food. The tastes for pens and tennis rackets are acquired by the use of these instruments, they are in no sense of the word instinctive; but once the habits of use are organized they demand the opportunity for expression, and satisfaction or its opposite will attach to their presence or absence.

Fear as a typical emotion. One of the significant examples of a strong negative attitude appears in the experience which we call fear. We sometimes speak of the instinct of fear. There is, indeed, in every animal a strong tendency to run away from everything that is strange or large or overstimulating. So delicately is the nervous system poised to protect the individual that when a strange or violent stimulation comes to the organs of sense there follows an overstimulation of all the active organs. This overstimulation is accompanied by an inner state of agitation. The inner agitation confuses all thought and is a source of displeasure just because the inner chaos is ineffective and incapable of arousing any coördinated forms of expression. The frightened man is proverbially not intelligent. The fact is that the frightened man is internally in a commotion, and his mind is blurred because he cannot cope with the situation. His motor processes are stalled or incoördinated, and his attitude is disagreeable and increasingly so the longer his inability to deal with the situation continues.

Fear is a form of displeasure, but unique as contrasted with the displeasure of rejecting an unacceptable taste or color. Yet so general in character is fear that it may attach to any violent form of excitement. Fear, which has been described as the most primitive form of human displeasure, does not disappear with modern life, but tends, rather, to become more general and more intense. To be sure, it attaches to new objects as man overcomes his first enemies, but it is one of the most common attitudes of life. Primitive man was afraid of an eclipse; modern man is not. Modern man is, however, thrown into a panic by an earthquake because it runs counter to all his established forms of behavior to have the solid earth under his feet begin to rock. The earth has been the base of all behavior, and one is at a loss to control behavior when this base of action changes. Not only so, but modern life contains new terrors which were not known in earlier stages of civilization. The embarrassment of appearing in public is one of the new inventions of civilization. That there is much superfluous excitement in this case is realized by everyone whose knees have trembled and whose pulse has gone to one hundred and thirty. The mental distress of the situation comes from the fact that these forms of reaction are ineffective, indeed are quite absurdly in the wrong direction.

How to change the attitude of fear. The common advice given to children to go directly and investigate any object of which they are afraid is in general good. The going and the handling of an object give the individual a form of reaction which is coördinated and normal as a substitute for the agitation and for the ineffective inner agitation.

Fear an emotion of complex beings. Kipling has made a tale out of the evolution of fear. The stupid, slow-going bullocks in a night stampede in the camp tell how they fight and criticize the elephant as a coward. The bullocks tell how they draw the guns.

"Then we tug the big gun all together — *Heya* — *Hullah !*
Heeyah ! Hullah ! We do not climb like cats nor run like calves.
We go across the level plain, twenty yoke of us, till we are un-
yoked again, and we graze while the big guns talk across the plain
to some town with mud walls, and pieces of the wall fall out, and
the dust goes up as though many cattle were coming home."

"Oh ! And you choose that time for grazing do you ?" said the
young mule.

"That time or any other. Eating is always good. We eat till
we are yoked up again and tug the gun back to where Two Tails
is waiting for it. Sometimes there are big guns in the city that
speak back, and some of us are killed, and then there is all the
more grazing for those that are left. This is Fate — nothing but
Fate. None the less, Two Tails is a great coward. That is the
proper way to fight. We are brothers from Hapur. Our father
was a sacred bull of Shiva. We have spoken." . . .

Whereupon the elephant who has heard himself accused
of being a coward replies as follows :

"Well," said Two Tails, rubbing one hind leg against the other,
exactly like a little boy saying a piece, "I don't quite know whether
you 'd understand."

"We don't, but we have to pull the guns," said the bullocks.

"I know it, and I know you are a good deal braver than you
think you are. But it 's different with me. My battery captain
called me a Pachydermatous Anachronism the other day."

"That 's another way of fighting, I suppose ?" said Billy, who
was recovering his spirits.

"*You* don't know what that means, of course, but I do. It
means betwixt and between, and that is just where I am. I can
see inside my head what will happen when a shell bursts ; and you
bullocks can't."

"I can," said the troop-horse. "At least a little bit. I try not
to think about it."

"I can see more than you, and I *do* think about it. I know
there 's a great deal of me to take care of, and I know that nobody
knows how to cure me when I'm sick. All they can do is to stop
my driver's pay till I get well, and I can't trust my driver."

.   .   .   .

Two Tails stamped his foot till the iron ring on it jingled. "Oh, I'm not talking to *you*. You can't see inside your heads."

"No. We see out of our four eyes," said the bullocks. "We see straight in front of us."

"If I could do that and nothing else you wouldn't be needed to pull the big guns at all. If I was like my captain — he can see things inside his head before the firing begins, and he shakes all over, but he knows too much to run away — if I was like him I could pull the guns. But if I were as wise as all that I should never be here. I should be a king in the forest, as I used to be, sleeping half the day and bathing when I liked. I haven't had a good bath for a month."[1]

Fear and pathology. The physicians who deal with mental pathology report fear as the most common form of modern mental breakdown. The fears of our present-day lives are not the fears of the forest, but they are subtle and disorganizing. They cannot be classified merely as unpleasurable agitations ; they arise from violent and disorganizing forms of disrupted nervous activity.

Parental love and altruism. Parental love for offspring has been described as an instinct. Here again we have to do with a complex attitude which can be understood only when one studies the forms of behavior which the parent cultivates. Nature has so organized the higher animals that they protect their young. Gradually the compass of these protective activities widens until a mother may be wholly absorbed in the care of her offspring. The evolution of many of the complex forms of social life is directly traceable to the efforts of parents to care for their young. Fiske, in a very interesting essay on the evolution of altruism, has shown how the care of the child has brought into the world a mental attitude wholly beyond animal instinct. Among primitive animals behavior was at first aimed at self-preservation. With the growth of parental solicitude has come a form of

1 Rudyard Kipling, The Jungle Book, pp. 284, 287–289. The Century Company, 1914.

behavior which is at times so strong that a mother will sacrifice herself and with supreme gratification undergo all kinds of hardships in doing for her child that which will protect him and promote his welfare. This in turn, as Fiske points out, leads to other altruistic acts and attitudes embracing companions and acquaintances. Cultivated modes of behavior may, as in this case, create mental values which are entirely unintelligible if we think only of individual self-protection.

Anger. Anger is a mental attitude which accompanies an effort to throw off restraint. There may be blind rage in which the angry man beats aimlessly at everything which is within reach, or there may be the subtle studied anger which step by step proceeds to the final attack. Watson has called attention in his experiments with infants to the fact that a new-born infant will be thrown into a rage if its movements are restricted. Hold an infant's head perfectly still and anger will appear.

Other emotions. The list of attitudes could be indefinitely amplified. Jealousy, shame, bashfulness, surprise, awe, reverence are all names of special attitudes which grow out of the efforts of the individual to deal in some active way with the world about him. They all reduce in the last broad analysis to pleasurable and unpleasurable experiences, but this general classification obliterates the distinctions which can be productively retained if, instead of merely trying to classify attitudes, one develops the formula of explanation which includes all the rich variety of human reactions to a complex environment.

Emotions as fundamental forms of experience. The foregoing paragraphs will be recognized by every reader as dealing with that aspect of experience which has always been referred to under the terms " feeling " and " emotion." The importance of the feelings must not be underestimated by the student of human life. Sensory impressions are of significance only as they arouse attitudes. It is the attitude which reveals the individual; and the attitude in turn is the result of organized modes of response. The paths in the nervous system along which sensory impressions travel to their motor discharge, the central agitations which arise in the nervous system as the sensory impressions are combined and recombined, condition experience in a way that cannot be overlooked by one who is interested in human nature. Human nature is what it is, not because of the impressions which come to the eye and ear, but because of the responses which are worked out through the central nervous system.

Higher forms of experience as related to behavior. Thus far we have been showing in a general way that attitudes are related to reactions. The full significance of reactions for individual mental life will become increasingly apparent as the subsequent discussions canvass the different types of organized behavior of human beings. We shall discover that there are lower forms of behavior and lower types of mental attitude, and that the development of higher forms of experience involves the development of higher and more complex forms of reaction. Indeed, the rest of our study will be a study of human reactions and accompanying experiences. The remainder of this chapter will be devoted to a study of some of the more primitive and more fundamental attitudes.

Feelings of organic type. Many of the most primitive adjustments of the motor organs of the body are internal adjustments and have to do with the well-being of the body itself. Accompanying these there is at all times a background of feeling which colors all experience. There is the buoyant feeling which one enjoys when he begins life on a bright, clear day and the feeling of utter depression of a foggy day. The reasons for such feelings can be understood from such experiments as the following. The muscles of a waking person are always under tension. Let the tension be tested under conditions of varying stimulation. The individual can be asked to show his muscular strength by means of a dynamometer or simple apparatus for measuring the strength of the grip. If such a test is made in a dark, silent room, and a second test with the same person is subsequently made in a room which is well lighted and full of sound, it will be found that more work can be done in the latter case than in the former. The additional light and sound have raised the nervous and muscular tone to a higher level, so that when the movement is undertaken, the motor impulses to the muscles have the advantage of the higher initial tension. It need hardly be pointed out that the conscious experience of the reactor is different in the two cases described.

Flexor and extensor movements related to characteristic attitudes. A second experiment is as follows : Let a person be trained to make an outward swing of the arm with his eyes closed. If a number of measurements are made, it is possible to determine with great accuracy the range of error of these movements. If the movements are made when the senses are in a quiet condition without special stimulation, they will not be of exactly the same length in successive trials, but they will not differ widely from each other. After these preliminary tests, let the reactor be given a strong bitter or sweet taste sensation. The result will be that the arm, in common with the other muscular organs of the body, will take on a different tension. The tension in the case of a sweet stimulus will tend to favor outward expansive movements ; the tension in the case of a bitter stimulus will tend to favor inward contracting movements. The result will be increased movements in these directions, even when the person tries to move as before. In short, bitter tastes and sweet tastes result in inner muscular tensions.

Changes in circulatory movements as parallels of conscious changes. One of the systems of muscles which is most noticeably affected by any change in stimulation is the system in control of the circulatory activities. If a recording apparatus is so adjusted as to give a record of the rate and intensity of the heartbeat, it will be found that there is a constant rise and fall in the rate and intensity of circulatory activity. The rise and fall can be shown in striking degree by using in the course of the experiment some marked stimulus, but even when no special stimulus is applied to the organs of sense, there is a continuous flux and change in the circulatory activities. Here, again, it is unnecessary to point out that consciousness is constantly changing, and that it changes most noticeably with the application of an external stimulus. Indeed, so close is the relation between activity and sensation in this latter case that it may safely be said that there is never a change in sensory excitation without a parallel change in circulatory activity.

Disappointment as negative emotion. Another case of this internal type of reaction is to be found in the fact that the body is from time to time thrown back on itself. For example, one starts to go about some ordinary task and finds that the energy he had mustered up for the work cannot be used because he cannot find the tools for his work. The energy which was to be expended in doing the work is thrown back into the body, and the inner agitation is accompanied by what we call in ordinary life disappointment. Here the nervous agitation is in the nature of a disagreeable stopping of movements which were originally directed outward but have suddenly been thrown inward.

External attitudes. There are many forms of reaction with an outward turn which are less emotional in character because the content of experience is less personal. We use in such cases terms like "satisfaction" or "interest." The man who makes a good stroke in golf enjoys it and gets satisfaction out of it, but he does not have so intense a personal experience as he has when he makes a bad stroke. The successful performance issues in a series of impressions and ideas rich in content; the unsuccessful act arouses violent internal circulatory reactions and unpleasant tensions of all the muscles of the body.

Attention as an attitude. There is one very general fact with regard to reactions to external objects. The individual either turns toward an object, looking toward it, reaching out for it, and bracing himself to deal with it, or else the individual turns away from an impression, neglecting it or actually rejecting it. The attitude side of these various forms of response is described by a general term, — the term "attention." One attends to an object or is interested in it, or in the other case he neglects it or exhibits a lack of interest or concentration on it.

Experiment to demonstrate tension. Attention is the attitude of reacting to an impression. The physical symptoms of attention are well known; there is the strained muscle, the fixed gaze, the leaning forward to catch the new impression which will in turn arouse more action. Much of the reaction exhibited in a state of attention is for the purpose of focusing the organs of sense on the source of the sensations. The infant is constantly trying to get into contact with everything for the purpose of getting more impressions.

All through life there is a tendency to move in the direction of an object which is in the center of attention. This is shown experimentally as follows: Let the person to be tested rest his hand on some recording apparatus which moves with very little friction. A board suspended by a long string and carrying a tracer at one end is a very good apparatus with which to make this experiment. Now let the subject close his eyes and think intently of his hand. The recording point will make short excursions back and forth, for there is no such condition as one of absolute rest of the hand muscles, and under the conditions arranged very slight movements are sufficient to produce a record. After noting the range and kind of movement which will be made when one thinks as steadily as he can of the hand, let the reactor think intently of some object at his right or left. Let him make an imaginary journey or draw in imagination some simple geometrical figure. The result will be that the movements of the recorder will be radically changed. There will often be a tendency for the new movement to take on a form directly related to the new subject of thought, but in any case there will be a change from the type of movement which appears when attention is concentrated on the hand, even if the form of the new movement is not directly traceable to the new experience. Fig. 45 shows the records of involuntary hand movements of the type described.

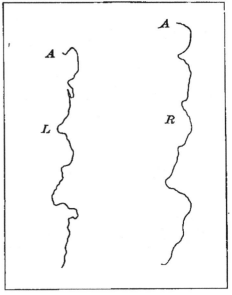

FIG. 45. Involuntary hand movements made by the right and left hands of an observer who is thinking of a building situated in front of him

The hands begin at the two points *A, A* ; the building lies in the direction of the movement which is here represented by the downward extension of the two lines. (After Jastrow)

Various forms of attention. Such an experiment reveals the reason for the use of words like " attention," "concentration," and " interest " as partial synonyms. The focusing of activity on an object arouses an emotional attitude ; hence we are justified in treating attention and feeling as closely related.

The explanation of attention will perhaps be understood most readily through consideration of those negative cases where the individual neglects the objects about him, as when we do not count the number of windows in a room. Here the impression goes into the nervous system, but is not made a center of any direct reaction. The impression is lost in the mass of reactions; it is not individualized. We say that it does not receive attention or arouse interest.

Sympathy with fellow beings. Such general comments on attention lead to the treatment of special cases. Whenever we see a fellow being trying to do something, we tend to share in the activity. The man who is lifting a weight arouses all who see him to like effort. The singer who is taking a high note will be followed by his audience with sympathetic muscular efforts. Attention in these cases issues in sympathetic action.

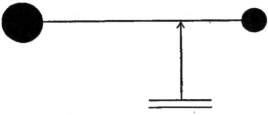

FIG. 46. Unæsthetical balance

The two black spots are evidently not well supported by the fulcrum shown in the figure. There is a restless feeling that the large figure should be supported by the observer

Sympathy involved in all recognition of objects. Sympathy extends far beyond one's fellow beings. All that we include under the term " æsthetical appreciation" belongs under the same heading. For example, let an observer look at an unsymmetrical drawing, such as that shown in Fig. 46. The long horizontal line with the black figures at its ends is not well supported at the fulcrum given in the figure. The feeling of lack of balance in this figure is directly related to an active tendency on the part of the observer to offer his support to the line as it carries the larger figure, and this tendency to action which is inspired by the figures is accompanied by a distinctly disagreeable experience, because it is continually ineffective in producing its purpose. Examples of the feeling of pleasure which comes from harmonious complexes can be derived from the study of Greek architectural forms. The Greeks recognized the fact that a column with perfectly straight lines is not an æsthetic object. Such a column always seems to be weaker in the center than at the extremities, where there are larger masses of matter. There is therefore a feeling of unrest inspired in the observer lest the column should give way in the center, where the tension is great and the material relatively reduced. The Greeks, accordingly, made their columns larger in the middle than at the extremities, and the result was that the observer, seeing the reënforcement at the critical part of the column, has a feeling of satisfaction rather than of unrest in looking at the lines. The term "sympathy" is not used here as a figure of speech. There is a real muscular tension involved in observing a column lifting a weight, and through this tension the observer enters into the situation as an active participator.

Illusion due to muscular tension. The presence of muscular tensions related to perception of weight can be demonstrated in certain special cases. If one prepares two blocks of exactly the same objective weight but of very different sizes, so that one is, for example, about a foot cube and the other three inches cube, the observer will find when he comes to lift these two blocks that the smaller block seems decidedly heavier than the larger one. The explanation of this fact is to be found in the muscular preparation of the observer when he first looks at the two blocks. The visual experience from the small block leads him to prepare to do a small amount of work in lifting it, while the visual impression of the larger block is recognized in terms of a totally different kind of muscular organization, which may be described by saying that the observer prepares to do more work in lifting the large block than he prepares to do in lifting the smaller one. When, with these differences of preparation, the observer lifts the two blocks, he finds that his preparation does not coincide with the demands forced upon him through his direct contact with the blocks. There is, therefore, a sharp disagreement between the original preparation based on vision and the subsequent experience dependent on touch. This disagreement expresses itself in the form of an illusion with regard to weight. This illusion is not due to sensations merely, but involves also preparation for active response. There can be no doubt that whenever one looks at any ordinary object of manageable size, he prepares to lift it. The preparation consists in an incipient act, and this act is the physiological parallel of an important phase of the observer's mental process of recognition.

Such muscular tensions common to many experiences. This illusion of weight and similar facts from practical life throw much light on the nature of the organization which was referred to when it was stated, in discussing the æsthetic attitude toward a column, that one sympathizes with the column in the work which it does in supporting the materials placed upon it. There is a certain direct perceptual estimation of the fitness of the column to do its work. That estimation expresses itself immediately in the muscular tension which is aroused in the observer as an integral part of the process of recognition. If the column is inadequate, the observer is led to a strained attitude of assisting it; if the column is adequate to its task, there is an attitude of satisfied recognition.

All consciousness a form of sympathetic attention. Thus we find that as human attitudes become more complex they are something more than feelings or emotions; they include also sympathies and discriminations which become parts of higher intellectual recognitions. When one sympathizes with a column, it is not a mere vague, general response; it is a discriminating response, bringing one into personal relations to the outer world. In all the higher stages of mental development one knows objects through one's sympathies with them.

The discussion of attitudes leads us thus to broad conclusions about the nature of consciousness. Consciousness is a function through which the individual attempts to put himself in harmony with the outer world. He translates the world into terms of his own responses and thus makes the objects outside of himself a part of his own inner life. After he has thus taken the outer world into his mental life, a new possibility arises — that of carrying back into the external world some of the rearrangements which are first worked out in the purely subjective sphere. The individual, by first fitting himself to the outer world, learns how to mold the outer world to meet his inner needs and desires.

Attitudes as related to higher processes of recognition. Psychology must study, then, those attitudes of feeling and sympathy by which the inner world absorbs impressions and makes them into personal experiences. It must then take up the higher processes through which inner experience is made effective in controlling the world from which impressions first came.

CHAPTER VIII

COMBINATION AND ARRANGEMENT OF SENSATIONS

Sensory experience always complex. The arrival of a sense impression in the central nervous system has been shown in earlier chapters to be only the first step in a series of processes in which this impression is combined with other sensory impressions and carried forward to a motor discharge. It is literally true that no sense impression ever comes into the central nervous system alone. Even if we think of only a single 'sense organ, we realize that it sends to the central nervous system at every moment a series of impressions rather than a single sensation. Thus, when the eye is stimulated by a colored surface, it is not a single sensation which arrives in consciousness, but a whole mass of sensations. The different parts of the field would yield various shades and intensities even if the receiving cells in the eye were all alike and all prepared to respond with absolute uniformity to the stimulus. But, as was shown in the chapter on sensation, various parts of the retina are different in their ability to receive impressions. The result is that a colored surface is the source of a most complex series of sensations.

The matter is further complicated by the simultaneous arrival of impressions through different senses. Thus we not only see a surface, we also touch it and may smell it or hear it vibrate. At any given moment there are impressions reaching the senses not from a single object alone but from various objects. As we look at a colored surface we receive touch sensations from contact with our clothing and from the floor on which we stand; we hear sounds from the next room and breathe in odors which have no relation to the colored surface.

Sensation combinations or fusions. In the midst of all this world of sensations there must be selection and combination. The individual works out, in the interests of practical life, certain units of experience in which sensations are fused with each other and distinguished from the rest of the world. For example, one sees an orange. What he really sees is a complex background in the midst of which there is a little patch of orange shade. He gets a mass of odors, but attaches a particular aroma to the particular patch of color. He is able, in the course of this attention to his experience, to recognize that the color and the aroma are nearer his right hand than his left. What he has done in thus fusing a group of sensations and locating the fused group on the right is designated in technical psychological language by the term "perception." One perceives objects; that is, one recognizes certain groups of sensations as belonging together and as different from the rest of the world.

Space not a sensation, but a product of fusion. In the process of perceiving the world the individual develops certain types of conscious experience which must be distinguished from sensations. Space is such a product of organized experience. Space results from the fact that sensations take on what we may call "togetherness." Togetherness is a product of fusion. The counterpart of togetherness is separateness. The perceived orange is distinguished from other objects. The whole complex of togetherness and separateness ultimately gets arranged into a general map or system. In this system there ultimately comes to be a right and left, an up and down. The world is now recognized as arranged in order.

Tactual space as a simple example of fusion. One of the earliest experimental studies in space perception dealt with the spatial arrangement of tactual experiences. In his effort to find some method of testing the sensitivity of the skin, Weber measured the distances which must lie between two stimulated points on the skin in different parts of the body before the points may be recognized as separate. He found that in much-used regions, such as the ends of the fingers, the lips, and the tongue, the distances which are necessary between points, in order that they may be distinguished, are very small, often less than a single millimeter; while on the upper arm or the middle of the back the points must be separated by three to six centimeters in order to be recognized as two. Furthermore, as has been abundantly shown since the time of Weber, there is the greatest uncertainty in the estimation of distances and directions in the regions where discrimination of points is difficult.

Subjective and objective space. On the basis of these facts we may emphasize the difference between external space and our recognition of space. Two millimeters of extension on the middle of the back are for the geometrician equivalent in all respects to the same distance on the finger. For the observer who perceives these two regions through the sense of touch, the recognition of the two distances is not a geometrical fact, uniform for all parts of the body, but a complex of varying experiences.

Perception and training. Experiments of the kind which Weber tried can be carried farther. Thus, it has been shown that after a little training regions of the skin where the discrimination was relatively difficult can be developed so as to permit of very much finer discrimination than that which was exhibited at first. In other words, without any radical change in the sensory conditions, practice will rapidly refine space perception. Again, if any region of the skin is stimulated by means of a continuous line rather than by two separate points, it will be found that the greater mass of sensations received from the line facilitates discrimination. A line can be recognized as having extension when it is about one third as long as the distance between two points which are just discriminated as separate from each other. The difficulty of discriminating two points when they are presented alone is not due to the character of the sensations from the points, but rather to the difficulty of discriminating them without the aid of a more complete sensory series derived from the stimulation of points between.

Development of spatial arrangements in the course of individual experience. In our search for an explanation of the facts of tactual perception of space, let us ask what is the course of individual development. Anyone who observes an infant recognizes that early in life there is the greatest uncertainty in locating stimulations on the skin. If the skin of an infant is vigorously stimulated either by some accident or by the efforts of someone who is interested in making an experimental investigation, it will be found that the infant moves its hands about in the most indefinite fashion, often failing entirely to reach the irritated spot. We can understand the infant's difficulty if we try to locate with precision some point which has been stimulated on the skin of the upper arm. The infant has sensation enough, just as we have when stimulated in an undeveloped region, but the sensation is not properly related to other sensations. It has no recognized relations which give it a definite place in a well-ordered sequence of tactual or visual qualities, because the well-ordered sequence has not yet been built up. An established series of relations of some definite kind is necessary before the sensation can enter into distinct spatially-ordered percepts. Until a definite series of space notions is developed, the sensation will enter only into vague fusions, and localization will be altogether incomplete. The change from vague to definite localization requires much experience and attention. Indeed, it is a fact easily verified that no sensation becomes definite in its relations until the practical needs of life demand such definiteness. The reason why an adult discriminates points on the end of the finger and not those on his back is that in the course of life he has been obliged to use his finger sensations. Use has led to an arrangement of points, to the development of what may figuratively be called a map. This map is developed by recognizing again and again the relation of a finger to the palm of the hand and of the palm of the hand to the elbow, and so on, until the various parts of the body are thought of as in a fixed relation. The map then takes on a kind of independence and remains in the mind as distinct from any particular sensations. The adult knows the parts of his body even when they are not actually stimulated at the moment.

Vision and movement as aids to touch. This process of developing definiteness in tactual localization has undoubtedly been very greatly facilitated by the presence of vision. Even in adult life one can often find himself making his experience of a tactual stimulation more exact and complete by looking at the point irritated, thus relating the tactual sensation to visual sensations. The process of localization of tactual sensations is also very largely dependent on movement. It is an empirical fact that the perceptual arrangement of skin sensations is most complete in the most mobile parts of the body. A number of careful experimental observers at one time explored the whole surface of the skin and showed that in any given region that part which is most mobile is the part on which points are most easily discriminated. Thus the hand is the most highly developed part of the arm ; the foot is the most highly developed part of the leg.

Tactual percepts of the blind. In some respects' the tactual perception of blind persons is more highly developed than that of persons who have vision. The blind are not supplied with better organs of touch, but they make more discriminating use of such experiences as they receive through the skin. They also make more use of movements than do normal persons, as may be observed in the fact that they restlessly explore every object which comes within their reach. The limitations of the space perception of the blind appear when complex objects are presented for recognition. When the mass of sensory impressions is great, the discrimination and fusion of these sensations become very difficult. This fact is strikingly illustrated by the history of the raised letters used in books for the blind. The most natural way of producing such books, and the way which was followed at first, was to print in raised lines the same letter forms as were used for persons who read visually. For vision the complex lines of ordinary printed letters offer no difficulties, because vision is so highly organized that it discriminates easily the ordinary printed forms. No one realized that touch being so much coarser than vision would discriminate forms less easily. Such proved, however, to be the case. The letters for the blind have, accordingly, been simplified until in one of the best and most recent systems the letters are made up entirely of points. These points are easy to distinguish and, being placed near one another, are also easy to recognize in groups.

Wundt on the tactual perception of the blind. The character of tactual perception in the case of the blind is thus illustrated and discussed by Wundt :

The way in which the blind alphabet is read shows clearly how the space ideas of the blind have developed. As a rule, the index fingers of both hands are used in blind reading. The right finger precedes and apprehends a group of points simultaneously (synthetic touch), the left finger follows somewhat more slowly and apprehends the single points successively (analytic touch).

Both the synthetic and analytic impressions are united and referred
to the same object. This method of procedure shows clearly that
the spatial discrimination of tactual impressions is no more immediately given in this case than in the case where vision was present,
but that in the case of the blind the movements by means of which
the finger that is used in analytic touch passes from point to point
play the same part as did the accompanying visual ideas in the
normal cases with vision.

Lotze's local signs. Another method of describing the tactual perception of space is that adopted by Lotze, one of the
earliest of the writers on physiological psychology. Every
point on the surface of the body gives rise, said Lotze, to a
tactual sensation which in addition to its general quality and
intensity as a tactual sensation has a peculiar and characteristic shading due to the structure of the skin at the particular
point where the stimulus is applied. Thus, if the same pressure is applied to the lips and the forehead, the resulting sensations will, in spite of general likeness, be slightly different
in the two cases, because there is soft muscular tissue under
the skin of the lips and hard bony tissue under the skin of
the forehead. These slight differences between tactual sensations which are due to locality lead the observer to arrange
his tactual sensations in certain systems or series. The qualitative shadings are thus transformed into spatial series. The
qualitative differences come to signify position and are consequently designated as local signs. Their character as *local
signs* is derived from the spatial system to which they are
referred; they are individually merely qualitative differences.

Inner tactual factors. The factors which enter into tactual
space percepts are probably derived in part from the inner
organs, such as the semicircular canals, the joints, and the
muscles. From the semicircular canals, as pointed out in
an earlier chapter, there is a constant stream of excitations
reaching the central nervous system with every change in
the position of the body. The limbs in their movements

give rise to sensations in the joints and muscles. While the child is exploring the surface of his body and attaining the degree of ability to discriminate points which is shown by Weber's experiments, he is also learning through muscle sensations to recognize distances away from the surface of his body by reaching for things about him. He is learning through the sensations from his semicircular canals that there is a fundamental distinction between " right side up " and oblique or inverted positions. He is learning through joint sensations to recognize how many steps must be taken to cross certain stretches of space.

Space not attached to any single sense. The striking fact is that ultimately all these different sensory factors are arranged into the same space form. There is not one tactual space, and another space for muscle sensations, and another for joint sensations. All are fused into a single system. The spatial order is a relational fact; that is, it is a product of the fusion or putting together of sensations. Whenever sensations are fused into the spatial relation they take on a character different from that which can be assigned to them when they are considered alone.

General conclusions regarding tactual space. From this survey of the facts of tactual space we have derived several important conclusions. Space is a complex. Space is not a sensation quality, but a relational form of experience. Tactual space is not explicable without reference to the general formula of organization which includes other sensations also.

We are, accordingly, justified in postponing the general explanation of space perception until we have taken up the facts regarding the arrangement of auditory and visual sensations in the spatial form.

Auditory recognition of location. Experiments on the localization of sounds may be made as follows : Let a sound be produced in the median plane, which passes vertically through the head from in front backward, midway between the two ears. If the sound is simple in quality, as, for example, a sharp click of some kind, and the observer's eyes are closed so as to eliminate vision and make him entirely dependent on hearing, the localization of the sound will in the majority of cases be erroneous. The sound will always be localized somewhere in the median plane, but its exact position in this plane cannot be recognized. If, on the other hand, the sound is moved slightly to the right or left of the median plane, it will be found that the observer can localize the sound with great accuracy. The explanation of the observer's ability to locate sounds coming from the side is simple and depends chiefly upon the fact that the observer receives from such a sound different intensities of sensation in the two ears. From all positions in the median plane the two groups of sensations received in the two ears have equal intensities, whereas the intensities of sounds received in the two ears from any position outside of the median plane are unequal.

Influence of movements in auditory experience of position. Undoubtedly here, as in the case of tactual space, the facts of movement are of great significance in organizing sensory experience. If a sound on one side of the head is more intense than the sound on the other, there will be a strong tendency to readjust the head in such a way that the stronger sound shall be made even more intense and the weaker group of sensations shall be made still fainter by the movement of the head. If a sound is in the median plane and there is difficulty in getting at its precise localization, there is frequently a noticeable effort on the part of the observer to bring the head into such a position that a more satisfactory determination of position shall be possible through a modification of the intensities of the sensations from the two ears. Often auditory perception issues in a movement which tends to bring the eyes toward the source of the sound. The same tendency which was noted in the discussion of tactual sensations to fuse various kinds of sensations into a single spatial system is obvious in this effort to supplement hearing by vision.

Qualitative differences and localization. The explanation which has been presented can be made more elaborate by giving attention to qualitative differences as well as to differences in intensity in the two groups of sensations received by the two ears. There can be no doubt that the external pinna of the ear modifies somewhat the character of the sound as it enters the auditory canals. If a complex sound strikes the pinna from in front, its quality will be different from that which would result if the same sound is carried into the ear from behind. As a result of these qualitative modifications produced by the external ear, we are able to localize sounds even in the median plane, provided they are of complex quality. The human voice, for example, in the median plane of the head, can usually be recognized with great precision as coming from a point in front or behind. This is due to the fact that the voice is complex in quality.

Distance of sounds recognized only indirectly. The discussion of the recognition of the direction from which sounds come may be supplemented by reference to the fact that the recognition of the distance of sounds also involves a large body of organized experiences. If one hears the human voice sounding very faintly in his ears, his frequent experience with voices and their normal intensity when the speakers are near at hand will lead him to recognize that the person speaking is far away. Furthermore, the qualitative character of the sound as well as its intensity is modified by the remoteness of its source, the elements of the sound being less distinct when it is transmitted from a great distance to the ear. The intensity and quality are, accordingly, both utilized in interpretations of distance so long as the sound is familiar.

Unfamiliar sounds difficult to locate. In contrast to the relatively easy estimation of the distance of a familiar sound, it is extremely difficult to estimate the distance of the source of an unfamiliar sound. An experiment may be tried by producing an unfamiliar sound, such as that which results from snapping a card in the neighborhood of an observer's head. Until this sound has become familiar the errors in estimation of distance will be very noticeable.

Visual space and optical illusions. If we turn from auditory space perception to visual experiences, we find a rich variety of examples which show how complex is the process

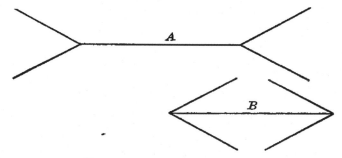

FIG. 47. Müller-Lyer illusion

The length of the horizontal line *A* is equal to the length of the horizontal line *B*.
(For further discussion of the figure see text)

of arranging sensations in a spatial order. There are certain cases of incorrect perception of length and direction of figures in plane surfaces, constituting what are known as geometrical optical illusions. These are especially clear examples of complex perception. Take, for example, the illusion represented in Fig. 47. The two lines *A* and *B* are in reality equal to each other, but the observer will recognize at once that they seem to be of different lengths. The retinal image of each line is distinct and clear; the apparent inequality cannot, therefore, be attributed to any confusion in the retinal processes; it must be attributed to some kind of perceptual complexity. The explanation of the source of this illusion has been the subject of much discussion, and it is probably true that no single statement will account for the apparent inequality of A and B. In a general way it may be said that one cannot look at A and B without including in his field of vision the oblique lines, and the oblique lines are such striking and unfamiliar additions to the horizontal lines that they are not neglected as they should be in perceiving the length of the horizontals. If, in addition to this general statement, we attempt to show in detail how the oblique lines affect the horizontals, there are a number of facts which may be noted. The oblique lines produce less of an effect upon some observers than upon others. This can be shown by making quantitative determinations of the intensity of the illusion. For this purpose one of the figures of the pair under discussion is made adjustable, and the observer sets it until it seems to him equal to the other figure. When the two seem equal they will be in reality different. The amount of difference can now be readily measured, and the results from various observers compared. Not only are the results of such measurements different for different observers, but the same individual will at various times give different results.

Effects of practice. One especially significant case of individual variation is that in which the observer deliberately sets about comparing the figures a great number of times for the purpose of becoming familiar with them. Three stages of change in interpretation show themselves in such a practice series. First, the observer takes a general view of the whole figure, as does the ordinary observer who looks casually at the illusion; he gets in this case a strong illusion. Second, the observer tries to look at the long lines and neglect the obliques; that is, he makes an effort to overcome the disturbing influence in a negative way. During this period of conscious neglect of the obliques the illusion grows somewhat weaker, but it does not disappear. Finally, in the third stage, the observer reaches the point where there is no need of an effort to neglect the obliques. Interpretation may be said to be so completely worked out in this stage that the obliques and the long lines fall into their proper relations without interfering with one another. Each is included in the percept, but in its true significance. At this stage the illusion is entirely overcome.

Percepts always complex. Such facts as these make it clear that a visual percept includes all the factors in the field of vision. If these factors are conflicting, they may result in grotesque misinterpretations. If, on the other hand, they are thoroughly assimilated into the percept, they

FIG. 48. Illusion of contrast

The middle portion of the short horizontal line marked off by the verticals seems longer than the equal distance marked off in the long horizontal line

take their appropriate relations and no longer disturb the total process of perception.

Contrast. A great many other illustrations could be brought forward to show the relation of one part of the visual field to all other parts. Thus, one cannot look at a line on a large blackboard and fail to be influenced in his estimation of the length of the line by the large surrounding space. Conversely, a line drawn on a small sheet of paper is always interpreted in terms of the paper as either relatively long or relatively short. Objects seem very different in size when seen outdoors and again in a small room. Fig. 48 illustrates this principle by showing a short central line as part of a long line in one case and as part of a short line in a second case, with the result that the central line seems to be of different lengths in the two cases.

Common facts showing size to be a matter of relations.
Other complications than those from the surrounding visual
field also influence one's perception of size. The natural
standards of size which depend upon familiarity and upon
the relations of objects to one's own body are constantly
influencing perception. Time and again descriptions have
been given by observers of the fact that a road seems
longer the first time one passes over it, when all the
sights are unfamiliar; and many have also referred to the
fact that places known in childhood always seem small when
revisited in mature life.

Physiological conditions of visual perception. The significance of all these facts for our understanding of visual space
is not hard to find. Putting the matter in physiological
terms, we may say that when series of visual stimulations
from a given line or figure reach the visual center, they find
there a larger series of excitations from other points on the
retina and a series of organized modes of response derived
from past experience. Each excitation takes its place in
this complex.

Psychological statement. Putting the same matter in psychological terms, we may say that every sensation becomes
part of a fixed order. This order or spatial arrangement is
something other than the sensations; it is a product of
perceptual fusion.

Photographic records of percepted movements. A clearer
understanding of the matter will be reached by considering
the results of photographic investigations, in which the path
of the eye movement in looking over certain illusory figures
has been determined. In Fig. 49 there is presented one of
the most striking of the illusions of direction. The long lines
are in reality parallel with each other, but the obliques are
far too distracting to permit the ordinary observer to recognize the true relations between the parallel lines. Fig. 50
shows another illusion of direction. The oblique lines are

parts of a single line, but seem to extend in slightly different directions because of the interrupting space between the

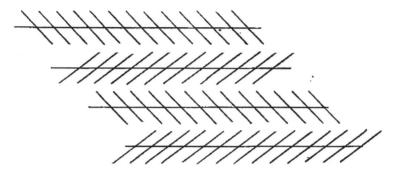

FIG. 49. Zöllner illusion

The long lines are parallel with each other

parallels. Fig. 51 shows the paths in which photographs indicate that the eye of an observer moved in attempting to look at the illusions discussed. In Fig. 51, *A*, the movement over the Zöllner pattern is shown. It is evident from the movements indicated in the photographs that the sensation factors are not fully mastered so as to permit coördinated movements along the parallel lines. The result is that though these lines give perfectly clear retinal images, they do not stand in their true relations in experience. The photographs show that often there is sufficient fusion of the sensory factors to permit a single movement in following a line, and this single movement is in the general part of the field of vision in which the line lies, but it is only a gross general approximation to the line. This corresponds exactly to the fact that the experience of the figure consists of a gross general perception of the long line and its obliques. One observer, after these preliminary photographs of his eye movements in looking at the Zöllner

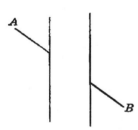

FIG. 50. Poggendorff illusion

A, B are parts of the same straight line

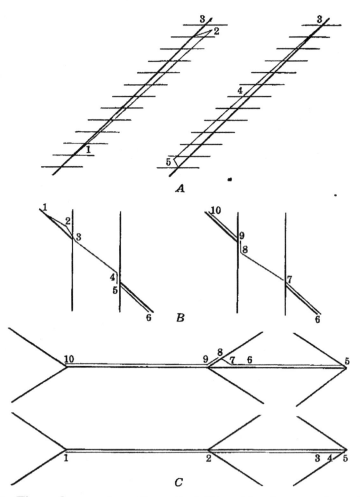

FIG. 51. These figures show the path followed by the eye of an observer
in examining certain of the foregoing illusions

In each of the figures the path of the eye movement is indicated by a supplementary line. The numbers placed along these supplementary lines indicate the points
at which a pause was made in the course of the eye movement. In Fig. 51, *A*, the
observer was attempting to follow the long line of the illusion. It will be noticed
that he departs from the long line, and at the extreme end of the movement, as at
2 and 5, makes a short corrective movement by which he again fixates the long
line. In Fig. 51, *B*, the distracting influence of the vertical lines is obvious, as is also
the difficulty of moving the eye across the open space in any such way as to reach
the point of interconnection between the vertical and oblique lines. In Fig. 51, *C*,
it will be noted that the eye movement is very free in that part of the figure which
is overestimated, and much restricted whenever the eye approaches one of the
acute angles. This is indicated by the frequent pause in 3, 4, 6, 7, 8, 9. In 8 it
will be noted that the eye is deflected from the horizontal line by the oblique

pattern, put himself through a series of quantitative tests with the figure. In this practice series he gradually overcame the distracting effects of the oblique lines, and the illusion disappeared. A second series of photographs taken after the practice series showed that his eye followed the long line with great precision. Photographs with other illusions show clearly the distracting effects of the additional lines as indicated in full in Fig. 46.

Relation between size and distance. When we study the relation of size to distance from the observer, we find a series of complexities even greater than those which have appeared thus far. In order to demonstrate this experimentally an observer should first secure an after-image through the steady fixation of some bright object. The after-image covers a certain number of retinal elements and may be considered as giving, as long as it lasts, a constant group of sensations. When the observer is looking at the object this mass of sensations will be interpreted as having a certain definite size and distance. When the same mass of impressions comes from the after-image, it can easily be related to different distances, and with each change in apparent distance it will take on a different apparent size. The change in distance can easily be produced by looking at various surfaces which are at different distances. The after-image will seem in each case to be on the surface at which the observer is looking at the moment, whatever the distance of that surface. The after-image will seem smaller when the surface on which it is projected is nearer than the original object from which the image was derived, and larger when the surface is farther away.

Definite optical relation between the distance and the size of an object and the size of the retinal image from this object. This series of observations makes it clear that the size of a retinal image does not determine the interpretation of the size of an object without reference to the additional fact of distance. A given retinal image, for the after-image on the retina remained the same throughout the series of observations, may be interpreted as a large object far away or as a small object near at hand. The optical principle which underlies this series of observations is illustrated in Fig. 52. In this figure the retinal image is represented by the inverted arrow *AB*, and the lines from the extremities of this image passing through the optical center of the lens determine the positions of various external objects, any one of which satisfies the image. It will be seen from this

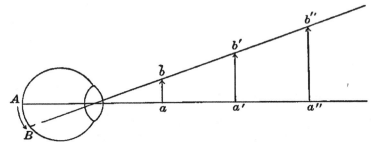

FIG. 52. The retinal image *A B* may be equally well related to any one of the objects *ab*, *a'b'*, *a''b''*

drawing that a succession of arrows outside of the eye, differing in length from each other, may all cast the same retinal image. This general principle is doubtless familiar to everyone when stated in the following simple terms: A small object such as the finger held near the eye can shut out the image of a large remote object, such as a tree or a building. When, now, the after-image in the experiment is projected to distances near and far away, its significance and perceptual interpretation are immediately modified, even though the retinal sensations are uniform in volume and distribution on the sensory surface of the eye.

Berkeley's statement of the problem of visual depth perception. These observations lead us to a problem which was so clearly stated by one of the early writers in the modern period of psychology that we may quote his statement in full. In a treatise published in 1709 Bishop Berkeley said:

> It is, I think, agreed by all that distance of itself, and immediately, cannot be seen. For distance being a line directed endwise to the eye, it projects only one point on the fund of the eye — which point remains invariably the same, whether the distance be longer or shorter. I find it also acknowledged that the estimate we make of the distance of objects considerably remote is rather an act of judgment grounded on experience than of sense.

Berkeley goes forward in the remainder of the "Essay toward a New Theory of Vision" to account for this process, which he calls a process of judgment. He draws attention to the fact that whenever one looks at an object near at hand he rotates his two eyes toward the nose so that the points of view from which he observes the object are different in the two eyes. He asserts that the convergence of the two eyes, as their inward rotation is called, gives rise to certain experiences of movement, which are utilized as interpreting factors.

Experiments on binocular vision. The researches of modern experimental psychology have confirmed, in general, Berkeley's explanation, though they emphasize more than he did the differences between the two sets of retinal impressions received in the two eyes. The fact that the two eyes contribute a complex of sensations through which we perceive distance has been abundantly confirmed. The reasoning involved is as follows: If distance is recognized as a result of a complex of sensations coming from the two eyes, then it should be possible to show that the recognition of depth is seriously interfered with by the withdrawal of any of the factors contributed by the two eyes. It is not possible to remove altogether the influence of both eyes, even when one is closed; hence, vision can never be reduced to strictly monocular vision, but the following simple experiment may be tried to show the dependence of the clear recognition of depth upon vision with two eyes. If an observer covers one eye and then attempts to bring his finger directly over some object which stands in front of the open eye, he will find that the ability to bring the finger directly over the object in question is very much less than his ability to do so under the ordinary conditions of binocular vision. A direct observation of the same general fact can be made if the observer will note carefully the difference in the apparent solidity and remoteness of objects when he observes them first with a single eye and immediately afterward with both eyes open. These observations show that the complete recognition of distance and depth involves all the sensory factors from the two eyes; whenever there is any disturbance of the normal conditions the result appears in incomplete perception, for the relational or perceptual process does not in such cases have its normal complex of content with which to deal.

Difference between the images in the two eyes. The contributions made to experience by the two eyes are different, as can be clearly seen if an observer will hold some solid object near the face and look at it, first with one eye open and then with the other. The difference between the two views in the two eyes can be briefly defined by saying that with the right eye one sees more of the right side of a solid object and less of the left side, while with the left eye one sees more of the left side of a solid object and less of the right side. These relations are made clear in Fig. 53. When the two retinal images from the solid object are received by an observer, they are immediately fused with each other into a single perceptual complex, as were the two groups of auditory sensations discussed in an earlier section of this chapter.

Stereoscopic figures and appearance of solidity. There is an apparatus often used for purposes of amusement, in which the principle that the appearance of solidity depends upon disparity of the two retinal images is utilized to produce the appearance of solidity even when no solid object is present. The apparatus in question is the stereoscope. Photographs are taken or drawings are made, corresponding in form to the retinal images which would be obtained by two eyes if they were looking at a solid figure or series of figures at different depths. The two drawings or photographs are then projected by means of the stereoscope into the two eyes of an observer in such a way that the right retina is stimulated by the image appropriate to the right eye, and the left retina is stimulated by the figure appropriate to the left eye. The observer, who thus receives the sensory impressions appropriate to solidity, will naturally fuse the two images and will see in space before him a solid object which, in reality,

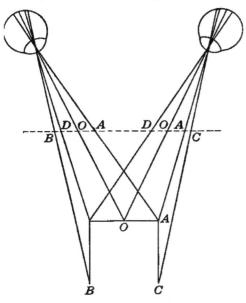

FIG. 53. Showing binocular parallax

The cube *BDAC* is held near the two eyes with the result that the right eye sees the surface *DA* and the right side of the cube, while the left eye sees the surface *DA* and the left side of the cube. If a plane is passed through the rays of light which enter the eye from the cube, as indicated by the dotted line in the figure, it will be seen that the retinal images of the two eyes contain each a distinct element. The eye on the left-hand side of the figure has a retinal image corresponding to *BD*, which is absent in the other eye. Further details will be obvious from the figure

is not there, but which is adequately represented by the two flat drawings projected into his eyes. A great many experiments can be tried with the stereoscope which make clear the significance of the two retinal images for the recognition of solidity and depth. It can thus be shown that the fused resultant, that is, the percept of a solid object, does not derive its characteristics from either one of the retinal impressions considered in itself, for each image so considered is deficient in solidity. The fusion is, in a very proper sense of the word, a compromise between the two different images, and there appears as a result of fusion at least one characteristic which neither figure had in itself; namely, the characteristic of clearly defined solidity.

Retinal rivalry. When the binocular images are totally different, as in certain experiments which may be arranged with the stereoscope, the observer finds that it is impossible for him to fuse the two groups of impressions. Thus, if he looks with one eye at a series of horizontal lines, and with the other at a series of vertical lines, he will see the fields in succession. The group of sensations coming from one retina will first be recognized in clear consciousness and will then fade out and give place to the sensations derived from the second retina. There is thus an oscillation in experience which is vividly described by the term "retinal rivalry." In retinal rivalry there is obviously a lack of fusion of the sensations. The artificial differences in binocular images here produced are so foreign to the experiences which present themselves in ordinary life that the observer is unable to fuse them into a single conscious process. If such strange combinations of sensations are to be in any way related, it must be in a temporal succession of mental activities rather than in a single spatial form.

Factors other than those contributed by the two eyes. The recognition of depth through the fusion of two groups of retinal sensations is not the only form of visual recognition of depth. Other factors of experience and other types of relation may enter into the complex. In every case, however, the factors or relations which contribute to the interpretation of solidity are, like the differences in binocular vision just discussed, complexes which get their significance and value not because of their sensation qualities but by virtue of the relations into which the sensations are brought.

Aërial perspective. The first facts to which reference may be made are the differences in colors and sharpness of outline which appear when objects are seen through different thicknesses of atmosphere. Remote colors are always dull and darker in shade than colors near at hand, and the outlines of remote objects are ill-defined. We are so trained in the interpretation of these general facts that in looking at a landscape we pay very little attention to color quality or to the lack of clearness in outline, but utilize these immediately for purposes of depth perception; that is, the sensations are not recognized as distinct facts in experience, but are allowed to serve their function, which is to indicate the position of the object from which they come. Let the observer carefully compare his experience of distant fields in the landscape with fields near at hand. He will find that the remoter greens are blue in cast, even though under ordinary circumstances his attention is not directed to these differences in color shades. The same truth is well illustrated by the fact that persons who have been accustomed to living in a moist atmosphere always misinterpret distances when they go to regions where the air is clear and free from moisture. Great distances seen through clear air are underestimated because of the small effect which the air produces in modifying the colors and outlines of objects.

Geometrical perspective and familiarity. Another important means of recognizing depth is through the familiarity which we have acquired with certain common objects. If a given object is carried farther and farther away from the eye, it will cast upon the retina a smaller and smaller image. If a man first observed at a distance of ten feet moves to a distance of twenty feet, the size of the retinal image and, consequently, the mass of sensations derived from this man will decrease one half. We seldom interpret such changes in the size of a retinal image of a familiar object as changes in the size of the object itself; thus, we never say that a receding man has dwarfed to half his original size. We have learned by long experience that most of the objects of our environment are permanent in size and that the changes in our sensations merely indicate changes in the position of these objects. In this way we build up an elaborate series of recognitions of differences in depth. How completely we depend upon this recognition of familiar objects for our interpretation of unfamiliar or undefined experiences will be recognized if it is remembered that the interpretation of the size and distance of objects in photographs is always uncertain unless some familiar figure, such as that of a human being, appears as a scale by which to gauge the sizes of the other objects.

Shadows. Another factor which is sometimes significant in giving rise to the interpretation of depth is found in the shadows cast by objects. The apparent solidity of a bank of clouds in the sky cannot depend upon binocular differences, because the clouds are too remote. They are also quite unfamiliar, and may be without color; therefore the methods of interpretation which we have described up to this point are quite inadequate to explain their apparent solidity. The shadows which they cast upon each other are, however, so clear in their indication of differences of position with reference to the sun that we immediately recognize a bank of shaded clouds as made up of parts differing in distance from us. The same principle of recognition of solidity is utilized in all flat drawings intended to represent solid objects. Such flat drawings can always be made to suggest solidity with vividness when they are shaded in a way corresponding to the objects themselves.

Intervening objects. Finally, we make use of the fact that near objects very frequently cut off our vision of remote objects. Thus, if a tree which can be seen in all of its parts cuts off a portion of a house or other object, we perceive the house not as divided by the tree but as standing behind it. Here again we interpret our sensations as indicating differences in position rather than differences in the objects themselves.

Depth a matter of complex perception. One cannot review this series of facts with regard to the visual interpretation of depth without being confirmed in his view that space perception is a process in which sensory factors are related to each other in the most complex manner. No retinal impression has its value for mental life fully determined until it is brought into relation with other sensations.

Relation to movements. As in the case of tactual percepts, so here there is a close relation between visual space and movements. In the first place, movements of the eyes are intimately related in their development to visual recognition of space. When an infant attempts to turn his two eyes on the same point of fixation, his movements are frequently so slow and irregular that they have the appearance, especially in photographs, of cross-eyed movements. Even in adult life it is shown by rapid photographs that the two eyes often move to a point of fixation in such a way that while one eye moves rapidly, the other comes up in an irregular, relatively slow movement. The development of a coördinated movement is thus seen to be the product of effort and concentration. That a coördinated movement has been developed at all shows how significant it is for the individual that he should acquire a unitary motor response to the complex of retinal sensations. The unity of response stands, indeed, in sharpest contrast to the complexity of the sensory factors. The organized ability to coördinate the two eyes depends on the development of a system in which each phase of experience, without losing its individual reality, is taken up in the single unitary system. Space and the coördinated system of ocular movements are thus seen to be very intimately related. The complex of movements has a unity which results from the union of all of the different phases of binocular movement into a single coördinated act. Space is also a system in which every point has a certain character of its own and at the same time has characteristics which attach to it as part of the general system.

General movements as conditions of fusion of retinal sensations. In the second place, the relation of visual space perception to organized behavior becomes clearer when it is noticed that the unity of visual percepts is demanded not only in the coördinations of eye movements but also in the coördinations of all forms of behavior which are guided by vision. If one reaches out his hand to grasp an object, his sensory impressions of the object will be derived from two eyes, but the reaction to be effective must be to all the sensations at once.

Space a system of relations developed through fusion. Our treatments of space perception in the sphere of touch, hearing, and vision bring us to a general conclusion that space is a closed system built up through the fusion of sensations and, further, that this system is closely related to bodily movements.

Movement and mechanical laws. The evidence that there is a close relation between space and bodily movement appears in the fact that space as we perceive it expresses those mechanical laws which govern all bodily movements. Human central nervous organization and related muscular movements are, from the very nature of mechanical law with which the movements must comply, capable of only a very definite system of developments. One cannot move his hand at the same time toward the left and the right. Left and right come to be, therefore, clearly distinguished directions in the organization of human responses to sensations. One cannot move his hand backward and forward in the same movement. As a result, all

sensations which are to be related to movements are ultimately assigned to places either in front or behind, never
in both positions at the same time. The child begins life
without a thorough organization of his movements and,
correspondingly, without any definite spatial forms of perception. The two develop together as he actively adjusts
himself to the world about him. Finally, as he becomes
master of his movements he finds that his perceptual world
also has taken on certain definite sequences of arrangement
which are so stable and systematic and so harmonious with
what he comes to know theoretically of mechanical law that
he can study the spatial system as he finds it in his perceptual consciousness and relate this spatial form of perception to his science of mechanics without the slightest fear
of finding any incongruity in the two groups of facts. It
should be noted here again that such a complete system of
space is much more than a series of sensations. Sensation
qualities are necessary as the factors with which the individual must deal; they constitute the material or content of
experience, but the spatial form of perception is a product
of perceptual fusion. Every sensation is related to every
other not because of its quality or intensity but because
every sensation must, in the organization of impressions,
take its place in a serial system before it can serve any definite function in individual life or have any clearly marked
place in consciousness.

Perception of individual objects. There are many forms
of perceptual fusion which supplement the fusions entering
into the closed system of space. To the ordinary observer
an object recognized through the two senses of taste and
smell is so unitary in character that he does not realize that
any fusion of discrete sensations has taken place. By a
simple experiment one can easily show that the perception
of any article of food involves a number of distinct sensations. Let the observer taste of some familiar substance,

such as coffee, and at the same time, by holding the nose, prevent the air from coming into contact with the olfactory organ, and coffee becomes a sweet liquid with little or no flavor ; even castor oil becomes an inoffensive thick oil under like conditions. Why is it that in ordinary experience tastes and odors are united? It is because, in spite of the separation of the gustatory and olfactory organs, there is a constant demand in life that tastes and odors shall be used together in guiding conduct. The whole inner organization of the individual is such that these different sensory qualities have a joint significance for perception and for behavior. There is a distinction on the qualitative side between tastes on the one hand, and odors on the other, because the sensory organs for the two qualities are different ; but there is the most intimate perceptual fusion to serve as a guide to conduct.

There are perceptual fusions in every sphere of sensation quite as compact as those of taste and smell and as various in character as the objects in the world about us.

Mere coexistence of sensations no explanation of unity in the percepts of objects. The physiological condition of this unity in the perception of single objects is not to be found in the sensory processes themselves, any more than was the physiological condition for the perception of space. The sensory processes derived from things are very different in type and in the points at which they are received into the central nervous system. The unity of perception is not to be accounted for by the fact that all the sensory excitations are in the brain together, for not all of the sensations that are in consciousness at the same time fuse into a single percept. When we recognize a single object we do so by distinguishing it from its surroundings as well as by fusing its various attributes into a single percept. Thus, one recognizes the book he is reading by distinguishing it from his hands and from the bookcase in the background.

Range of fusion determined by practical considerations.
Again, as in the treatment of the fusion which leads to
space perception, we must appeal to the central coördinations which are worked out under the stress of practical
demands. One fuses sensory factors into the percept of a
thing because he can adjust himself to certain aspects of
experience in a single act. Thus, one speaks of a bookcase and its contents as a single object when he merely
wishes to name over the articles of furniture in his room.
He distinguishes the separate books as objects when he
wishes to take them out and use them. The range of one's
experience of a thing is thus seen to depend not on sensory processes but on the practical motives which lead to
the synthesis -of more or less comprehensive groups of
these sensations into single phases of experience.

Changes in percepts through repetition. The fusion of
factors into single groups becomes easier after repetition.
Thus the expert rifleman comes to recognize at once the
movement of his game, the distance of the game from
himself, and the wind which will' influence his shot, factors
which might have coexisted indefinitely without being fused.
All this he has acquired as the result of repeated efforts to
shape his conduct in accordance with the demands of his
total environment. Indeed, such a case of acquired fusion of
widely divergent sensory factors may very frequently involve
in its earliest stages conscious effort to adapt action to whole
groups of sensations. The unity is made more and more
compact as repeated efforts are undertaken to recognize the
factors together, so that ultimately the perceptual unity, which
began in a conscious relating of factors, becomes a synthetic
unity of the ordinary type ; thus, we learn to see pen and
hand and paper together when we learn to write, until all
the factors which enter into the act of writing and its conscious control are unified, and the final consciousness seems
very simple, although it is a complex of many factors.

Parallel development of perception and habit. Discussions of perceptual fusion might be carried over directly into the discussion of habits so as to show that the development of organized perception and the development of organized activity always go hand in hand. The training of eye and hand in any technical art, of ear and vocal cords in singing or speaking, of ear and hand in playing a musical instrument, go together in practical experience. The expert in every line not only acts more skillfully but he sees or hears more skillfully and comprehensively. Perception is discriminative and complete just in so far as the factors of experience are organized into wholes appropriate for individual reaction. Our present purposes, however, can be fully satisfied without a complete study of habits. The perceptual fusion involved in the recognition of an object is one phase of organization ; habit is an expression of this organization and will be taken up in a separate, later chapter.

Time as a general form of experience. Before leaving the subject of perception it is important that we consider briefly a form of arrangement which has often been regarded as similar in character to the space form ; namely, time. Time, like space, involves a relation between several factors of experience. Like space, it is not a sensation quality. It is even more general in character than space, for it is not merely a form of perception ; it is also, and indeed chiefly, a form of the indirect, or memory, experiences. A percept is always in the time series, but it is always in that portion of the time series which we call "the present." It will, accordingly, be appropriate for us to discuss in this connection some of the attributes of "the present," leaving the other phases of time consciousness to be taken up in connection with memory.

Experimental determination of the scope of "the present." "The present" is not a single point of experience ; it is a group of experiences. Some experimental evidence as to the possible length of "the present" may be gained as follows: Tap rapidly on the table at intervals of half a second or less, producing a series of sounds, and find how many taps of this kind can be grouped into a single easily apprehended unity. The observer will have little difficulty in determining the limit of such a series if he will simply listen to the taps and refrain from counting. A short series of five or six taps will leave behind in consciousness a feeling of perfect definiteness and ease of apprehension. If such a series is exactly repeated, or if a second slightly different series is sounded, the observer will be in no doubt as to the likeness or unlikeness of the two series. If, on the other hand, a series of twenty or thirty taps is sounded, the observer will recognize that at a certain point in the series a state of confusion sets in. The series is no longer apprehended as a unity, but has a vaguely defined massiveness which seems to elude the mental grasp.

Scope of "the present" and its varying conditions. The ability of the observer to group together a series of experiences is radically modified when the series itself is changed. Thus, if every third tap is made stronger than the others, or if it is given a slightly different quality, as in a series of musical notes, the scope of the immediately recognized group will be much increased. If the taps come irregularly, either in point of interval or in point of intensity or quality, the scope of the unitary group will be decreased.

Time relations in verse and related systems of experience. All these facts appear in such practical forms of time perception as those which are utilized in making up English verse. The recognition of the successive feet in poetry is facilitated by grouping the sounds into simple compact groups. The character of each group is determined by variations in intensity, quality, and content in such a large number of ways as to satisfy the demand for novelty in experience, while at the same time retaining very fully the characteristics necessary for temporal uniformity in the successive groups of factors.

Time arrangement as conditioned by the rhythmical changes in nervous processes. To find a precise physiological basis for the time grouping of experience will require the discovery of processes which are much more general than those which constitute the physiological basis for space perception and for general perceptual unity as exhibited in the recognition of objects. Indeed, we must go far enough, as indicated above, to recognize that the conditions of temporal discrimination are involved in indirect memory processes even more than in perception. Such a general characteristic is to be found in the fact that all nervous processes are constantly fluctuating in intensity because the inner nervous condition is never in equilibrium. The nervous condition is a living process, now rising to a higher intensity, now declining to a low intensity. This can be seen if an observer will pick out in the constellation Pleiades a faint star which is just visible, and watch it for a time. He will find that it disappears and then reappears for an interval, only to disappear again. The rhythmical change is here so complete that it is perceived as a change in the object. A like fluctuation of intensity is present in all sensory impressions, even if the sensation is so strong that its decrease in intensity does not cause it to disappear entirely.

Perception more than the flux of sensations. In addition to the fluctuations in experience which result from the conditions in the nervous system, there are changes which arise from the relation of the observer to the object. For example, as one makes his way down the street he sees some object for a moment and then loses sight of it until he comes once more to a point from which he can observe it. In all this flux of experience action must be based on a recognition of the permanency of objects which transcends present sensations. We project our fluctuating sensations into a series which provides for time changes which are not changes in the things themselves. Thus we find new evidence that experience is organized out of sensations but goes far beyond sensory qualities and intensities in the attributes which it exhibits. Time is not a sensation; it is a form in which sensations are held because the mind recognizes in objects a permanency which extends beyond present personal experience.

SUMMARY

Discussions of perception. The discussion of perception may be closed with a brief summary. Perception involves, first, a spatial order; second, the compact fusion of sensations into percepts of separate objects in the world; and third, the beginning of a temporal order. The spatial arrangement is intimately connected with movement, being the arrangement given to sensory factors under the mechanical demands for characteristically different reactions to different sensory factors in the total mass of experience. Fusion of sensations into separate recognitions of objects is, like spatial arrangement, related to activity, for all those phases of sensory experience will be fused together which require one and the same response. Finally, time recognition depends on the flux in experience which comes to be recognized as a flux not interfering with the permanency of objects.

CHAPTER IX

HABITS

Organic retentiveness. Up to this point only casual reference has been made to the fact that the nervous system is constantly undergoing structural changes as a result of use. When an impulse passes from cell to cell, it leaves behind a path which makes it easier for some new impulse at a later period to pass along the same course. In this way it is also made easier for later impulses to be brought together. Very soon the effects of past experience become so complicated that it is impossible to picture them in detail. Thus, when one learns the name of an object, there must be traced through the nervous system a series of paths which make it possible in all later experience for the percept of that object to arouse the tendency to articulate the name. Or, to take another type of example, when one has thought of Europe and Asia as parts of a great continental mass, it becomes easier in all future experience to couple these two ideas in thought.

The facts referred to in the last paragraph are grouped together under such general terms as " organic memory " or " retentiveness." It is one of the most important facts about the nervous system that it is highly retentive. As a result of this retentiveness, present action of any part of the nervous system is explicable only in small measure by the impressions of the moment. The present impression is received into a network of paths which carry the impulse here and there in accordance with past experiences through traces left behind by such experiences.

Remoter conditions of retention. Considered in a large way, all structures of the nervous system are the results of past development. The coördinations which the child inherits result from racial experiences, and no individual can face the world without reflecting in all of his instinctive attitudes the fundamental experiences of his ancestors.

Ordinarily we do not think of these remoter effects of experience. We use the terms " memory " and " retention " to refer to those phases of personal experience which we consciously connect with our own past contact with things and people. When the ordinary man uses the term " memory," he thinks of a reinstatement as nearly as possible of some situation experienced at an earlier date. One remembers what he saw and did yesterday. For the psychologist this is only one case of retention and revival. From the doings of yesterday there come over into to-day many influences which are difficult to observe directly. There is skill of hand which is the product of a slow and systematic learning process ; there is accuracy of spatial reference which makes it possible for the individual to put his hand with precision on the object before him or at the right or left. There are modes of attention ; there are attitudes of fear and anger, all of which come out of the past development of the individual but are ordinarily not recognized as due to nervous retention.

Before taking up the cases of memory which are usually recognized as coming under that name, it will be well to study those less noticed forms of organization which bring the past into the present and affect the present without being recognized through introspection.

Instincts. The simplest cases of this type are the instincts. As was pointed out in an earlier chapter, every individual is born with certain main outlines of his nervous structure provided through inheritance, exactly as the other structures of his body are provided through inheritance. If an individual has arms and legs, he will also have the nerve fibers to connect the muscles of these extremities with the spinal cord. The structure of the sense organs is also provided through inheritance, and, as has been made clear in earlier discussions, there is little or no change in the character of these organs in the course of individual experience. Inheritance, however, goes even further than to provide these main structures. The central organs themselves are, to some extent, mapped out at the beginning of individual life. The result of this central organization is that at the time of birth the muscles of the body are not merely under the general control of the nervous system, they are under the control of organized centers which are able, to a certain extent, to coördinate the activities of different parts of the body.

Protective instincts. Illustrations of instincts occur in the life of any animal and in the early life of human infants. For example, if a young bird hears a loud sound, this sound not only discharges itself through the nervous system, but because of the internal organization of the nervous system the sound will discharge itself into the muscles of the whole body in that form of behavior commonly described as feigning death. The individual bird does not 'recognize the significance or value of its behavior, at least the first time it executes it. The act can therefore not be explained as due in any way to individual intelligence. Furthermore, the same form of action appears in all members of the species. The organization which controls the activity has been worked out in the course of the experience of the bird's ancestors as a form of protective movement to be put into operation whenever the animal is threatened by an approaching enemy. To say that the young bird which performs this movement is cognizant of danger and assumes an appropriate attitude would be to invert the true relations exhibited in the situation. The mode of behavior is immediate and depends directly upon the external stimulation plus the inherited organization. The attitude of fear results from the action which takes place without the animal's control or choice. The inner experience of fear is just as much determined through heredity as is the ability to hear the sound through the ear or the ability to respond to the sound with the muscles of the body.

Food-taking instinct. Other typical illustrations of organized instinctive modes of behavior may be drawn from a study of the human infant. One of the most fundamental instincts of the infant is the instinct of sucking. Any young mammal responds to a small object placed between its lips by a complex form of reaction which nature has provided as the only possible means of supporting the animal's life during a period when individual experience is not sufficiently mature to guide it in securing its own food. The form of consciousness which accompanies this instinctive behavior is, of course, a matter of speculation, but it seems highly probable that the experience of the infant is one of emotional excitement and of satisfaction when the act finds some appropriate object on which to express itself.

Instincts established through selection. The process by which the instincts have been evolved is most elaborate. In the later stages of animal evolution those members of a species which do not exhibit the highly organized instincts of protection and food-taking perish. It is easy to see how the instincts are perpetuated through natural selection. In somewhat the same fashion we can imagine how, through a long regressive series, those nervous systems were gradually selected which provided the forms of reaction most favorable to the preservation of life.

Delayed instincts common. In treating of human instincts the matter is somewhat complicated by the fact that a great many instincts are present only in incipient forms at the beginning of life and are fully matured at a relatively late period. A good illustration of such a delayed instinct is found in the tendency of the young child to walk. That this tendency is inherited is shown by the fact that it will mature, even if there is little or no individual practice. The common development of the young child is a mixture of maturing instincts and ambitious efforts on the part of the child himself and of those surrounding him to hasten the development which would naturally come, even if no exertions were made in that direction. Certain interesting cases are on record which show that children who for one reason or another had never made any individual effort to mature this mode of activity suddenly exhibited it under suitable conditions in a fully developed form. Young animals have frequently been experimented upon in a way to show that their modes of locomotion are wholly instinctive, even though locomotion develops only at a relatively late period in life. Thus young birds which have been incubated in isolation and have been caged until they reached full maturity will fly with the natural mode of flight of their species as soon as they are liberated.

Impossibility of distinguishing instincts from later-acquired forms of behavior. As there are instinctive modes of behavior which develop somewhat slowly during the early years of life, it is impossible to draw a line and say that every form of activity which matures after a certain period is independent of direct hereditary organizations. It is equally impossible to say, on the other hand, that the inherited tracts in the nervous system are in no wise modified in the course of individual experience. Indeed, it is always true that on the foundation of inherited coördinations there is built up a system of refinements and modifications which constitute the characteristic mark of the individual.

Habits from instincts and from independent conditions. Instincts are sometimes simplified in the course of use; at other times they are united into larger systems of action or are broken up into their elements and recombined into new types of composite activity. We turn, then, to the consideration of these processes of activity which are related to instincts merely as outgrowths and may therefore be treated as the products of individual experience. Those modes of behavior which depend upon individual experience are called habits. In order to make clear the relation of habit to instinct, it should be pointed out that not all habits grow directly out of single well-defined instincts. For the purposes of our discussion two classes of habits may be distinguished: first, there are habits which develop out of instincts; second, there are habits which develop by a process of selection from among the diffuse activities which appear whenever there is no definite mode of instinctive behavior which serves as a foundation for development. We may refer to these two types of habits as habits developed from instincts and habits developed from diffusion.

Development of habit through conflict of instincts. An illustration of a habit developed from instincts is found in the case in which a child develops a certain definite attitude toward certain animals. This attitude of the child can in many cases be shown to have originated out of a conflict between two tendencies. There are two fundamental instinctive tendencies in every child, indeed in every young animal. Every young animal tends, on the one hand, to run away from any strange or unusually intense stimulation. A large object moving toward the eyes, a loud sound attacking the auditory organs, or a strange odor or taste will stir up in a young animal a mode of action of the protective type. There is, on the other hand, among all of the higher animals an instinct toward contact with members of the same species and with related forms of animal life. Thus, young birds naturally tend to keep close to any member of their species and to other objects which are in any way similar to members of their own species. So also do young mammals. Young puppies and young kittens are extremely fond of companionship, and even certain of the more solitary animals naturally herd in packs or in small groups, especially when young. The human infant exhibits both of the two fundamental instinctive tendencies which have just been described. When, accordingly, the child is for the first time confronted by an animal, its reaction may be one of withdrawal or one of friendly contact. Which of the two natural tendencies is actually selected will depend upon a variety of circumstances. If the instinct of flight or protective activity is strong, either because the individual child is disposed to react in this way more emphatically than in the direction of social contact or if the instinct of protection is rendered especially pronounced by some accident of excessive external stimulation at the particular moment, then the instinct of fear will dominate and the social instinct will be suppressed. In such a case the specialized habit will begin to form in the general direction of fear. Sometimes the attitude is so thoroughly determined by the first contact with the animal that all through life the individual tends to follow the initial impulse received at the first experience. There are persons who have a very strong attitude of fear for cats and dogs, which attitude has become a fixed individual habit after being selected from among the various possible instinctive modes of response which existed through inheritance at the beginning of life.

Nervous development concerned in the selection of instincts. The nervous mechanism involved in a habit which has resulted from selection among instincts is relatively easy to explain. We need only to assume that the stimulation which is given at the first experience has two possible lines of discharge, either one of which would be through a well-defined instinctive tract. The conditions of the first encounter carry the stimulation in question into one of the two instinctive channels, and thereafter this selected channel becomes the natural and easy path of discharge for the stimulus whenever it recurs. The habit is, accordingly, dependent upon individual experience only in the one respect that individual experience determines which of the possible instincts shall be selected.

Habit as a modified instinct. A second somewhat different type of derivation of habit from instinct is found in cases in which the final mode of activity is not along the line of any single instinct, but is a compromise in which one instinct is modified by conflict with other instinctive tendencies. Suppose, for example, that the human infant who naturally tends to be afraid of an animal is encouraged by circumstances to assume a friendly attitude toward the animal of which he is naturally afraid. His attitude and mode of reaction may be modified to a greater or less extent, so that instead of expressing the full tendency of his instinct to run away, he may have merely a suppressed internal recoil from the animal, while all of his grosser protective movements are modified. Many of the human instincts are probably thus somewhat reduced in intensity and in their form of expression. Darwin argued at length that the expressions of human and animal emotions are in many cases simply reduced instinctive forms of behavior. Many of the facial expressions in human beings are, according to his view, remains of early forms of activity in the jaw and mouth muscles, which once accompanied real combat. The changes in circulation and respiration which come with fear and embarrassment are to be regarded as partial expressions of certain fundamental instincts. For example, when we are frightened there is for an instant a pause in all the internal activities preparatory to the violent activities necessary to flight, and after this first pause there comes a rapid beating of the heart which originally accompanied flight. When in mature life one refuses to indulge in flight, he may, nevertheless, have all the internal activities. If, however, he persists in refusing to run, the inherited tendency may, through this fact, be gradually overcome even to the point of disappearance.

Importance of heredity in explaining consciousness. Such examples as these tend to emphasize heredity. The individual is seen to begin life with a large stock of possible habits and instinctive attitudes. His final attitudes are determined in kind and degree by the circumstances of individual life, but a great number of the fundamental possibilities in human nature are given at the beginning of life. We may say, therefore, that an individual is born with a large stock of attitudes quite as much as with a large supply of organs of sense and forms of possible sensory experience. The inherited attitudes are not specific in their application until after individual experience has worked out the application, but they are native and explicable only in terms that recognize their fundamentally hereditary character.

Diffusion a mark of lack of organization. Turning now from the habits which are developed through the selection and modification of instincts, we come to the habits which cannot properly be traced to any single instinct or group of instincts. Let us suppose that a stimulus or a combination of stimulations is introduced into the nervous system of the child but finds no specific channel of discharge open to it through inherited organization. This stimulation will produce an excitation which will be very widely distributed throughout the whole nervous system, because it has no specific channel of discharge and because, as free energy, it must be transmitted through the nervous system until it finds a discharge into the active organs. The stimulation will ultimately issue through the avenues of motor discharge into the active organs of the body, but instead of issuing in a well-coördinated series it will be distributed diffusely and irregularly and will affect a great number of muscles. An example of the diffuse distribution of stimulation in mature life is seen when one is suddenly startled by an unexpected loud noise, and there follows a general contraction of the muscles throughout the whole body. Such a strong stimulus breaks over all of the bounds of organization in the central nervous system and is distributed diffusely throughout the body. A diffuse distribution of the stimulation is clearly a disadvantage to the individual. The state of the organism after the stimulation is such that the individual is not well adapted to his environment, his activities are not concentrated in any single direction, and he is altogether unprepared to meet the future demands which the stimulation may impose upon him. Furthermore, it can easily be observed that the mental attitude which accompanies such diffuse activity is quite as unorganized as the bodily attitude, and this, also, is an intolerable condition for any individual. The process of modifying such a diffuse reaction, of developing definite and precise attitudes on the mental side and well-coördinated movements on the physical side, is a long, complex process, carried out by the organism and by consciousness with the delays and complications which appear in every process of natural development.

Development of habit from diffusion. If we take a form of activity which has little or no instinctive background, such as the activity involved in writing, and observe the early stages of the effort to develop this type of activity into a habit, we discover the characteristics of a diffuse activity. It will be found, first, that movement is excessive in both extent and intensity. The child who is learning to write moves not only the necessary muscles of the fingers and hand directly engaged in writing, but the muscles of the other hand as well. He also moves the muscles of the face. The diffusion of the excitation throughout the whole organism is one of the most obvious facts to be observed in such a case. In the second place, the elements of movement which are present are not coördinated into harmonious wholes. The various muscular contractions involved in the earliest attempts at writing seldom enter into such relations that there is economy in their several activities. This will be apparent if one observes the way in which the fingers and the hand act during the child's formation of series of letters. There must always be a movement of the hand during writing to carry the fingers across the page. In the child's writing the fingers are used as long as they can be used without any coöperating hand movement. The hand is brought into play only after the fingers have become so cramped that they can no longer make lines. When this cramping of the fingers reaches such a point that it can go no farther, the finger movement is altogether suspended for a moment and the hand is moved forward in a distinct and relatively separate act. The writing then proceeds as before, the fingers being used quite to the exclusion of the hand. This obvious lack of combined activity of the hand and fingers illustrates a general fact which is also exhibited by the incoördination of the learner's several fingers in relation to one another. The thumb and first finger do not at the outset coöperate with each other in the harmonious way in which they should. For example, at the beginning of an upward stroke, as in the written letter *l*, the first finger presses downward against the pencil or pen more vigorously than is necessary and, as a result, the thumb is called upon to do an excess of work in order to overcome the unnecessary downward pressure of the first finger. There is thus a lack of harmony and even a certain degree of interference in the organs which are directly involved in the activity. The explanation of diffusion and incoördination at the beginning of development is similar to the explanation of the general diffusion of the activity throughout the whole muscular system in the case of a sudden loud noise. In both cases the nervous impulses which excite the muscles do not follow definite channels. In the case now under consideration the channels are not yet developed, while in the case of the loud sound they are not able to confine the strong discharge to definite paths.

Undeveloped movements. Another characteristic of an undeveloped movement is one which is closely related to its incoördination, and consists in the fact that the various phases of movement are all of brief duration, not being united with each other into a continuous series. If one examines the writing of a child, he finds that the lines, instead of being continuous, fluent lines, are made up of short, irregular parts. The direction of the movement in these short, irregular parts is very frequently away from the general direction which the movement should follow. We may say that the movement is a succession of efforts to produce the line rather than a sequence of coördinated muscular contractions appropriate to the general movement. When the movement develops, as it does after practice, the different elements are bound together in such a way that their sequence cannot be detected; they are no longer separate factors. The adult who begins to write the letter *l* does not make a series of separate movements as the pencil is carried along the upward stroke. He does, however, make a series of muscular contractions. The transition from the irregular succession of separate movements to a series of contractions constituting phases of a single complex activity, which, however, is thoroughly unified, results from the coupling together of a series of nervous tracts which provide for the proper temporal distribution of the motor excitation.

Diffusion analogous to all forms of overproduction. It is clear from the foregoing study of the characteristics of an undeveloped activity that nature approaches this problem of development in the same way in which all the problems of development are approached; namely, through excessive productions and selection of the proper elements. Since the child does not have the proper nervous organization to control his movements, nature has provided that he shall make a superabundance of movements involving all of the different parts of the body, even those which are not directly concerned in the final activity. If, in this excess of movement, certain factors accomplish the end toward which the individual is working, these successful constituents of movement will gradually be emphasized and the unsuccessful constituents will gradually be eliminated, until finally diffusion gives way to a limited number of precise and well-defined combinations of activity. If the selected factors are repeated together a sufficient number of times, the nervous activities involved in each particular phase of the movement gradually become connected with each other.

Conscious correlates of habit. The conscious accompaniments of action which has grown habitual are easily described. There is a feeling of familiarity when one is trained to respond to sensations ; there is a definiteness of discrimination which makes one's percepts sure and clear. Too often the psychology of habit has been guilty of the statement that habituation leads to unconsciousness. This is not the case. When we can deal skillfully with any situation, we have an attitude of attention and of assurance wholly different from the attitude of indefinite excitement which accompanies diffusion. The skillful man is the discerning man ; his discernments may disregard certain factors and emphasize others, but, on the whole, he will give attention to that which is most important in guiding action.

Instinct, habit, and mental attitudes. The reader will be able without detailed discussion to see the relation of this chapter to the earlier chapter which deals with mental attitudes. All mental life exhibits natural likes and dislikes, acquired sympathies and antipathies, forms of attention and interest. These are related, as was shown before, to modes of reaction. We now see how these tastes and interests are developed as a part of the individual's adjustment of himself to the world. Some tastes are traceable to inherited instincts, others to acquired habits, and so on through the list. The important fact for psychology is that past experience comes over into the present in the form of fundamental attitudes and tendencies. The introspective observer is likely to make the mistake of thinking that his likes and dislikes are the products of his present thinking, when in reality they come to him from a remote past, even in some cases from his racial inheritances.

Applications of the doctrine of attitudes to social science. What is shown by these few examples is of the greatest importance for the social sciences. Social life has developed innumerable habits in the individual. We pass each other on the right; we accost our friends on the street; we gather about the table and take our food in an orderly way. In these and a thousand of the customs of social life we record the experience of the past. At the moment we find ourselves in sympathy with our surroundings. Indeed, we should be most uncomfortable if our surroundings did not call for those forms of behavior which are laid down by habit in our nervous systems. Personal habits and social customs have thus come to be two aspects of a single line of development. Here again we are often too much in the midst of the experience itself to see how our social attitudes came into being and what is their real character.

CHAPTER X

SPEECH AS A FORM OF BEHAVIOR

Speech as a highly important special habit. Among the habits developed by human beings none is so elaborate as speech; none is so intimately related to the higher levels to which human experience attains. Speech is evidently a form of muscular behavior, as can be readily observed if one notes the movements in the thorax, larynx, and mouth during articulation. So complex, however, are the mental processes related to the movements involved in speech that we ordinarily overlook entirely the physical side of the process and think of speech only as one of the higher forms of mental activity.

Speech and ideas closely interrelated. There would be logical justification for a postponement of the discussion of speech until after the description and classification of ideas and of those thought processes which develop with the evolution of language. Speech would then be treated, as it is in the thinking of most people, as a product or expression of higher intelligence. But speech is more than a product of thought; it is the instrument which makes thought possible; or, differently expressed, it is the kind of reaction which is essential to the higher attitudes of discrimination and comparison. Just as the processes of perception are not merely receptive but involve reactions, so the higher thought processes are active and depend for their character on those forms of behavior which make up the speech habit. We are justified, therefore, in discussing speech before treating of ideas, even though we shall have frequent occasion in this chapter to refer to the higher mental processes before we have described them in detail.

Speculations regarding the nature and origin of speech. Speech has from the earliest history been recognized by man as a unique power. It is the distinguishing characteristic between Greek and barbarian, between Hebrew and gentile. In more emphatic degree, it is the mark of distinction between man and his nearest relatives in the animal kingdom.

Long before there was a science of human nature, man speculated curiously as to the source from which language came. His first answer was that the Deity gave it to him by a special act of creation.

The special creation theory. The special creation theory of the origin of language ignores, however, certain facts which are too obvious to be set aside. It ignores the fact that animals have the ability to make certain vocal sounds which they utilize for purposes of communication with one another. We cannot explain how it is that animals have modes of expression so closely related to human language without, at the same time, recognizing the natural origin of language itself. Furthermore, the processes of human expression are constantly undergoing changes and developments which are so natural and so definite in their character that it seems probable that language has always been evolving just as it is at the present time. If the principles under which language as we know it is developing can be ascertained, it is reasonable to project these laws back of the historical period and to assume that the beginnings of language were also under the regular laws of development. The creation theory has therefore gradually given way to various theories which attempt to give a naturalistic explanation of language.

The imitation theory. It has sometimes been held in later speculation that language originated from the tendency to imitate sounds. This theory, while it would explain certain of the special forms of words, cannot give any adequate account of the way in which an individual develops the power of turning imitation to the special ends of speech. There are a number of different animals that are capable of a wide range of imitation, but they have never developed a language, as has man. This is clear evidence that the essence of language is not to be found in imitation, but rather in the use to which the imitative power is put.

The interjection theory. It has also been suggested that language developed out of the interjections which man naturally used in his most primitive stage of development. If he was astonished by any sudden stimulation, he naturally gave forth ejaculations in response to the sudden excitation. These ejaculations, it is said, came gradually to have the power of calling to mind the situations to which they belonged and ultimately became the means of communication. Here again the objection to the theory is not that it seems improbable that man began with simple forms of expression, but that the theory does not explain how these simple forms of expression acquired a meaning and importance which they did not have at the beginning. What is needed, rather than a formal description of the first expressions used by primitive man, is a consistent psychological explanation of how the ejaculations came to have significance for mental life and to serve as the vehicles for elaborate thought processes.

Roots of language in natural emotional expressions and their imitation. The psychological explanation of language begins with a general reference to the statements made in earlier chapters. Every sensory stimulation arouses some form of bodily activity. The muscles of the organs of circulation and the muscles of the limbs, as well as other internal and external muscles, are constantly engaged in making responses to external stimuli. Among the muscles of the body which with the others are involved in expressive activities are the muscles which control the organs of respiration. There can be no stimulation of any kind which does not affect more or less the character of the movements of inspiration and expiration. In making these general statements, we find no necessity for distinguishing between the animals and man; so far as the general facts of relation between sensations and expression are concerned, they have like characteristics. That an air-breathing animal should produce sounds through irregularities in its respiratory movements when it is excited by an external stimulus, especially if that stimulus is violent, is quite as natural as that its hair should rise when it is afraid or that its muscles should tremble when it is aroused to anger or to flight.

Imitation. The important step in the development of language is the acquirement of the ability to use the movements of the vocal cords for purposes other than those of individual emotional expression. The acquirement of this ability is a matter of long evolution and depends in its first stages upon social imitation. The importance of imitation in affecting the character of animal behavior appears as soon as animals begin to live in packs or herds or other social groups.

Other imitative communications of animals and man. So far as communication through imitation is concerned, there is no reason why attention should be confined exclusively to the forms of activity which result in sounds. All animals imitate the activities of other members of their species on a very large scale. The stampede of a herd of cattle is an excellent illustration of the importance of the tendency toward imitation. The frightened animal which starts the stampede does not consciously purpose to communicate its fright to the other members of the herd; it is performing a natural act of its individual life. Incidentally, it affects all those about it by arousing in them a violent form of imitative activity. The stampeding herd may have no consciousness whatever of the original cause of fear in one of its members; the real cause of the stampede and of the resulting excitement in the herd is the example of the one frightened animal. Thus we see that the activity of an animal takes on, because of the reaction of its social environment, a significance which the original act never could have had unless it had been imitated.

Value of sounds as means of social communication. What is true of activity in general is true of activities which result in sounds. The sound produced by the activities of the vocal cords can impress itself readily upon the ears of some other animal, more readily by far than the visual impression of trembling or of general muscular tension. If, now, the animal which hears the sound has itself produced this sound or one closely resembling it in quality and intensity, there will be a natural tendency for the sound stimulation to arouse in the second animal a sympathetic response. Witness the tendency of all the dogs in a community to bark together or of all the roosters to begin crowing together when one gives the signal. The result of imitating the sound will be to throw the imitating animal into an emotional state very similar to that of the animal which first made the noise. This result will be more likely to follow if the two animals are closely related in their organization and types of activity. There will be relatively less tendency to sympathize with an animal of entirely different organization and habits, for the activity aroused through imitation in the listening animal will not agree in character with the activity of the animal which sets the example. Thus, one can judge from his own experience that there is very little possibility of arousing in a human being the mental state which appears in dogs or cats through imitation of the sounds which they produce. In general, imitation of sound is valuable as a means of arousing sympathy only between animals sufficiently related to each other to have similar modes of producing sound.

Limitation of forms of animal communication. Given the similarity of organization which makes imitated sounds significant, we have a type of communication provided which is widely utilized in the animal world. The food calls and the danger signals of birds are significant to other members of the flock. Such calls have definite natural relations to the organized responses of all members of the species. It is to be noted that these calls do not constitute a language in the sense in which human sounds constitute a language, for the bird calls are incapable of conveying definite ideas, such as ideas of the kind of food or the particular kind of danger discovered by the animal which makes the sound. The sounds serve merely to arouse certain attitudes. An animal can induce in its fellows a tendency to fear and flight by means of cries which in the history of each member of the flock have been associated with fear, but the animal can go no farther in its communications than to arouse emotional attitudes.

The first stages of human articulation like animal cries. There are stages of human infancy which are closely related to the stages of animal life thus far described. The human infant does not at first make sounds as the result of any conscious desire to communicate its feelings to those about it, much less does it use its sounds for verbal discussion of the details of its conscious experiences. The infant makes noises exactly as it swings its arms and legs, because the muscular contractions which produce these noises are instinctive motor expressions related through heredity to the stimuli which arouse them. Later there appears a strong tendency to imitate others of its own kind, and this imitation may serve to put the infant in some contact with its social environment and give it a medium of communication comparable in character to that which we find in animals. This is not language, however, for imitation alone is not enough to develop language. Further processes must take place before the full development is effected.

Articulations selected from the sum of possible activities. While imitation applies to many different forms of activity, such as those of the limbs or face, a moment's consideration will make it clear that the activities which produce sounds have a number of unique advantages as vehicles of imitative communication. The ability to produce sounds depends largely upon the animal itself and very little upon external conditions. Contrast sound with visual impressions. Visual impressions are cut off in the dark; they are cut off by intervening objects and by a turning of the head of the observer. Sounds travel wherever there is air; they are as easy to produce in the darkness as in daylight; they can easily be varied in intensity. For these reasons they come to be the chief means of social communication, even among the animals. The result is that the vocal cords and the ability to discriminate sounds are highly developed long before the development of language proper.

Evolution of ideas and speech. The advance which human language makes beyond animal communication consists in the fact that human language relates sounds to ideas as well as to emotional attitudes. This step cannot be taken until ideas are present in the minds of both parties to the communication. We find ourselves, therefore, at this point involved in a perplexing circle. Human mental processes as we know them are intimately related to language. Even when we think about our own most direct experiences, we use words. Yet these words are not explicable except when we assume complex ideational processes as the necessary conditions for their development and interpretation. Did human mental advance result from the development of language, or did language result from the development of ideas? The only answer to this question is that language and ideational processes developed together and are necessary to each other.

In describing the first stages of the development of true language we may assume, therefore, that both speaker and auditor have reached a stage of development where it is possible to have higher nervous and conscious processes.

Such higher processes are to be contrasted with mere emotional attitudes. For example, if one sees his fellow being pointing in a certain direction, there is a strong tendency to turn and look in the same direction. There will result in this case not an emotion but a common attention to some object. The gesture of pointing is, accordingly, a mode of communication which rises to a higher level than does the cry of fear or the food call. Its development opens the way for a higher system of communication.

Gestures and broad scope of attention. Still higher is the gesture that depicts some elaborate act. Thus, when a man is hungry he will point to his mouth and make the gesture of taking up food and carrying it to his mouth. This simple gesture will not be made by an animal, because the animal has only a limited range of attention. If the animal thinks of food, it cannot entertain any other ideas. It spends all its mental energy seeking food rather than trying to communicate with some other animal. In human life there is breadth of attention exhibited in a gesture. The person who makes a gesture includes in his experience the person with whom he wishes to communicate, plus the idea which is to be communicated. The animal may have a simple idea but not the complex of ideas involved even in gesture.

This ability of man to have two centers of attention can be explained anatomically by recalling that man has great masses of cerebral tissue within which impulses can be worked over. The animal has only a little brain tissue, and any impulse received in the brain must be discharged very soon in the form of a motor impulse. The hungry animal must act at once in the effort to remove hunger. Man, on the other hand, has enough brain tissue to hold the impulse in suspense, unite it with impressions from his fellow beings, and act in a complex way with full regard both to his fellow beings and to his hunger.

Gesture, or gesture language as it is called, is thus seen to be not merely a complex form of behavior but one which expresses a new type of relationship between the reactor and his environment. Gesture is a social form of behavior involving attention to persons as well as to objects. Indeed, gesture supersedes the more direct forms of attack on objects.

Evolution of gestures in direction of simplification. The earliest forms of social communications undoubtedly included much gesture if, indeed, they were not limited altogether to gesture. The term " natural sign " has been used in describing these early gestures. The gesture was so full and pantomimic in character that the interpretation was almost as direct as in the case of an emotional expression. The gesture could be interpreted by anyone who had passed through an experience at all like that of the person making the gesture. All that we need to assume by way of explanation of gesture is the law of social imitation which was stated in earlier paragraphs and the higher power of reviving ideas.

The later development of gesture language brought with it a reduction of the gesture so that it became a mere remnant of the earlier act. This reduction to a simpler act was possible within the group of those who had learned to communicate with each other. Thus, instead of requiring the full pantomime to communicate the fact that one was hungry, it came to be enough that one pointed in the direction of the mouth. A mere clue served to arouse the idea. This stage is reached when both the parties to the communication have developed the power of supplying the ideas needed for interpretation to such a high level that it is very easy to call out the idea by the slightest hint.

Speech a highly specialized mode of behavior. This development, which made it less and less important that the gesture be a full pantomime, opened the way for a selection of certain particular forms of activity which became the vehicles of communication and were wholly set aside for that purpose. The vocal cords were not available as organs for communication of ideas so long as the ideas had to be depicted in full by means of elaborately imitable gestures. But as the need of gestures diminished and the power of supplying ideas increased, the vocal cords proved increasingly useful as special organs of social communication just because they were not otherwise used. The hands which were used for communication during the period when gesture was evolving were in demand for the direct practical activities of life. When two individuals wish to communicate with each other, it is often extremely inconvenient to suspend all other activity, to lay down what one may be carrying, to come where one may be clearly seen, for the purpose of holding a parley. The vocal cords, on the other hand, are not required for the practical purposes of life. They are easily disconnected in their action from the general mass of the muscles and, therefore, very naturally became the organs for a system of social activities.

One of the most primitive forms of vocal art is the work song. This illustrates strikingly the relation of vocal reactions to handwork. The workers secured social coöperation through the song, their hands in the meantime being occupied in practical work.

Consequences of specialization. The fact that speech thus separates itself from other forms of bodily activity and becomes a highly specialized system of behavior brings with it a number of important consequences. First, it is possible for speech to develop to a high level without involving the corresponding development of any of the practical arts. What is sometimes called pure verbalism may result. Thus a student may acquire mere words and not have any power of applying the words which he repeats to other forms of behavior.

Second, the specialized character of speech results in the sharp differentiation of one local language from that of other sections. Ultimately each language grows so far from the parent root that it is wholly unintelligible except to those who are trained in its special forms.

Third, there is a possibility that ideas will be attached to sounds so loosely and ambiguously that the two parties to communication will drift far apart in their interpretations while using one and the same sounds.

Speech an indirect form of behavior. Speech as a form of behavior thus lacks that direct relation to the outer world which most habits exhibit. It takes on a highly artificial character. Its uses are controlled by social convention rather than by natural necessity. We may therefore very properly describe speech as an indirect, conventional form of behavior.

Evolution of writing. The stages of evolution of speech which have been described in the foregoing paragraphs are exemplified in essentially the same sequence, though in slightly different form, in the evolution of the art of writing.

Writing at first direct in form. The earliest stages of writing were those in which pictographic forms were used; that is, a direct picture was drawn upon the writing surface, reproducing as nearly as possible the kind of impression made upon the observer by the object itself (see Fig. 54). To be sure, the drawing used to represent the object was not an exact reproduction or full copy of the object, but it was a fairly direct image. The visual image was thus aroused by a direct appeal to the eye. Anyone could read a document written in this pictographic form if he had ever seen the objects to which the pictures referred. There was no special relation between the pictures or visual forms at this stage of development and the sounds used in articulate language. Concrete examples of such writing are seen in early monuments, where the moon is represented by the crescent, a king by the drawing of a man wearing a crown. An example of this stage of writing is also supplied

by the ancient Chinese forms shown in the upper line
of Fig. 55.

**Images reduced to lowest terms as powers of reader
increase.** The next stage of development in writing began
when the pictographic forms were reduced in complexity
to the simplest possible lines. The reduction of the picture
to a few sketchy lines depended upon the growing ability of
the reader to contribute the necessary interpretation. All
that was needed in the figure was something which would

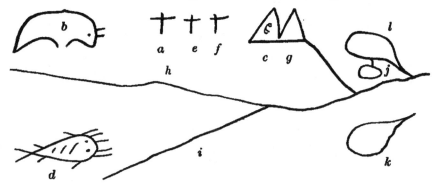

FIG. 54. An Ojibwa love letter, recorded and explained by Garrick Mallery
in the Annual Report of the Bureau of Ethnology, 1888–1889, p. 363

The writer, a girl of the Bear totem, *b*, summons her lover, who belongs to the
Mud Puppy totem, *d*, along the various trails indicated, to the lodge, *c*, from which
the beckoning hand protrudes. The inclosed figures at *l*, *j*, and *k* are lakes. The
crosses indicate that the girl and her companions are Christians. "The clear indications of locality," writes Mallery, "serve as well as if in a city a young woman had
sent an invitation to her young man to call at a certain street and number"

suggest the idea to the reader's mind. The simplification
of the written forms is attained very early, as is seen even
in the figures which are used by savage tribes. Thus, to
represent the number of an enemy's army, it is not necessary to draw full figures of the forms of the enemy; it is
enough if single straight lines are drawn with some brief
indication, perhaps at the beginning of the series of lines,
to show that these stand each for an individual enemy.
This simplification of the drawing leaves the written symbol with very much larger possibilities of entering into

new relations in the mind of the reader. Instead, now, of
being a specific drawing related to a specific object, it
invites by its simple character a number of different interpretations. A straight line, for example, can represent
not only the number of an enemy's army, but it can represent also the number of sheep in a flock, or the number
of tents in a village, or anything else which is capable of
enumeration. The use of a straight line for these various
purposes stimulates new mental developments. This is
shown by the fact that the development of the idea of the

FIG. 55. Ancient and modern Chinese writing

The upper line shows ancient forms of Chinese writing; the lower line shows the
derived modern forms. Reading from left to right, the characters signify "sun,"
"moon," "mountain," "tree" (or "wood"), "dog"

number relation, as distinguished from the mass of possible
relations in which an object may stand, is greatly facilitated
by this general written symbol for numbers. The intimate
relation between the development of ideas on the one hand
and the development of symbols on the other is here very
strikingly illustrated. The drawing becomes more useful
because it is associated with more elaborate ideas, while the
ideas develop because they find in the drawing a definite
content which helps to mark and give separate character to
the idea. Striking examples of the simplification of form
in order to facilitate the writing of symbols are shown in
Figs. 55 and 56.

Written symbols and their relation to sounds. As soon as the drawing began to lose its significance as a direct perceptual reproduction of the object and took on new and broader meanings through the associations which attached to it, the written form became a symbol rather than a direct appeal to visual memory. As a symbol it stood for something which, in itself, it was not. The way

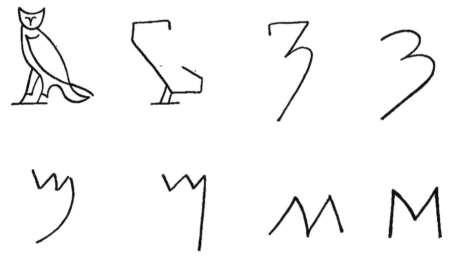

FIG. 56. Derivation of the Roman letter M from the ancient Egyptian hieroglyphic owl

The four forms in the upper part of the figure are Egyptian forms. The first on the left is the usual hieroglyphic picture of the owl, or, as it was called in the Egyptian language, *mulak*. The three remaining upper forms are found in the writings of the Egyptian priests. The first form on the left of the lower series is an ancient Semitic form. Then follow in order an ancient Greek form and two later Greek forms.

(From I. Taylor's " The Alphabet," pp. 9, 10)

was thus opened for the written symbol to enter into relation with oral speech, which is also a form of symbolism (see Fig. 56). Articulate sounds are simplified forms of experience capable through association with ideas of expressing meanings not directly related to the sounds themselves. When the written symbol began to be related to the sound symbol, there was at first a loose and irregular relation between them. The Egyptians seem to have established such relations to some extent. They wrote at times with pictures standing for sounds as we now write in rebus puzzles. In such puzzles the picture of an object is intended to call up in the mind of the reader not the special group of ideas appropriate to the object represented in the picture but rather the sound which serves as the name of this object. When the sound is once suggested to the reader, he is supposed to attend to that and to connect with it certain other associations appropriate to the sound. To take a modern illustration, we may, for example, use the picture of the eye to stand for the first personal pronoun. The relationship between the picture and the idea for which it is used is in this case through the sound of the name of the object depicted. That the early alphabets are of this type of rebus pictures appears in their names. The first three letters of the Hebrew alphabet, for-example, are named, respectively, *aleph*, which means "ox," *beth*, which means "house," and *gimmel*, which means "camel."

The alphabet. The complete development of a sound alphabet from this type of rebus writing required, doubtless, much experimentation on the part of the nations which succeeded in establishing the association. The Phœnicians have generally been credited with the invention of the forms and relations which we now use. Their contribution to civilization cannot be overestimated. It consisted not in the presentation of new material or content to conscious experience but rather in bringing together by association groups of contents which, in their new relation, transformed the whole process of thought and expression. They associated visual and auditory content and gave to the visual factors a meaning which originally attached to the sound. Pictures thus came to mean sounds rather than objects (see Fig. 56).

Social motives essential to the development of language. The ideational interpretations which appear in developed language could never have reached the elaborate form which they have at present if there had not been social coöperation. The tendency of the individual when left to himself is to drop back into the direct adjustments which are appropriate to his own life. He might possibly develop articulation to a certain extent for his own sake, but the chief impulse to the development of language comes through intercourse with others. As we have seen, the development of the simplest forms of communication, as in animals, is a matter of social imitation. Writing is also an outgrowth of social relations. It is extremely doubtful whether even the child of civilized parents would ever have any sufficient motive for the development of writing if it were not for the social encouragement which he receives.

Social system as source of the form of words. Furthermore, we depend upon our social relations not merely for the incentives to the development of language but also for the particular forms which oral and written language shall take. It is much more convenient for a child born into a civilized community to adapt himself to the complex symbolism which he finds in the possession of his elders than to develop anything of the sort for himself. It is true that tendencies exist early in life toward the development of individual forms of expression. A child frequently uses a certain sound in a connection which cannot be explained by reference to social usage. It may be a purely individual combination, or a crude effort to adopt something which has been suggested by the environment. This tendency to give sounds a meaning might prove sufficient to work out a kind of language, even if the individual were entirely isolated from his fellows; but the natural tendencies are very early superseded by the stronger tendencies of social imitation, and in the end the social system completely dominates individual development, dictating in all cases the forms of words.

Social usage and the domination of individual thought. In adopting the forms of expression used by those about us, we are led to take up certain general social forms of thought which ultimately control the whole mental life. The effect of this social influence is so far-reaching that it is quite proper to say that an individual is, in a very large measure, the creation of his social relations, at least in the higher phases of his mental life. The fundamental forms of direct activity, which constitute the personal habits by which we have succeeded in adapting ourselves to the demands of the physical world, are to a certain extent unsocial. They are, to be sure, alike in different individuals because they have grown up, as was shown in our earlier discussion, under the demands of a common physical environment. Our forms of space perception, for example, are not the creations of our own individual caprice but rather the arrangement which we have given our sensory experiences in our effort to fit ourselves to a world which dictates these space relations to us. Since we have all grown up in the same space world, our space ideas are alike. The community of social ideas expressed in language is of a different type. Even the direct, relatively unsocial forms of perception are influenced by these higher social forms of thought. If, for example, there is no word in a certain social environment for long spatial distances except a word which refers to a certain number of days' journeys, it is not likely that the individual will feel any tendency to discriminate fifteen miles from seventeen. His attitude in this matter will be determined by the attitude of his social environment, and he will neglect in his thought, as do those about him, the finer details of distance. Similarly, if there are no names for certain forms of property rights, it is not likely that the individual will, of his own initiative, recognize these forms of right as belonging to those who constitute the social group with him.

Social ideas dominate individual life. The history of thought has been, in large measure, the history of the development of certain social ideas which could be marked with definite names and made subjects of thought, because they were so marked. Consider for a moment the difficulties which would be experienced in conducting any train of thought with regard to the forces of physical nature if there were no names for the different forces and no fully developed definitions to give each name clearly recognized character. If it is true in a general way that general tendencies of thought have been dependent upon the development of words to express ideas, it is still more true in the case of the individual that his mental tendencies are very largely determined by the forms of social thought expressed in words. A child who has had his attention called to certain colors and who is, at the same time, given a name for these colors is more likely to identify them in later experience than if no name had been given. The name serves as an incentive to the concentration of attention upon a particular phase of experience which would otherwise be lost in the general mass of sensations. Without the word the possibility of dwelling upon the single phase of experience in thought would be small. This is the reason why the retention of facts in memory is so closely related to the naming of objects.

Experimental evidence of importance of words. Some experimental evidence can be adduced to show that names are of great importance in this respect. If one is confronted with a large number of pieces of gray paper ranging from black to white, and is asked to discriminate as many of these different grays as he is able to recognize with certainty, it will be found that he can distinguish ordinarily about five classes of gray shades. He can distinguish the very dark from those which are medium dark, the very light from those that are medium light, and he can place between the dark and the light grays a middle shade which he is not disposed to classify as either light or dark. Beyond this fivefold discrimination he will find that he is very uncertain. If, now, after making this test under ordinary conditions, the individual is allowed to examine the various shades of gray and to adopt a series of names or numbers for them, it will be found that he can notably increase the range and certainty of his discrimination. The names furnish, as stated above, definite means of concentrating attention upon slight differences which existed from the first but were not noted in experience. Furthermore, when these slight differences have been discriminated and marked by the attachment to them of definite names, they become permanent additions to the individual's equipment and can be retained more easily than they could be as mere unnamed sensation qualities.

Number terminology as a device for recording possessions. One of the best illustrations of the significance for mental life of the creation of a terminology is found in the ease with which a developed individual uses numbers. In general, it may be said that primitive languages have only a very meager number terminology. Savage tribes have frequently been known to have no number terminology reaching above ten, and in some cases tribes have been reported with a number terminology not reaching beyond three. There are certain forms of direct perceptual experience which can be utilized up to a certain point instead of the developed number system which we now have. If a herdsman has a herd of cattle for a period long enough to become acquainted with its individual members, he can recognize the size of the herd by recalling the individuals which make it up. If one has material possessions which can be heaped together, he will come to estimate his wealth directly through the general impression made upon him by collecting all of his wealth at a single point. As soon as the direct recollection of each individual possession came, in the development of human wealth, to be too cumbersome a form of representation, and the collective image became too vague to be relied upon, man naturally endeavored to devise a method of recording his property and retaining it in consciousness in some simplified form. Instead of trying to remember every one of his possessions, he adopted some system of tally. At first he began counting off on his fingers each different article which he wished later to be able to recognize, or he adopted in some cases one of the more elaborate methods found among savages who use pebbles or shells. The Latin root which appears in our word " calculate " and all related words is the word for pebble, and indicates that the early forms of computation among the Romans consisted in the use of pebbles.

Symbols for groups of tallies. As soon as the system of enumeration became complex, there naturally arose the necessity for grouping the tallies so that they could be easily surveyed. The method of grouping the tally marks in a system convenient for recognition is suggested by the five fingers on the hand, and this is often adopted, even by savage peoples. A clear indication that this grouping appeared in the natural tally systems can be seen in the symbols used by the Romans to indicate numbers, for in this system the number five and the number ten are crucial points in the notation, and show the adoption of a new group symbol to include many individual symbols in a more compact form.

Parallel growth of number names and system of ideas. As the number system was worked out into a system of major and minor groups there was a tendency to develop a system of articulation directly related to the tally system. Number of the primitive tally form probably developed just as did writing, without reference to speech. The creation of words which should express number was slow, as indicated by reference to savage language, because in this case the symbolical system needed to develop to a high degree before the demand for corresponding articulation was felt. As soon as the demand for articulation became sufficiently pressing, the words appeared, and they show distinctly in their character the tendency toward groups. Further than this, the names for successive tallies came to be the means, not only of referring to individual marks but also of referring to the serial arrangement of these marks. Thus, the names "one," "two," "three," etc. are not significant merely as names of tally marks ; they have also each its special significance as the name of a special position in the total series.

Development of arithmetic depends on an appropriate system of numerals. The advantage to the child who finds a complete number terminology developed is very great. The more perfect this terminology for purposes of expressing quantitative relations, the more complete and rapid will be his initiation into the forms of thought which the terminology expresses. The historical illustration of this fact is to be found in the acceptance by European nations of a system of notation which was imported from the East in the Renaissance period. The written number symbols which had been used by the Romans were crude and rendered any forms of arithmetical manipulation extremely difficult. The Arabic system was so much more complete and economical that it immediately took the place of the older and cruder symbolism. How long it would take an individual child to acquire independently anything like the mathematical ability which, with the aid of his social environment, he acquires through the adoption of the developed Arabic number system can hardly be imagined. Certain it is that his forms of thought are now dominated by the social system into which he is born, and this system was in turn borrowed *in toto* from non-European nations.

Social world unified through common forms of thought. There is in this acceptance of the social system not only an economy which operates to the advantage of the individual, but there is the additional fact that the individual becomes thereby a part of the social whole in a fashion which is significant for society as well as for himself. We are bound together as intelligent beings by the common systems of tradition and language to a degree which makes us no longer centers of merely individual adaptation, but rather parts of a general organization which has a certain unity and exercises a dominating influence over many individuals. This social unity perpetuates customs and practices so that we have, in addition to the bodily structures which we inherit, a social heredity which guides us in the activities of personal life. Language is the chief medium for this social heredity.

Changes in words as indications of changes in individual thought and social relations. It is in connection with the development of social institutions that we find the most radical changes in human language. If an individual comes upon a new idea and coins a new word for its expression, the new word gains standing and comes to be a part of the permanent language of the community only when others feel the same necessity as the inventor of the word for this new means of expression. When, therefore, we have a long history of variations in any word we may depend upon it that there has been a corresponding series of social as well as of individual experiences related to the word. The detailed history of words is a detailed history of individual mental attitudes toward the world, and at the same time a detailed history of the social relations in which individuals have joined.

Illustration of change in words. It will not be in place in this connection to enter into any elaborate linguistic studies, but one illustration may be used to indicate something of the character of the psychological and social study which grows out of the history of words. In his " English Past and Present," Trench gives an account of the development of the word "gossip." This word was originally used at baptismal ceremonies and referred to the sponsor who stood for the child in a way analogous to that in which to-day the godparent stands as sponsor for the child. The first three letters of the word "gossip" are derived directly from the word "God," and the second part of the word, namely "sip," is a modification of the word "sib," which is even now used in Scotland to indicate a relative. When the social institution of baptism was a matter of larger community significance than it is to-day, the word was needed to express the relationship of the individuals involved in the ceremony; but being a general form of expression rather than an image of a particular individual, it came easily to refer to other phases of social contact than that which was primarily thought of in connection with the baptismal ceremony itself. The worthy sponsors of the child unquestionably indulged, even in the early days of the ceremony, in certain exchanges of information with regard to other members of the community, and this social function which the individual served was very readily connected with the word coined to refer primarily to the religious function. As the religious ceremony came to be less and less elaborate, and there was a decreasing demand for reference to the religious function, the word gradually drifted over to the second phase of meaning. It is probably true that the aberration of form, which appears in softening the d in "God" to an s, made this transfer of meaning easier. Indeed, as we have seen at various points in our discussions, words become true symbols only because they are simplified so as to take on easily new types of relation. Thus, the word "gossip" ultimately lost its original meaning and came to signify something which it signified only very vaguely to the minds of those who first used it. Furthermore, it is clear that this transfer of meaning is directly related to the development of the social institution with which the word was connected. The mental attitude of the individual who uses the word to-day and the social character of the institution are both entirely different from the attitude and institution of earlier times.

Words as instruments of thought beyond immediate experience. Other illustrations of the developments which take place in language can be found in the introduction of new words with new inventions and new discoveries in science. Once the habit of using words is thoroughly established in a community or individual, it furnishes an easy method of marking any experience which it is desired to consider apart from the general setting in which that experience appears. If to-day a civilized individual wishes to think of certain relations such as the physical force of gravity, or the economic facts of value, and to consider the bearings of the factors which enter into these relations, he will devise some word or phrase by which to mark the relations and hold them clearly before his thought while he considers all of the facts. There comes to be thus a system of experiences which we are justified in describing as constructed in consciousness for the purpose of guiding attention; these constructs have, as contrasted with ordinary mental images, very little content. Indeed, the reduction of the content of thought to the lowest possible minimum is the tendency of all mental evolution. The child has undoubtedly a more concrete imagery than the adult. The adult finds as he learns to use words fluently that the imagery which at first was necessary to explain them falls away. The result is that great ranges of thought can be much condensed; as, for example, when all the cases of falling bodies are thought of at once under the single term " gravity." In the discussion of habits it was shown that as experience becomes more completely organized into habits, the memory content and even the sensory contents receive less attention. An organized attitude is substituted for a complex of content factors. In somewhat analogous manner, words may be regarded as means of epitomizing consciousness, while they permit the highest type of ideational elaboration of experience. The widest variety of content factors may be related to words; that is, the use of a word is often cultivated under the guiding influences of concrete content, as when the child builds up the idea of animal through direct perceptual contact with dogs and horses. After a time the concrete memory images attached to the word fade out and leave the word as a substitute, as a minimum content to which (as when the man condenses his whole attitude towards all kinds of animals into a single compact experience) an elaborately organized meaning may attach.

Images and verbal ideas. When, therefore, we ask what it is that a person thinks of in his use of a word, we shall certainly go astray if we attempt to answer that the word calls up all of the concrete experiences with which it has been connected and with which it may be connected. For example, let the reader ask himself what presents itself in consciousness when he sees the word "animal." It would be still better if, instead of choosing some word thrown into the text as an isolated illustration, we should ask the reader to give an account of the mental experiences through which he passed when he observed one of the words that came in the course of the general discussion. For example, what was called up a moment ago when the eye passed the very definite word "text"? The answer to these questions with regard to the content of consciousness at the moment of recognition of words will certainly not be that the mind is filled with trains of concrete images.

Mental attitudes as characteristic phases of verbal ideas. The consciousness of a word has sometimes been described as a feeling or an attitude, and such a description as this unquestionably comes nearer to the truth than does the explanation of meaning through images, which has sometimes appeared in psychological discussions of this matter.

A general term such as "animal" or "text" turns the thought of the reader in one direction or the other without filling the mind with definite contents. The content of experience arises rather from the total phrase or sentence; the single word indicates only the direction in which this content is to be sought, or in which it is to be applied in some future stage of mental activity. For example, if I say that all animals are subject to man's dominion, there is much more of attitude in the whole experience than there is content. We look down upon the animals; we feel their inferiority; we recognize ourselves as above them. The attitude of mind experienced is the all-important fact. There is an experience of personal elation, which may perhaps be worked out into imagery, if one contemplates it long enough. Thus, one may turn the thought into images by thinking of himself for the moment as the representative man looking down upon the animals gathered as he saw them in childhood in some picture of Adam naming the animals. But all this concreteness in one's description of the animals and of himself is recognized as too picturesque to be true to ordinary experience. We can stop and fill out the attitude with appropriate imagery if we like, but we do not ordinarily do so. The truer statement is that the idea comes as a single simple attitude and prepares one to go on from a position of superiority to some appropriate sequent relation. The value of the words lies in the fact that they carry experience forward, furnishing only so much content as is necessary to support thought without overloading experience with all the detail.

Other illustrations of thought relations. Again, take another illustration which shows that there may be nicety of shading in our thought relations without much content. If we use such a word as "savage," we are likely to take an attitude of superiority somewhat analogous to that taken toward the animals, but flavored more than the former idea with a concession of equality. If we speak of higher beings, such as angels, we assume an entirely different attitude, without necessarily giving ourselves the trouble to fill in any definite content. Indeed, the content of any thought referring to the higher beings is recognized everywhere as more or less of a makeshift, in that we fill in the unknown with such images as we can borrow from ordinary life, the images being symbols, not true representations.

Concrete words. All this has been expressed by certain psychologists in the statement that general ideas are in essence nothing but dispositions toward activity. Here we have a formula which is very closely related to the formula which we derived in our discussion of the development of percepts. There are, undoubtedly, direct motor habits and consequent attitudes in connection with many concrete words. It is, on the other hand, probably not true that the bodily attitude assumed when we think of the word "animal" is anything like a complete bodily attitude such as would be assumed in the presence of animals in concrete experience. The mental attitude aroused by the word probably has as its direct physiological parallel a bodily movement which is a much-reduced resultant of earlier direct attitudes. It is in its present form merely a faint reverberation, significant not for direct adaptation but merely as a step in the development of a general and perhaps very remote form of activity. The present attitude is one of those indirect forms of human adjustment which render the experience of man freer and more ideational than the experience of the animals. The bodily movement in such cases is symbolical and transient, assumed merely for the sake of carrying the individual forward into a more complete state which lies beyond.

Examples of words arousing tendencies toward action. The matter may be made clear by considering what happens when by means of words one is told that he is to go first to the right until he reaches a certain place, and is then to turn toward the left and go straight ahead. There are clearly certain tendencies toward direct bodily movements aroused by the words " right " and " left " and " straight ahead." These tendencies toward movement, it is true, are not significant as present adaptations to the environment ; they are significant merely because they give the thinking individual a certain tendency, which may, indeed, work itself out later in a much more fully developed and concrete form, but is at present a kind of suppressed, incipient form of action. If one has thought out a series of movements toward the right and left, he will have developed within himself a form of behavior which, on the presentation of the appropriate stimulation in the form of the signpost or building at which he is to turn, will serve as a sufficient preliminary organization to arouse a significant and concrete form of behavior. The preliminary thought attitude and faint bodily expression serve, therefore, in a tentative way to aid subsequent direct adaptations.

Abstract words. If, now, we choose as our illustration not words of direction but abstract phrases, such as the phrases by which men are exhorted to patriotism, obviously the emotional stirring which one feels as the result of these exhortations is by no means adequate to explain the true significance of the word " patriotism." A man cannot become truly patriotic by going through the inner stirrings which this word arouses. Indeed, in not a few cases vague emotional responses check rather than promote the development of true interpretations because the vague response satisfies the need of the mind for experience but gives no complete or adequate content. The trouble with the emotional response lies not in the fact that it is emotional but in the impossibility of its expressing fully the whole significance which the word must carry. Such an abstract term as that under discussion can be made potent for direct bodily organization only when it is supplied through proper settings with some definite and final purpose of an active kind. To be truly patriotic one must be

aroused to some definite form of public service. The final
purpose will then be like the concrete words "left" and
"right." The abstract word taken alone is the expression of
a relation. If it is treated as a final factor of experience, it
will dissipate itself in vague emotional reactions.

To take still another illustration : If in the course of a
scientific discussion one is told that a certain problem needs
very much to be investigated, the word "problem" will arouse
within the individual some kind of a responsive attitude which
can be described in a general way as an attitude of hesitation,
of turning hither and thither in the search for a solution. But
the conscious process will be more than the attitude of hesitation and turning, for it will have a form and significance
determined by the whole train of ideas into the midst of which
this attitude of hesitation and turning is injected. Thus, if
the problem is in geology, the attitude of inquiry will be very
different from that which would be assumed if the train of
thought related to astronomy. We may therefore speak of
the attitude aroused by the word "problem" as wholly relational in its character. Another way of expressing the matter
is to say that the attitude is in the world of ideas for the time
being rather than in the world of practical adjustments. We
mean by such statements as these that the attitude is merely
a temporary step in the process of ideational organization ; it
is not an immediate reaction on any object. It is an indirect
and elaborate phase of adaptation ; it has value and significance because of the turn which it gives to the ideational
process rather than because of the concrete imagery or
reaction to the world of things.

Contrast between concrete images and abstract ideas. The
indirectness of verbal forms of consciousness and of the related nervous processes involves, as has often been noted in
discussions of language, certain dangers of possible malad-
justment. Concrete images and direct forms of experience
cannot, because of their limited nature, be turned in very

many directions. Verbal ideas, on the other hand, especially if they are abstract, are capable of a great variety of connections because they are so meager and schematic in individual content.

Besides this, there is a disadvantage in the use of abstract terms in that two individuals, while they may start with the same general tendency of attention, may, in the course of the use of the words, drift apart, without being as clearly conscious of their divergence from each other as they would be if they dealt constantly with concrete percepts. It is a much more definite method of interchanging ideas to demonstrate the objects themselves, or to demonstrate some concrete representations of the objects, such as pictures or models. If one does not have pictures or models, he naturally tries to correct the errors which are likely to creep in when he is using words, by calling up from time to time as concrete an image in the mind of his listener as it is possible to evoke by the use of words. We all of us feel the relief in any continued discourse when a figure of speech, or an illustration, is used. The figure of speech gives us a fairly concrete image with which to deal. The image in this case may be remote from the immediate subject of thought, it may be related to the present discussion only as a kind of rough analogy, but the presence of some characteristic which illustrates and renders concrete the abstract discussion is a relief in the midst of abstract relational terms and furnishes the means of correcting possible tendencies toward divergence of thought between the speaker and the listener. An illustration is even more definite in its character, and so long as it calls up in the minds of the speaker and listener the same kind of concrete images, it is a direct corrective of the possible looseness of verbal thought and verbal communication.

Particular images as obstructions to thought. How far one should be picturesque in his language, and how far one should, on the other hand, use terms which are not related to definite mental pictures, is a matter which must be determined by the demands of the particular situation at hand. It would be quite impossible in any generalized science like physics continually to deal with concrete illustrations. If the scientist speaks, for example, of the general law of gravity, he cannot be dealing with all of the specific cases of gravity known to his experience, nor can he feel himself bound to a single illustration. He may come back to the single illustration in order to hold his verbal idea true to the concrete facts, but he should cultivate the ability to get away from the concrete cases into the wider sweep of thought which is covered by the general word.

Ideas or indirect forms of experience characteristic of man. In concluding this discussion of language it will be well to reiterate that human life has taken on, through the development of indirect modes of consciousness and behavior, an aspect which differentiates it altogether from the life of animals. The consequences for human nature of the evolution of a mode of reaction such as speech is, are unlimited in importance. The full significance of this unique mode of behavior will become increasingly apparent as we canvass in detail the problems of ideation and abstraction.

CHAPTER XI

MEMORY AND IDEAS

The problem of describing ideas. Throughout the last chapter reference was made to ideas without any effort to describe in full these important phases of experience. It now becomes necessary for us to take up the treatment of ideas and of the complex processes of thought which are made up of ideas.

The way has been prepared for this discussion by the conclusions reached in all earlier chapters. Let us review briefly the essentials of our earlier studies. First, animals develop inner states in their efforts to respond to sensory stimuli. Second, the higher animals become increasingly able to carry on elaborate internal readjustments. Corresponding to these elaborate readjustments are certain complexes of sensations and certain attitudes which gradually grow more and more highly differentiated. Third, the inner organization of man and his closest relatives in the animal world is such that experience is progressively recorded in the form of habits of reaction and corresponding mental states.

We are now ready to ask what is the form of this inner enriched mental life which man develops in the course of experience. Our popular language is well supplied with words referring to these products of experience. We say that man stores up in memory ideas and thoughts. We speak of recalling the past, of images in the mind, of an inner world of thoughts and thought relations.

Ideas not derived from present impressions. In all such phrases as the above there is a sharp contrast between present sensory impressions and the experiences which are brought over from the past. There is also a recognition of the overwhelming volume of past experiences. The individual faces the world of the present moment with a mind set and prepared through long training. What we call intelligence is not the impression of the moment but a body of experiences drawn out of the past.

Ideas as revivals. Let us consider some of the simplest types of ideas. If one closes his eyes and thinks of the scene which a moment before impressed itself upon his vision, he will recognize that his consciousness is filled with a substitute for direct visual sensations and percepts; this substitute is called a memory image. When one thinks of an absent acquaintance, the memory image may contain factors which are substitutes for direct auditory impressions of the voice. When one thinks of a rough surface without touching it, the image contains substitutes for tactual factors and their perceptual organization. These illustrations serve to emphasize the scope of the word "image," which it will be seen is used not merely for vision but also for all spheres of experience.

Advantages of relative independence of sensory impressions. Before taking up any of the details regarding the character and laws of memory images, it will be well to dwell briefly upon the great advantage to the individual of possessing these substitutes for direct impressions. The mind supplied with memory images is relatively independent of contact with objects; the images may serve as the basis for attitudes and for reconstructive organizations which may be of the highest significance in individual life. A commonplace illustration of this advantage is seen whenever one runs over in his mind the various places in which he has been and where he might have left a lost object. More complex illustrations may be drawn from the mental activities of an inventor who thinks out many combinations, thus using the images in consciousness as substitutes for real objects. To be sure, there are certain disadvantages which connect themselves with these advantages. The inventor can make more mistakes in this imagery than he could if he tried to fit together real things, and one's false memory of where he left his property may lead him far astray. But taken in the large, the freedom from the necessity of always waiting for direct impressions is one of the great superiorities of the higher forms of mental life.

Individual variations in imagery. One of the most important statements to be made in the description of memory images is that different individuals show great differences in the character and vividness of their memory images. Some years ago Galton asked a number of individuals to test their mental imagery by calling up as definitely and fully as possible the familiar objects of the breakfast table. After the memory image had been called up, the observer was requested to state how clear the mental image was in color and form and other characteristics. Some of the observers said that they recalled objects with a vividness and detail altogether comparable to their perceptual experience. These Galton called good visualizers. Others described their memory images as extremely vague and hazy. Still others, who were between the extreme classes, stated that their mental images were restricted in extent and were relatively fainter than the percepts themselves but, nevertheless, fairly comparable in general character to direct sensory experiences. Galton's tests have frequently been repeated, and his results have been fully corroborated. Furthermore, it has been found that persons who have faint visual images have, in some cases, vivid auditory images. Some persons have vivid tactual imagery or vivid memory of movements. The blind, for example, can have no visual memories; their memory consciousness must therefore be filled by a totally different type of content from that which exists in the mind of the normal individual.

The accidents of individual experience and mental imagery.
Not only is the type of memory very different in different
individuals, but the special contents differ according to the
accidents of individual experience. Thus, if two persons
have looked at the same scene from two different points of
view, their imagery will be different; certain near and vivid
factors for one person will be vague and remote for the
other. Then, too, individual attitudes react upon the contents of experience to determine the character of imagery.
If an especially pleasing or disagreeable color has been presented to a given individual, it may continue in his memory
for a long time, while a second individual looking at the
same color, but not greatly pleased or displeased by it, may
very soon forget it altogether.

Dependence on vividness and recency. In spite of individual differences in mental imagery, there are certain general statements which apply to all persons and all types of
memory. All other conditions being equal, memory depends upon the vividness and recency of the sensory impression. It should be noticed that memory does not depend
on intensity but on vividness. If intensity results in the concentration of attention upon the impression, then intensity
may indirectly help to fix the impression; but a faint
impression upon which attention has been centered will
continue in memory long after the disappearance of an impression which passes without attention. The recency of an
impression is also a matter of importance. Careful quantitative tests show that impressions fade with relative rapidity
at first and at a very gradual rate later. We forget many
impressions entirely in the first few moments after they are
received. What we retain beyond the first brief period is
more likely to continue as a relatively permanent addition
to the content of consciousness.

The training of memory. Much may be said with regard
to the scope of memory and with regard to the possibility

of increasing the scope of memory by training. It is doubt-less true that the ability to retain impressions differs greatly with different individuals ; some retaining many impressions and carrying them forward through long periods, others having little or no ability to retain. So clearly marked are these natural characteristics of different individuals that the changes produced through practice are relatively small. In-deed, Professor James asserts that there is no possibility of changing the degree of natural retentiveness through train-ing. This statement has been shown to be out of harmony with the, facts, for there are evidences of increase in the scope of memory through training. Nevertheless, Pro-fessor James's statement is probably much nearer the truth than the popular assumption that memory can be radically changed through practice.

Retention as distinguished from recall. Another general fact regarding memory is that experiences are not actively recalled without some present impression or related memory which serves as the motive or occasion for the exercise of memory. The mere retention of an impression is not the whole of memory. For example, at this moment there must be retained by every reader of these words hundreds of proper names. There is no motive for the recall of most of them. If one should find in the text, however, such a phrase as "author of the Iliad," one of the proper names would be recalled and memory would become active for that one name. This name might in turn suggest other memories. The fact that memories are thus linked together and that active recall is always a matter of a train or sequence of processes was noticed long ago by Aristotle. He described the principles of memory, or, as they were later designated, the laws of association. There are two general principles of association which we may note : first, the principle of association by contiguity ; and, second, the principle of association by similarity or contrast.

Association by contiguity. When one thinks of the letter *A* he is very likely to recall also the letter *B*, because the two have so often followed each other in experience. The first line of a poem suggests the second; the sight of one of two intimate friends suggests the other. In general, when two experiences have been intimately related in earlier experience, the appearance of one is likely to serve as a sufficient motive for the recall of the second.

Association by similarity. When one sees a face which has eyes, or nose, or mouth like those of another person, the like feature is in many cases enough to recall the absent person. In such a case as this the two faces now associated need never have appeared together in the past; it is enough that they contain the same feature. This relation between two experiences having a common factor is evidently a more complex fact than association by contiguity, for it involves a sufficient analysis or concentration of attention upon a single feature to separate it from its

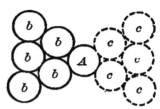

Fig. 57. Association by similarity

The full-drawn circles represent the elements of the present experience. Of these elements *A* attaches itself also to the system of elements represented by the dotted line circles. *A*, when taken with the circles *b, b, b,* constitutes the present experience; *A*, when taken with the circles *c, c, c,* constitutes the recalled experience. *A* is obviously the center of relations between the two systems

present surroundings and make it the link of connection with a group of experiences not now present. The diagram in Fig. 57 represents the situation. The circle *A* represents a single feature of the face now seen; *b, b, b* are the other features. In a past experience, *A* has been part of a system of features of which *c, c, c,* were the others. If *A* becomes the subject of special attention, it can revive the elements *c, c, c,* and thus detach itself from *b, b, b* the features of the present complex in which it stands. In general, then, whenever a factor of experience now present has appeared in earlier experiences in a different combination, the earlier combination may be recalled through association by similarity.

Association by contrast. Association by contrast will be clear after the foregoing discussion of association by similarity, for no contrast can exist without like elements. One may contrast a candle and the sun because they both give light, or the moon and a coin because they are both round, but in each of these cases the basis of the contrast is a common factor.

New products evolved in ideation. Thus it is seen that memory images do not represent merely the traces of earlier experiences, but by continual association and readjustments memory images change their character and in the later stages show quite as much the effects of readjustments in mental life as the results of initial impression. When two ideas have been associated by contrast, there is an analysis which tends to break up the original memory images and bring to clear consciousness one element of the associated ideas together with what we may properly call the new idea of contrast. When the idea of contrast arises, the descriptive term " image " becomes less appropriate than it was for the simple ideas with which the discussion began.

Ideas not all images. The idea of contrast is an idea of a higher type. It is very difficult to state what is the content of such an idea. It is a kind of shock of difference, a feeling of intellectual opposition. Indeed, there are many psychologists who insist on the use of the term " imageless thought " in describing such an idea. They mean by this term to draw attention to the fact that the mind deals at these higher levels not with definite revivals of sensory content but with certain tendencies of consciousness which are to be sharply distinguished from memory images. Perhaps the best description which can be given will be by the use of an analogy. The mind is calling up a series of images when suddenly it turns in a new direction. The abrupt turning is a real experience, often very vivid and important for all later thinking. Just at the moment of turning there must have been an experience. What was the experience of turning? It was an experience which linked together two images, but it was not in itself an image.

Tendency to revert to imagery type. The more complex ideational experience becomes, the more elements there are which must thus be described as imageless. On the other hand, it is to be noted that there is a tendency to develop devices by which the mind can mark and hold steadily before it these imageless ideas. When one has had the experience of contrast, one tends to mark the experience by a word which will give it enough content to make it a stable unit in thought.

Advantages of indirect forms of experience. All these statements draw attention to the fact that ideas are, more than any other phase of experience, flexible and subject to inner readjustment. Thus, even when dealing with revivals of perceptual experiences every person has his own peculiar image depending on his point of observation and his personal powers of retention. Courts of law are familiar with this fact and attempt to eliminate by comparison of much testimony the purely personal elements which always attach to a memory image.

The flexibility of ideas, as has already been pointed out, may be of great advantage because it puts the individual in possession of a device for thinking out changes in the perceptual world. When men put together ideas, they do so because ideas are flexible. If they get them put together in a productive way, they often make up a model to which later the hard material world may be made to conform.

We are brought by this statement, as we have been several times before, to a recognition of the distinction between direct and indirect modes of adjustment to the world. The physiological conditions necessary to the formation of ideas are undoubtedly provided for in the nervous processes which go on in the association areas of the cerebrum. In the lower animals, where the association areas are small or lacking, there is little evidence of ideas. In these animals sensory processes pass to motor discharge with greater directness than in man. In like manner the infant seems to be wholly absorbed in percepts. This is related to the fact that the tracts in the association areas are the latest to develop, the process of development being, as noted in an earlier chapter, distinctly traceable for a period after birth.

Animal behavior direct and perceptual, human behavior indirect and ideational. The significance of the evolution of the association areas can be seen by contrasting the modes of human behavior with the modes of behavior exhibited lower in the scale of life. If an animal is aroused to anger by some stimulation, it responds by directly attacking the source of the stimulation. If an animal is pleased by some form of agreeable excitation, it makes clear its pleasure in an immediate reaction. There is in animal life very little delay or indirection in response. When we contrast all this with human life, we are impressed by the fact that man's activities are most of them indirect. They require more time to mature. Thus, if a man sees an object passing before him, he may be thrown into a long train of thought rather than into a direct series of activities. The long train of thought is possible because man has a complex central nervous system through which the impression may circulate before it passes out as a motor impulse. Or man's action may be indirect in another sense, as was shown in the chapter on speech. Instead of attacking the object directly, he may call his neighbor and talk the matter over with him, ultimately arriving at a mode of action only after a long series of verbal preparations and plans which are indirect and related only in the most remote fashion to the object which yielded the original impression.

The world of ideas comes ultimately to be a world of superior importance. Its laws of association are free and independent of the world of things. One can think of the cities of the country as belonging together because in the mind cities are associated, while in reality they are held apart by great stretches of territory.

Influence of ideas on things. The result of the evolution of this inner world of ideas is that man ultimately puts together not only in his mind but in his actual conduct elements of the world which would never have been put together except for the laws of mental association. The laws of association are thus made to dominate the world of things.

Tool-consciousness. Take, for example, the invention of tools. Primitive man was cut by a stone or torn by a thorn. Did he merely cry out with pain as an unintelligent animal might? Not at all. He saw that the sharp edge which had injured him might be of great use to him if it could be brought into new relations. So he picked up the stone and plucked the thorn and put them to the uses which he saw first in his own mind and afterward realized in material readjustments.

Knowledge of nervous process limited. It must be frankly admitted that this discussion has carried us beyond our knowledge of the conditions in the nervous system. We know in a general way what association areas are, but we do not know the details of their organization. We know ideas introspectively more intimately than we know their objective conditions.

Traditionally, psychology has begun with ideas and given less attention to those lower and simpler forms of experience with which we dealt in earlier chapters. For this reason the science of psychology has suffered in its relations to the biological sciences. Either ideas have been thought of as facts wholly apart from bodily life or they have been declared in a vague way to be dependent on laws of physical being. Psychology has oscillated between a purely theoretical spiritualism and a crass materialism. The mind has been regarded either as wholly distinct or as part of the bodily phenomena.

Consciousness as product of evolution. The view to which our study has led us can be expressed in evolutionary terms. Gradually the animal world, in working out its reactions to the environment, has evolved an inner world conditioned by indirect and tentative reactions. This inner world is social in many of its characteristics; that is, it is a world through which individuals of the same type are drawn into sympathetic communication. The inner world is one in which ideas as substitutes for things are rearranged. The inner world is thus distinct from the lower levels of bodily adjustment, but is at the same time a part of the economy of individual relation to the world and is directly evolved out of the efforts at direct adjustment.

Such an explanation of the place of consciousness in evolution gives us the fullest justification for our emphasis on those aspects of ideas which are not copies or reproductions of sensory impressions but new modes of rearranging experiences.

We shall continue our discussion, accordingly, with a treatment of the changes produced in experience through the most elaborate rearrangements in ideas.

CHAPTER XII

IMAGINATION AND THE FORMATION OF CONCEPTS

Adaptation through ideas. The animal adapts itself to its environment by cultivating better modes of direct reaction, such as greater speed of running or greater skill in the use of its teeth or claws. Gradually there appears in the highest animals a new mode of adjustment in the tendency to organize into social groups. The social group is a protective device which gives the individual greater strength than he can cultivate in his own individual organism. As soon as the social group evolves there must grow up, and there do grow up, types of activity designed to hold the group together. In man this latter phase of evolution culminates, and social coöperation becomes one of the dominant facts in life. No longer does man compete with his enemies by cultivating greater and stronger muscles; he meets the struggle for existence by social coöperation. His reactions on the world are in large measure indirect. He invents a world of social forms which can be described only by saying that it is an artificial environment of human making.

In a very real sense this means the evolution of a new type of adaptation. The competitions of human life are at a new level, wholly different from those of animal life. The character of this new type of adaptation can be studied through an analysis of one system of human behavior such as commerce, which has no parallel whatsoever in the animal world.

Early stages of barter. In the earliest stages of exchange the parties to the transaction demanded direct contact with the objects bartered. Even at this primitive stage much self-control and much regard for social relations are exhibited. The fact that men will barter at all proves that they have cultivated ideas to the extent of refraining from mere brutal seizure of that which they desire and to the extent of realizing the possibility of giving up one thing for another. Barter involves in its crudest form some powers of thought and some attention to social relations. But barter is always perceptual in its demand that the commodities to be exchanged be directly accessible in tangible and visible form.

Barter perceptual. The stories of primitive barter which show the savage duped by the gaudy color of cheap wares bear eloquent testimony to the fact that perception is at this early stage not yet replaced by ideas.

Standard values. After barter began to be understood and widely practiced, there was cultivated a desire for uniformity; that is, for standard methods of exchange. Some commodity more durable in its qualities than the rest began to serve as a common standard to which all transactions were referred. Among hunting tribes all barter is standardized in terms of furs. In grazing communities sheep and cattle become the standards. Through the use of such standards, ideas of uniform value were developed, and the mere showy perceptual characteristics of objects receded into the background.

Symbolic values. The next step in exchange comes when some very permanent commodity takes on symbolic value. Wampum is prized not alone because it is a beautiful string of shells but because it serves as a counter and may be passed around as a promissory note for future delivery of a stipulated number of pelts or tents or arrows. By the time this stage is reached we must assume high powers of association. Wampum has value now because it calls up ideas and because the social group in increasing measure guarantees the ideas connected with the symbol.

As with wampum, so with the metals. The ideational values are finally marked on the metal. Then comes the paper substitute for the metal and finally the various forms of commercial credit of modern commerce. One has only to represent to himself the scene which would follow if a bank note were offered to a savage hunter in exchange for game to realize how far from direct perceptual experience modern commerce has gone.

Evolution from perception to ideas. This sketch of the evolution of barter into commercial exchange could be paralleled in every field of human action. Manufacturing with machinery has replaced the simpler direct contacts of primitive life. Travel by borrowed power of animals and finally by mechanical forces has largely replaced migration of the savage type. Sanitary regulations and settled modes of urban life have replaced the life of the forest and the wilderness.

How has all this evolution come about? There is one and only one answer. Man has learned to combine and recombine ideas, to call on his neighbor for coöperation and for the further comparison of ideas, and to meet the needs of life indirectly rather than by direct perceptual responses.

Higher controls of conduct. The transformation of life thus outlined has not gone on without bringing about the most radical internal changes in the mind of man. To the direct and vivid emotions which accompany instinctive reaction have been added trains of ideas which lead to deliberate forms of behavior. Human nature has become complex. There is an element of animal life and of primitive devotion to perceptions in every man. We shall never outgrow instincts or our native impulses to seize the things about us. But above and beyond these direct modes of adaptation there is the higher world of ideas. In dealing with this higher world a new type of experience has been evolved. There are new pleasures which come from the fitting together of ideas. There are new forms of displeasure which come from the clash of ideas.

Ideational attitudes. For example, there is a shock when one hears a profane word which is little less than the shock from a physical blow. The name of the Deity has associated itself in all experience with the attitude of reverence, and when this name is taken out of its proper associations and used in a reckless fashion, the emotional recoil is violent.

Other examples can be drawn from the cultivated demands for the use of proper grammatical forms. The child gradually learns that a plural noun demands a plural verb. The shock which comes from hearing a violation of this rule is quite as unpleasant as the shock from a sharp, cold breeze striking the skin. Furthermore, the inner muscular recoils in the two cases are not unlike. Both involve, among other factors, an interruption of respiration and a change in the rate of the heartbeat.

Ideas as substitutes for impressions. When we speak of the world of ideas as a real world, all the foregoing considerations must be kept in mind. Ideas are real in prompting behavior and in giving directions to our acts. Ideas may be followed by habitual reactions until they come to demand these reactions quite as much as do things seen through the eye or heard through the ear. Ideas may influence the train of attention quite as much as percepts. For example, the man who is lost in thought does not attend to the object coming toward his eyes. In short, ideas have values comparable in all respects to percepts and in some respects quite superior.

Imagination as reorganization of ideas. In this chapter we shall discuss some of the changes which take place in this world of ideas, for it is important if we are to understand the world in which man lives that we shall know the laws of change in his world of ideas. In an earlier connection the laws of memory were discussed. It was there shown that in some measure the mind holds its ideas fixed and brings them back under proper conditions so that past experiences may operate in present surroundings. When ideas are thus carried forward, they are called memories in the strict sense, or sometimes they are called images. It was pointed out in that earlier treatment of the matter that memories undergo a change in experience. We now turn to the more elaborate types of such change. For these types of change there are a number of names. Sometimes ideas are described as imaginations. This term is used to indicate that a mere rearrangement of elements of memories has been made. One imagines a horse with wings. The source of the idea " horse " is memory, likewise of the idea " wings," but the union of these two sets of ideas is an act of the imagination. When the combinations which go on in consciousness are purely capricious, we speak of fanciful imaginations. When, on the other hand, recombinations of mental processes are worked out systematically and coherently, we speak of scientific imagination. Thus a dragon is a fancy ; the imagination of a Columbus or a Watt is scientific and constructive.

Personifying imagination. One of the most primitive forms of imagination is that exhibited by savages when they attribute to inanimate objects the personal characteristics which they find in themselves. The savage never thinks of thunder or of the wind without putting back of it in his imagination some personal agency. This form of constructive thought is the simplest which could originate in a personal consciousness. An emotion of anger is a more direct explanation for a natural catastrophe than is some abstract statement referring to physical force. To modern thought the myths of early peoples seem like the play of the most capricious imagination ; to the mind untrained in the forms of critical scientific imagination nothing could be more natural than a myth. Even the trained mind derives pleasure from the personification of objects, because it is easy to use the factors from personal experience in all manner of combinations.

Imaginations occasions of useless activities. Early man was led by his imaginations to undertake many useless forms of activity. Thus, he attempted to propitiate the personalities which his own mind had put into streams and mountains and trees. There was no direct evidence that his imaginations were not in conformity with the facts, and hence the imaginations went on increasing in complexity until they broke down by their own incoherency.

Critical tests of imaginations. This reference to the fanciful imaginations of primitive man introduces us to the discussion of the more productive forms of imagination in which the mind does not weave together factors of experience capriciously, but under the guidance of conditions which limit the freedom of the constructive process. When imagination is used for purposes of practical construction, or for the later purposes of science, its products must be subjected to critical examination by the individual who develops them. A first principle of criticism of imagination may be described as the principle of empirical test through application. The constructs of imagination may be used to guide activities, and if the activities are not successful, it will obviously be necessary to go over again the combinations which were worked out in consciousness and to revise these combinations with a view to making them more suitable bases for action. We may speak of this form of criticism as the practical or empirical test of imagination. If, for example, a given individual finds that he must get across a certain stream, he is likely, if he has time and the necessary mental development, to consider first in imagination the means by which he can get across. He determines in thought that it would be possible by bringing together certain appliances to make the passage easy. If, on trying the expedients which have suggested themselves in his thought process, he finds that the idea is a good one, his imagination receives the confirmation which comes from practical utility. If, on the other hand, his imagined device breaks down when put to the practical test, he will be led to further considerations of a more elaborate character, in order to correct the deficiences which have been shown by the practical test to exist in his imagination.

Empirical test often inapplicable. There are many ideal constructions which cannot be subjected directly to practical tests. For example, in the course of human history man has constantly been trying to reconstruct in imagination the process of the development of the earth on which he lives. Our modern science of geology is an elaborate effort to reconstruct the history of the earth. Obviously, the ideas reached by geology cannot be tested by any single practical act. Man has developed, accordingly, a system of criteria by which he tests the validity of his ideal constructions, even when these ideal constructions are not directly intended for the practical uses of life. These theoretical criteria, as we may call them, can be shown to grow out of the nature of experience itself.

The test of internal agreement. It is demanded by every human consciousness that the elements of any given idea shall be harmonious. We have seen that it is true of perceptual processes that they have unity and arrangement, such that all of the conflicting qualitative factors are provided for in a single experience through the arrangement of the elements of experience in spatial and temporal series. Thus, even in perceptual consciousness, a certain coherency and harmony are required of the elements before they can enter into the percept. Still more when we come to the constructs of imagination is there a demand for harmony of relations among the factors which are presented. Thus it would be difficult to think of one physical substance as subject to gravity and another as not. If any factor or relation is recognizably incongruous with the system of experiences into which it is introduced, then that system of experience will have to be rearranged until the whole organization is adapted to the reception of the element which was out of harmony with the other elements, or else the incongruous element will have to be rejected. Thus, if all substances fall toward the earth and smoke rises, we must devise an explanation. Scientific imagination, when not susceptible to practical tests, is thus nothing more nor less than the effort to develop an elaborate system of congruous ideas.

The criterion of coherency a product of development. Primitive man does not have this criterion of the harmony of all of the elements of thought as fully developed as does modern science. This is in part due to the limitations of primitive experience : as when a savage believes thunder to be a voice because he knows little of either the thunder or of the mechanism which produces the voice. It is in part due to a general uncritical attitude : as when in Greek mythology the earth is borne upon the shoulders of Atlas because attention was not ordinarily concentrated on the necessity of supporting Atlas.

The demand for coherency as exhibited in constructive scientific ideas. It cannot be asserted that the criterion of harmony among the elements of imagination is applied with full success even in modern science, but examples can be given without limit of its application. Thus, it is quite impossible for us to think of the earth and the sun as related to each other without, at the same time, conceiving of some kind of bridge between the earth and the sun. Science has therefore developed the notion of the ether as a continuous substance between the earth and all other points in the universe. The ether is not a factor of direct experience in any form. It is demanded in scientific considerations in order to make the idea of the solar system and of the universe a coherent thinkable idea. Ether may, accordingly, be called a product of imagination. This statement does not deal with the question of its objective reality; it merely asserts that ether comes into scientific experience in response to a demand for harmony in the ideational system, not through perception.

Uncritical imaginations. The extent to which imaginations are criticized depends upon the development of the individual who possesses them and upon the type of ideas under examination. A good illustration of the dependence of criticism on individual development was given above in discussing the myths of primitive peoples. Another may be found in the imaginations of children. It has frequently been said that children are more imaginative than adults. This statement is based on the observation that a child will imagine many things in connection with its toys and derive a great deal of satisfaction from these imaginations, when an adult would be so clearly conscious of the falsity of the imaginations that he would derive little pleasure from them. This observation does not show that the child is more imaginative than the adult, but it shows that the imaginations in early life are not subjected to any careful criticism. Almost any mental combination is accepted by the child and enjoyed for the moment without serious criticism. Indeed, the child's experience is often like the savage's, too meager to make it possible for him to construct any systems of thought that shall constitute the basis for the criticism of his particular imagination. Furthermore, many of the child's activities are not sufficiently serious to constitute practical tests for his imaginative constructs. As life goes on and the systems of thought become more and more closely united with each other, and the practical demands of individual existence come to be more strenuous, the indulgence in fanciful imaginations unchecked by criticism becomes less common than it was in early childhood.

Literary imagination and the canon of coherency. An illustration of the way in which the products of imagination may be subjected to different kinds of criticism is to be found in the case of literary forms. Literature is an effort to construct through the exercise of imagination a system of thought which deals with human interests and human activities. If this constructive process purports to be held closely in agreement with certain records, we call it historical in character, and we demand that it shall conform to the canons of congruity with all the legitimate records of the period in question. If the construction is, on the other hand, confessedly free from any particular reference to definite situations, we call it imaginative literature and recognize its product as fiction. Even in this case we demand of literature that it shall have relation to experience. A wholly unnatural creation has no justification, even in fiction. The particular circumstances which are grouped together may be circumstances which never were brought together in the course of human history or individual life, but the principles of combination must be recognizable as principles in harmony with the general nature of human experience.

The canons of criticism in literature are by no means as clearly definable as are the canons of criticism in scientific thought. The reason for this is that literature includes wide variations in types of individual experience and consequently permits laxness in the demand that the imagined experiences shall conform to the particular type of any individual's life. It is not difficult for us to accept certain rather grotesque and unusual combinations, provided these combinations of experience are referred to periods in time or points in space remote from those with which we are ordinarily in contact.

The uncritical forms of thought which preceded science. The beginnings of what we call scientific thought are obscure, because the careful comparison of scientific ideas is preceded, at times by much practical adjustment of activity to the environment and, at other times, by much uncritical speculation. The practical effort to adjust one's activities to the world leads to certain systems of ideas. Thus, the child always looks for the causes of the happenings which come into his experience long before he formulates in clear, explicit thought the statement that every event has a cause. When he hears a noise, he has a vague notion of something back of the noise. In the same way men must have sought causes in practical life long before there was any science. They also had ideas which they used in the constructive activities of life, such as ideas regarding the strength and durability of certain building materials. In addition to these practical ideas there were speculative ideas. Superstitions of all kinds flourished in the uncritical thought of primitive man. If a bird flew across his path, he thought of infinite varieties of good or ill. There is a certain sense in which all these superstitious and practical ideas constitute the beginnings of science. They furnished the thought material which, when sifted and organized into systematic form, constitutes science. The methods for sifting and organizing this thought material are the essential additions to mental life which came with science.

First sciences limited to facts remote from life. When the systems of coherent ideas began to emerge from the original chaos of practical and superstitious constructs, it is striking that the facts remote from individual control were the earliest to yield to the organizing endeavors of thought. It was possible to construct a system of consistent scientific ideas regarding celestial movements, because these remoter facts were far enough from individual life to be observed without perplexing minor incongruities. The nearer facts of any situation are too full of variations to fall into anything like an harmonious system without the most elaborate ideational reconstruction. Thus, a science of social relations and a science of mental processes could develop only after man had become so thoroughly devoted to the forms of scientific thought that he could follow facts in long series, could deliberately assume some attitude other than that of direct personal relationship, and, consequently, could trace out certain abstract relations in the midst of the complex of varying elements.

Scientific concepts. Let us consider one of the scientific constructs built up in the course of the development of physical science. Such a construct is called a scientific concept. An example of such a concept is that of the atom. Man found, as he examined the bodies about him, that these bodies underwent certain changes which were indicative of unperceived characteristics. It was important to understand these characteristics in dealing with the bodies for practical purposes. For example, water freezes, stones crumble, metals expand and contract with changes in temperature. Man must have noted many of these changes and many of their conditions very early in his dealings with such substances, but he had no direct means of observing what went on in the mass of the matter itself. He therefore set about, at least as far back as the early Greeks, trying to form some idea of the changes which must take place within the substance, in order to explain the changes which he observed. Certain of the Greek thinkers drew upon the forms of experience with which they were familiar — namely, their experience of composite matter made of separate parts — and formulated the concept that all substances are made up of particles which are separated by intervals of space. They concluded, further, that the particles which they assumed as the elements of the substance must be capable of greater and less separation from one another, as in expansion and contraction, and also that they must be capable of rearrangements, such that the appearance of the whole substance is modified without destroying the particles. Through such considerations as these, some of the early scientists came ultimately to refer to the smallest particles of any given substance as atoms, and to describe these atoms as separated from one another by space, and as constituting by their composition the observed body. The physicist or chemist to-day uses this very valuable concept in his thought about substances; he constantly refers to atoms, although he never expects that he will be able to see an atom, or to test the validity of his mental construct by the sense of touch. Indeed, the atom is an idea needed by science just because science has to bring together into an harmonious ideal system more than can be discovered in any single inspection or handling of an object.

Validity of concepts. When such statements as these are made, some persons think that the validity of the scientific concept is seriously called in question. On the contrary, there is no higher guarantee for any form of knowledge than that it is demanded in order to render congruous the whole system of experience. As we have seen, in all of the earlier discussions of perception and ideation, experience has many higher phases which cannot be resolved into direct sensory elements. The validity of space as a form of experience cannot be called in question because it is a relational rather than a sensational phase of experience. For similar reasons, the construction of a concept is justified as a result of a higher organization of experience. The method of arriving at such an ideal construct is indeed indirect; but the concept has all of the validity which belongs to experience as an organized system.

Abstraction. When ideas are completely under the control of the individual, they may be arranged according to principles which are set up by thought itself. Thus, one may decide that it is desirable to group together all round objects or all hollow objects. There then arises an idea of roundness or of hollowness which is called an abstract idea. The term "abstract" means that something has been "cut off." When we think of roundness alone, we neglect color and position and weight. We can cut off the one quality and make it a subject of attention because the power of thought has been developed to the point where inner motives are stronger than external motives.

Generalization. Furthermore, whenever the mind reaches the stage where it can select and concentrate on single aspects or attributes of experience, it can at the same time group together under each selected attribute many individual cases. This is called the power of generalization. Thus, once the mind has fixed on roundness as a selected attribute of objects, it can bring together and group in one class the earth, a ball, an apple, etc.

Abstraction and generalization are valuable not merely as feats of inner control; they make possible highly developed forms of conduct. If one can select and hold steadily before the mind one aspect of an object, conduct can be made more effective through concentration than when the observer is distracted and confused by an effort to deal with unanalyzed complexity.

We shall find ourselves coming back to this topic later when we take up volition as the highest form of behavior. The more fully ideas are abstracted and generalized, the more conduct will be guided by inner motives. The man who sees values in objects and decides to be thrifty is guided by an abstraction and is so far forth acting in response to an inner motive.

Judgments and reasoning. After a concept has been formulated, it may become part of a still more complex mental process which includes several ideas. Thus, when two concepts are related as in the statement " The sun is the center of the solar system," the whole process is termed a judgment. When two or more judgments are united for the purpose of setting up an even more complex combination, the whole process is called reasoning. An example of reasoning is as follows: The sun is the center of the solar system; any central body in a system of this type must have a controlling influence over the other members of the system; hence we should look for the control of the sun over the earth and the other planets.

Logic. It is not in place here to give an account of the various types of judgment and reasoning. It is the function of the science of logic to study the complex processes of thought and to develop the rules under which the validity of these processes may be tested. We must content ourselves in an introductory treatment such as this with certain comments which will serve to call attention to the psychological character of these complex forms of ideational experience. Perhaps the best single topic with which to introduce a psychology of logic is the topic of belief. Let us consider, therefore, what is meant by the statement "I believe a certain conclusion to be true."

Primitive belief. The first and most direct case of belief is that in which I assent to any combination of ideas because my natural tendency is to accept combinations of ideas when there is no reason to deny what is presented. The psychological fact is that ideas which stand together in the mind unchallenged by other experiences are accepted as coherent and acceptable. Thus, when I was a child I believed in Jack the Giant Killer and Jack and the Bean Stalk because my experience was too limited to deny these stories.

Belief after hesitation. A higher form of belief comes after one has hesitated. In such cases the statements are not immediately accepted. This means that they arouse series of associations which suggest various conflicting forms of statement. At this stage there is a restlessness, and other forms of statement are tried; other authorities are cited. It may be that one goes out and tests the conclusion by practical behavior. If the first opposition is broken down by one or the other of these influences, there results in the end a waning of the suggested contradictions.

Belief a positive psychological fact. There can be no doubt that belief in all these cases is something more than the mere hearing of certain sounds or the mere coupling together of certain ideas. When we say that the idea is accepted, we undoubtedly refer to some positive physiological process. Belief is related to the fact that a sensory impression goes through the nervous system to some form of positive expression without being opposed. If it were checked by encountering some current opposing it, we should be restless and the feeling would be one of hesitation. Assent is a genuine process of a positive type. Such a positive process will usually issue in a definite motor response. It may be that the motor process is a mere nod of the head or an inner emotional twinge. The important fact is that the nervous process issues in a positive discharge. The motor discharge may be in itself insignificant, but the fact that it occurs and the fact that it is positive in character give to experience that special turn or coloring which we designate by the term " belief."

Spurious verbal belief. Such considerations lead to brief comment on what is called mere verbal assent. It is possible for one to give assent carelessly by merely repeating what he hears. Many students accept what they find in books in this way. The motor paths leading to the speech centers seem to be stimulated directly by the eyes as they read, or by the ears as they hear. Reaction is of little value in such cases. It is a kind of shunt circuit. The impression does not get mixed in the association areas with any forms of ideation which confuse or interrupt the direct transmission to the speech center. The result is a specious belief and a useless form of nervous and mental reaction. There is nothing more fatal to true mental organization than this short-circuiting of the eyes and ears to the vocal centers. It is one of the penalties which man pays for the development of an indirect mode of behavior.

Habitual belief. Another highly developed form of belief is that which comes from the organization in individual life of certain habitual modes of response. Thus the physicist learns, in spite of sensory testimony to the contrary, to think of every substance as porous. He finds that his beliefs are all conditioned by conformity to this cultivated idea. If any remark is made or any fact turns up which runs counter to this accepted principle, the new proposal will be rejected. Beliefs are thus not unlike the fundamental emotional attitudes. They are very real factors in thought, though they are not made up of memory images.

Religious belief not instinctive. Certain writers, impressed with the similarity of beliefs to emotional attitudes, have regarded certain well-established beliefs, such as religious beliefs, as instinctive. The belief in the Deity, in immortality, in the certainty of moral categories, is held by these authors to be no less primitive in human nature than the fundamental desire for food, for physical comfort, and for companionship. On the other hand, it is held by others that such beliefs are the results of developed systems of ideas.

Sentiments not instinctive. The latter formula, which is the more defensible, suggests the explanation of many of the so-called sentiments and tastes of later life. They are connected with acquired modes of behavior. Certainly, if one studies the life and practices of savages, he finds a striking parallelism between behavior and tribal belief. The savage practices certain customs, and they come to have for him the sanction of the highest religious demands. So in civilized life as well. The sanctions of society are bred into our very beings until we believe in the necessity of social conformity.

Social life and the higher mental processes. Efforts have been made in the recent literature of sociology and psychology to explain social institutions as the products of instinctive tendencies. The argument of this chapter is that belief which grows out of systematic thinking, while it may have the appearance of an instinctive emotion, is in reality the product of the highest types of mental activity. Social sanctions are evolved through association and comparisons of ideas and through the evolution of modes of social behavior. Society may rest on instinctive tendencies, but its forms and operations are all worked out through the use of language. Everywhere in social life one finds abstractions, now of a higher type, now of a lower. Social life is a product of thought and ideation, not of blind instinct.

Fields for the application of psychology of ideas. This chapter must close with these mere outlines of discussions of the higher mental life. That there is a field for a psychological study of all the higher forms of appreciation is indicated by what has been said. This matter will be touched on again in a later chapter dealing with the applications of psychology.

There is a psychology of invention in which the individual is studied at those critical moments when a new set of associations is being evolved within him. There is a psychology of education which must distinguish between learning of a true type and learning to repeat words out of books. There is a psychology of social theory and social conduct. The formula for all of these is a formula of organized mental processes leading to various forms of expression. If the student has grasped the import of this general formula, he will be able to unravel the particular types of organization which appear in each of these spheres.

CHAPTER XIII

THE IDEA OF THE SELF

The idea of self sometimes regarded as matter of direct knowledge. Among the ideas which are built up in practical life and refined by scientific study, there is one which is of special significance to the student of psychology. It is the idea which each person has of himself. So significant is this idea for our ordinary thought that it has sometimes been described in terms which imply that one knows oneself directly as though through some kind of immediate perception. One is supposed to look within and there find an inner reality which is known and recognized without any of the ordinary steps that enter into the process of knowing reality.

Idea of self a concept. That the self is a being which can be directly perceived is, however, contradicted by all the facts of development. The child does not know himself until after he has had a series of experiences. Even the adult has something to learn about himself with each new turn of conscious life. The idea of self must therefore be described as a concept which matures in the course of experience just as does any other scientific or practical idea.

First stages of personal development not self-conscious. Let us attempt to formulate what we know of the most primitive stages of experience, in order that we may arrive at some notion of what consciousness is like before there is any recognition of the self. The simplest forms of animal behavior, as has been repeatedly pointed out, do not indicate any clear marking off of impression from expression. The activity which follows upon impression is so direct that there is no time for the interpolation of any factor, either in the nervous system or in consciousness, between impression and expression. Much the same kind of situation appears when we examine the human infant. There is an inherited mechanism in the instincts which supplies appropriate responses to stimuli, and as a result there is little or no consciousness of any kind involved in reacting to the impression — certainly no recognition of one's own personality. Sensation and response blend in an experience which is overwhelmingly emotional in character and not at all capable of distinguishing one factor of the situation from another. Such experience includes no separate idea of oneself.

Gradual discrimination of self from things. The development from this point is toward the discrimination of phases of experience. Probably there is a gradual differentiation of the sensory elements from one another and of the sensory elements from the individual's attitudes and responses. As soon as things begin to be recognized, there must be a tendency to formulate all one's feelings and attitudes into a kind of personal unity or self. The construction of such a personal core or self in contrast with things is a slow and complex process.

Child's early notion of self largely objective. Undoubtedly, a child's contact with his own body is very important in building up some early crude distinctions between impressions and attitudes. When the child handles his own feet, he finds that the impression he receives, and the attitudes into which he is thrown by the double stimulation of two parts of his body, are entirely different from the impressions which he receives and the simpler attitudes into which he is thrown by the stimulation of one of his members through some external object. He thus comes to distinguish between his body and the external world. The body is a part of the world with characteristics different from the other factors which he recognizes through his senses. There is probably some ground in this fact for the statement that the child's earliest recognition of himself is of the nature of a percept and relates to his physical organism. The relatively objective character of the experience of self at this stage is shown by the fact that, in addition to his own body, the child attaches to himself, as a part of what he calls himself, the possessions which he comes to recognize as his individual property. The external world is broken up into the *meum* and *tuum*, and the general notion of that which belongs to the individual himself is gradually distinguished from that which belongs to others, but the *meum* is not primarily a subjective fact. It is looked at through consciousness, but that consciousness is very little self-consciousness in the purely subjective sense in which we use that term in mature life.

The idea of self as related to discrimination between the objective and subjective. Such considerations as these tend to show that the idea of self is a product of discriminative analysis rather than a fact of immediate perceptual consciousness. So far as we understand immediate consciousness in its early stages, there appears to be little or no ground for assuming that there is present any complete discrimination of the self on the one hand and things on the other. Even in mature life the distinction between the self and nonself is not always drawn. The man who is hurrying to catch a street car has a vivid experience, but it is not nicely analyzed. The hungry man with food before him is little more self-conscious; if, indeed, any more self-conscious, than the animal which spends all of its time and energy in the eager pursuit of food.

The self discovered by contrast with not-self. What brings any individual to a clear recognition of himself will probably depend upon the accidents of individual fortune. The struggle of personal interests with some unyielding objective fact may accomplish it. The development of an idea of some other self, opposed in interest to the self, is often a powerful incentive to the recognition of one's own self. Historically, it has repeatedly been pointed out that the national spirit, which is analogous to personal self-consciousness, often grows out of some contest. In like fashion, the clear idea of the self undoubtedly rises out of some contest of opposing interests.

Social consciousness and self-consciousness. The conflict of interests may take a purely social form, as in the use of language. One sees that all the words referring to spatial directions, for example, center about one's own body. One finds that active or passive verbs have reference to some person. One finds, in short, that one's own expressions are arranged and organized around a different center than are the expressions of every other human being. So impressive does this contrast between individual attitudes become that ultimately, when we find ourselves in agreement with others, we are impressed with the agreement, as in earlier cases we were impressed by the differences, in mental attitude. The result is that our contact with the social world is a constant stimulus to the development of a more and more clearly defined recognition of the self. The child undoubtedly comes to self-consciousness through his use of language more than through any other means.

The self at first not a scientific concept, but a practical concept. Some idea of the self, based upon discrimination of one's own attitudes from the attitudes of other persons, is developed in a wholly unscientific way by every individual, just as the discrimination of the individual body and of one's personal possessions from the rest of the physical world arises naturally in the course of personal life without any effort at systematic definition. Beyond this natural discrimination one may attempt to cultivate a more highly refined formulation of his personal attitudes and personal characteristics, and yet not pass directly into science.

Cultivated self-consciousness. To illustrate certain cases in which self-consciousness takes a form other than the scientific, we may refer first to literary criticism. If a reader begins the criticism of any piece of literature, he will constantly be contrasting the impression which the author intended to produce with the personal attitude aroused in himself through the statements which he reads. There will thus be a certain social contrast between the individual and the author, and this is deliberately cultivated for the purpose of refining and critically elaborating one's own taste. In some cases this may take the form of an effort to conform personal tastes or attitudes to the standards which have evidently been adopted by great masters. There is here an unquestionable tendency to refine self-consciousness at the same time that one cultivates attitudes toward the objective facts.

The religious motive for self-consciousness. Another illustration of the nonscientific cultivation of the concept of the self will appear if we refer to the attitude which is assumed by many individuals in the contemplation of their own origin and destiny. The religious attitude has undoubtedly contributed more to the definition of self in the minds of unscientific individuals than any other system of thought or activity in the world's history. One here asks himself how fully his own personal attitudes conform to what he understands to be the demands of the laws governing his destiny. The system of laws, which he accepts as a system of higher law, may be derived from very different sources; but in any case, whether it be the religious faith of the savage or the systematized theology of the most highly cultivated devotee of an elaborate religious system, there is always in religious thought and aspiration a comparison between the demands of the religious system and the demands of individual interest and feeling. The notion of the self comes to have a compactness and importance under this system of religious self-examination which it could never attain by mere social contrast with the experiences of other individuals or in the presence of physical objects. Questions of ultimate destiny arise, and these are answered in terms of a self which is much more highly elaborated than the bodily or material self upon which man concentrates his attention in the early stages of individual life or the primitive stages of mental development. We find, however, many indications, as we look into savage customs, of a curious mixture of the primitive bodily self and the religious self. The savage always protects with great care the bodily remains of those whom he would serve, and he mutilates and destroys the body of an enemy. The bodily self is here recognized as the tangible aspect of personality.

Scientific idea of personality. As contrasted with these unsystematic efforts at self-realization, the science of psychology aims to build up a thorough idea of the nature and relations of the self. The self becomes for our science a being whose laws of organized life must be discovered and explained.

The self can be fully described and understood only through studies of the type which have been outlined in the foregoing chapters. The self is a being which perceives and forms concepts; it remembers and expresses itself in regular habits. It is characterized by emotions and by elaborate ideational forms of thought. The self is, however, not merely a chance collection of percepts and habits and ideas. There is one attribute of the conscious self which stands out as of paramount importance. The self is a unity. It expresses itself now in one direction, now in another, but in all its various manifestations it is an organized unit. Whatever conscious states the self possesses are modified by virtue of the fact that all aspects of individual consciousness are united in the one being.

The only analogy which can be used in expounding this type of being is the analogy of life. The living being is an organized unity.

The chief item in the concept of life the abstract idea of organization. Such statements as the foregoing are confusing to certain students of science. They profess to know what an atom or an object is, but they say of life that it is not a scientific entity because it is not simple, and they say of conscious selves that they are not entities in any such scientific sense as are atoms and physical forces. Some chemists, for example, would reduce life to mere coexistence of atoms in a complex molecule of protoplasm. It is, indeed, true that there is a chemistry of protoplasm. The significant fact, however, is that once the molecule of protoplasm became organized it began to exercise functions which were absolutely new. It began to reproduce, to contract, to show irritability, and to take in foreign particles and transform them into new molecules of protoplasm. The world began to take on a new aspect when protoplasm came into it. One cannot continually look backward to chemical elements in treating of protoplasm; he must look forward to the effects produced by protoplasm.

Unity of self. So it is with a conscious being. Such a being is conditioned by sense organs and central nervous processes, but a description of these conditions does not exhaust the account. The self has become through organization a unit in the world, capable of affecting in some measure the doings of this world.

The self as an efficient cause. A conscious being is, accordingly, different from a being not endowed with mind just in the degree in which the conscious being can produce effects which depend on consciousness. To deny the reality of the conscious self is to repudiate a scientific concept which is as fully justified as the concept solar system.

Self as a valid scientific concept. Yet certain writers deny the right of science to deal with the idea of self. They say that the self is never seen as is the object which gives us a visual impression. They say that physical reality can be known, but the knowing self is something intangible and unapproachable by scientific methods. The difficulty in the whole situation is that the individual who is trying to explain and understand himself sometimes loses sight of the central fact of his own mental life, as he explores the conditions which surround this central personality. The central personality is taken so much for granted that scientific description tends to deal with all that leads up to personality, and there it stops, finding its chief subjects of thought in these surrounding facts rather than in the central result of all the organized conditions. Some day the historian of thought will write it down as one of the curious fallacies of immature science that certain physiologists, biologists, and even psychologists, were satisfied to call their own personalities mere by-products, without essential significance in the world, just because they did not find consciousness capable of description in the regular scientific formulas adopted for the discussion and explanation of external reality.

One hardly knows how to find phrases in which to answer those who hold consciousness to be less real and potent than physical forces. Certainly, nature has protected and conserved consciousness throughout the whole development of the animal kingdom. Certainly, the world is different because consciousness has been evolved. Certainly, consciousness is no less real than are its conditions; and, finally, consciousness is certainly much more directly approachable to the student of science than is matter.

Concept of unity. These are the statements which describe the psychologist's concept of the self. Such a concept is no less clear and well established than the concepts of all science. Indeed, it is from one's own ideas of himself that the notion of external unities is derived. When one comes back time and time again to the same object and recognizes it as familiar and attributes to it a continuity which goes far beyond anything he can observe through his senses, he is projecting a concept of unity derived from his own experience into the world of outer realities. When science thinks of the earth as a unity, or of the universe as a unity, this is a concept, not a percept. The same kind of comprehensive generalization appears in the practical and scientific study of self. It is probably not true that animals recognize their own unity. Experience with them is, as it is with us, a succession of interrelated events, but the survey of the total succession is not possible in the undeveloped animal consciousness. It is probably not true that children have any broad view of the unity of their personalities. The ability to remember is one of the most significant special experiences from which we derive the content with which to construct a broader self. The ultimate recognition of the most comprehensive unity is a conceptual rather than perceptual fact, even after memory has made its full contribution.

The self a concept. One must be satisfied with a scientific description of the self. One can never see the self directly. To demand that the details of the total unity be filled in with a concrete image or illustration is to demand even more than natural science would demand, if it required a direct perceptual representation of its ultimate substances, such as the atoms.

CHAPTER XIV

DISSOCIATION

Disorganized personality in contrast with normal self.
The discussions of the last chapter, as well as the detailed
description of mental processes of various types, show how
essential is the concept of self unity. This lesson is power-
fully reënforced by considering certain abnormal states in
which the unitary self gives way to disintegrating forces and
leaves the self broken down and unable to play its part in
the world.

Illusions and hallucinations. Every form of mental pathology or abnormality is in some sense a case of malorgani-
zation or disintegration. There are certain mild cases of
irregularity which may be classed as forms of maladaptation,
rather than distinctly pathological cases. Such are, for example, our geometrical illusions. As we saw in our earlier
discussions, an illusion is always an incomplete organization
of the sensations presented to the observer. Defects in organization may be carried very much further in the case of
a person who has what are known as hallucinations. An
individual may, for example, have an irritation upon some
part of the skin which, under normal conditions, would be
neglected or, at most, treated as an inconvenient excitation
of the part; but if the organizations of mental life are unstable because of some general diseased condition of the
individual, this excitation in a certain part of the skin·may
become the center for a most abnormal combination of experiences and may lead to the development of a distinctly
abnormal type of interpretation. Everything that suggests

itself to the mind may be made subservient to this stimulation, until finally the person constructs an imaginary world, giving the abnormal excitation a value and importance which, in normal life, it could never have had. He may come to believe that he is made of glass or stone, or he may think that someone is attacking him with poisons or acids. These illustrations will serve to make clear what is meant by the statement that abnormal mental experiences are always experiences which result from irregularities in organization, and commonly involve more or less disorganization or dissociation of the elements which should be combined.

Sleep, the influence of drugs, hypnosis, and insanity as forms of disorganization. We may examine three distinct cases of dissociation in order to make clear in detail what is meant by mental disorganization. First, there is in sleep a form of normal suspension of central nervous activity which has been provided by nature for the purpose of recuperating the individual. This nervous condition is accompanied by a temporary interruption of normal conscious processes. Second, there are certain forms of dissociation and partial reconstruction which are very similar in character to sleep, but do not serve the purposes of recuperation as does normal sleep. The conditions here referred to may be induced by the use of drugs or by certain other devices, conspicuous among which are the methods of inducing hypnosis. Finally, the dissociations and partial reconstructions, which are temporary in hypnosis and after the use of certain drugs, may appear in a great variety of relatively permanent forms in the different types of insanity. One or two of these typical forms of insanity will be referred to later, in order to exemplify the conditions which result from permanent disorganization.

The physiological conditions of sleep. The physiological conditions which present themselves in the nervous system during sleep are not fully understood, but their general character can be described with sufficient clearness for our purposes. In the first place, the condition of fatigue in the nerve cell has been found to be a condition of somewhat depleted tissue in the cell body. There are also certain chemical changes resulting from fatigue. These are demonstrated by the different degrees to which fatigued and normal cells respectively take on the coloring substances which are used in staining microscopic sections of the tissue. The protoplasm of the fatigued cells, as seen from Fig. 58, is in part exhausted as a result of the processes of stimulation through which they have passed. Sleep must be a condition in which these cells are supplied with nutrition and return to their normal state of energy and activity. During the period of sleep, each cell seems to be capable of insulating itself from the neighboring parts of the nervous system. There are some extreme conditions, probably pathological in character, in which the dendrites of the nerve cells curl up and form,

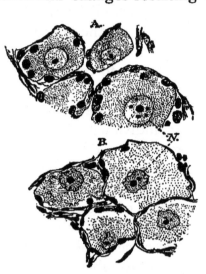

FIG. 58. Fatigued cells

Two sections *A* and *B* from the first thoracic spinal ganglion of a cat. *B* is from the ganglion which has been electrically stimulated through its nerve for five hours. *A* is from a corresponding resting ganglion. The nuclei *N* of the fatigued cells are seen to take a darker stain and to be very irregular in outline. The general protoplasm of the cell bodies is also less uniform in density in the fatigued cells. (After Hodge)

instead of extending branches, little knotty balls across which stimulations cannot easily pass. This curling up of the dendrites is probably a very much more radical change than occurs under the ordinary conditions of sleep. The synapses, or interlacing of fibers, which connect a cell with other cells or incoming fibers, are interrupted in most cases, not by any gross movement of the dendrites but rather by some chemical change in the tissue which makes it difficult for the stimulation to pass across from one cell to another. There are known chemical substances which affect primarily the synapses and prevent stimulations from being transmitted from cell to cell. All of these indications go to show that the nerve cell, when it enters on the process of recuperation, tends to give up its normal transmitting function, and devotes itself for the time being to the processes of building up tissue.

The closing of avenues of stimulation in sleep. The external characteristics of a sleeping individual are clearly intelligible in terms of the physiological changes which have been described. In the first place, the individual becomes less and less susceptible to stimulations from the outside world. This means that when any form of external energy acts on the nervous system, it finds the nervous system relatively inert. The receiving organs are closed and their cells are probably in a chemical condition unfavorable to any vigorous activity. Even when stimulations are received at the periphery and are transmitted to the central nervous system, they make headway through the tissues with the greatest difficulty. They do not follow the well-defined paths which are used in normal life, but are diffused throughout the whole organ.

Various degrees of dissociation. The condition of the individual need not be a condition of complete sleep in order to show this inertness of the nervous system. There are many conditions of fatigue in which the nervous system shows, before sleep sets in, more or less of a tendency to resist external stimulation. Furthermore, the different stages of sleep are by no means equal in their degree of dissociation. This has been shown by experiments in which the amount of noise necessary to arouse a sleeping individual has been made the measure of the intensity of sleep. The result of such experiments is to show that a person goes to sleep rapidly and profoundly during the early part of the night, and from this time on gradually comes back to a condition of susceptibility to stimulation. Fig. 59 shows a sleep curve of the kind which results from these experiments.

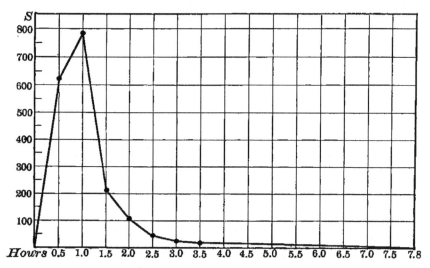

FIG. 59. Curve showing the intensity of sound necessary to awaken a sleeper at different periods of sleep

Along the horizontal line are represented the hours of sleep; along the vertical, the relative intensities of sound. Thus, at the end of the first half hour an intensity of sound somewhat over six hundred is necessary to awaken the sleeper. At the end of two hours the intensity of sound is approximately one hundred. The curve indicates that the sleeper falls rapidly into a profound sleep and then gradually comes into a condition of very light slumber preceding for a long time the waking. (After Kohlschütter)

The curve rises rapidly, indicating, as stated, that the amount of stimulation necessary to arouse the nervous system increases rapidly in the early hours of sleep; it falls off gradually toward the end, indicating a gradual waking of the subject.

Dissociation in the central processes. Not only are the cells of the sleeper's nervous system impervious to external stimulation, but they are uncoupled in such a way that the stimulations which succeed in entering the nervous system do not follow the ordinary paths of discharge. This uncoupling of the central nerve cells does not take place in equal degree in all parts of the nervous system. The large cells of the spinal cord are able to resist the effects of fatigue, and the spinal cord may be said never to sleep under normal conditions. For this reason, stimulations which reach the spinal cord from the surface of the body are always transformed into reflex impulses and sent to the muscles of the trunk and limbs. The spinal cord is in this case uncoupled, not within itself, but only with reference to the higher centers. The reflexes are very much simpler in form and more likely to appear under these conditions than when the stimulus has an open path to the higher centers. Thus a cold or uncomfortable hand will always be moved reflexly in sleep. The medulla, like the cord, seems to be able to resist, to a great extent, the tendencies toward fatigue, for many of the organic processes, such as circulation and respiration, are maintained through the nerve centers in the medulla, while the rest of the nervous system is closed to external stimulation and to any well-ordered activities.

Dreams as dissociated groups of ideas. One effect of the uncoupling of the various nerve tracts in the organs of the central nervous system above the medulla is that any processes which take place in these higher organs because of strong stimulations, or because of some abnormal excitability in the nervous system, are fleeting and irregular. The higher centers probably do not all of them sink into the same degree of inactivity even in a normal individual, and the slightest abnormality may result in a heightened activity in certain parts. The facts of consciousness which correspond to these irregular, detached activities in the central nervous system during sleep are easily understood when it is recognized that the nervous system is acting not as a single organized system but as a disorganized group of centers. To put the matter in terms of experience, one may say that an idea which presents itself during sleep is not related to the general body of ideas by which the experiences of ordinary life are checked and held under criticism. If, in ordinary life, the idea suggests itself to some individual that he has enormous possessions, he is immediately reminded by the evidences of his senses and by the familiar surroundings and limitations of his sphere of action that the idea is merely a subjective imagination. If, on the other hand, one should have this idea in his dreams, under conditions which would remove it from all restricting relations, it would obviously be compelling in its force and would be accepted by consciousness as an unqualified and unlimited truth. It would be dissociated from the other ideas which fill normal consciousness, and this dissociation would determine its character in such a way as to make it distinctly different from the processes of coherent thought built up in normal life.

Dreams impressive only because they are uncriticized. It will be seen from such considerations as these that a mature individual is brought in his sleep into a condition somewhat similar to that exhibited in the irregular and unrestrained imaginings of children. The young child constructs imaginations and is quite unable to criticize them because of his lack of experience and because of the lack of organization within his experience. The lines of organization are not laid down in the child; in the dreaming adult, though systems of ideas have been built up, they are for the time being interrupted, and the processes of mental life lapse into unsystematic and uncritical forms. There is, for this reason, a certain freedom from all kinds of restraint, which accounts for the highly erratic character of dreams.

Motor processes suspended by dissociations in sleep. The third characteristic of sleep follows naturally from these which we have been discussing. Muscular movements are almost completely suspended in normal sleep. The muscles relax more than they do in any condition of waking life, just because the nervous system sends only very much reduced stimulations to the muscles, and, as we have repeatedly seen, the muscles are quite unable to perform their work when they are not stimulated by the nerves. The few straggling stimulations which succeed in getting through the nervous system to the muscles are lower reflexes or they are irregular and without coördination. The movements which appear are, therefore, often more incoherent than the fleeting dream experiences which accompany the activities in the central nervous organs. Indeed, in most cases, any intense movements of the muscles during sleep indicate a distinctly abnormal condition and are closely related in character to the irregular coördinations which appear in certain forms of drug poisoning.

Narcotic drugs dissociative in their effects. The discussion of the phenomena which attend the use of drugs will aid in the understanding of what has been said about sleep. It is a familiar fact that certain narcotics produce a condition very closely related to sleep. The narcotic drug closes the avenues of sensory reception, reduces central activity or renders its processes irregular and incoherent, and suspends muscular contraction. If the drug is taken in a relatively small dose, so that its effect upon the nervous system is slight, these various effects may be produced in slight degree only. The effect in this case will be most marked in the irregularity of ideas and in the incoördination of the movements.

Effect of alcohol on the nervous system. A familiar effect of a drug is the intoxication which is produced by alcohol. The chemical condition of nerve cells and consequently the relations between them are in some way affected by alcohol, and the stimulations are interrupted or become irregular in their transmission through the tissues. The fact that a man under the influence of alcohol sees things moving irregularly, or sees them double, depends upon the incoördination of the muscles of the eyes. The fact that he is unable to walk steadily shows the incoördination of the muscles of the legs. There is a corresponding irregularity in the flow of his ideas; and his credulousness for the ideas which suggest themselves to him is analogous to the ordinary credulousness of a dreaming sleeper. The imperviousness of such an individual to the stimulations of the outside world is also a well-known fact.

Overexcitation is also dissociative. In the case of any one of the drugs which produces dissociative conditions in the nervous system, the condition may be overcome by the ordinary processes of recuperation by which the organism throws out the drug. In some cases the effort of the organism to restore the normal condition leads to a reaction which is abnormally intense. We may then have for a time, as a result of reaction to the drug, a state of hypersensitivity and a more vigorous activity within the central nervous system and in the muscles. The dissociating effects of such intense activity in the nervous system may be, so far as consciousness and muscular coördination are concerned, quite as abnormal as the depressing effects of fatigue or complete suspension of nervous activity. Thus, if the stimulations coming to the central nervous system are much increased in their intensity because the nervous tissue has been thrown into a condition of heightened activity, there may be an irregularity in the central nervous processes due to the abnormally strong currents of excitation and to the impossibility of restraining these currents of stimulation within the ordinary channels of connection and discharge. The disorganization here is like the disorganized behavior of a stream that overflows its banks.

Toxic effects of certain diseases. There are certain conditions produced in nature which are quite analogous to those which are produced by drugs. Such conditions appear in fevers when the organism is under the influence of certain toxic substances produced by the organism itself or by bacteria lodged in the body; under such conditions the nervous system is rendered hypersensitive through the chemical action of these foreign substances on the tissues. The delirium of the fever patient presents clearly the picture of too intense activity in the central nervous system, and the muscular activity of such an individual is directly related to his irregular and excessive central processes. Such a person may also be excessively sensitive to slight sounds or other irritations of the organs of sense.

These negative cases as evidences of the relation between normal consciousness and organization. These different cases show the relation between nervous organization and mental organization, and by their negative characteristics confirm the discussions of the preceding chapters, in which it has been maintained that normal mental life is a continuous process of integration and organization.

Hypnosis a form of dissociation closely allied to sleep. The condition known as hypnosis has long been the source of superstitious wonder, and much has been said and written in regard to it which would tend to increase the mystery which attaches to it. In many respects it is a condition closely related to normal sleep. On the other hand, it has certain peculiar characteristics which differentiate it from ordinary sleep. These peculiarities can, however, be fully understood under the formula adopted in explanation of normal sleep, provided that formula is slightly modified to include certain specialized forms of dissociation.

Hypnosis as partial dissociation. While normal sleep involves the uncoupling or dissociation of the nervous elements, especially of the type which suspends activity in the higher centers, hypnosis involves a dissociation which is partial and leaves a part of the higher centers in action. To put the matter in simple terms, we may say that in normal sleep the cerebrum is dissociated from the lower centers, and all the centers in the cerebrum are dissóciated from each other; whereas, in hypnosis only a part of the cerebrum is dissociated from the lower centers. The remaining part of the cerebrum continues to carry on its activities and, indeed, profits by the cessation of activity in the dormant portion, for the active part of the nervous system is, in such a case as this, supplied with an unusually large amount of blood, and its activity may reach a much higher level of intensity, because of this superior nutritive supply and because of the concentration of all of the nervous activity in one region. Such a crude statement as this is undoubtedly too simple in its terms, and yet it represents the situation in principle.

Methods of inducing hypnosis. The way in which the condition of partial or hypnotic dissociation is produced in the nervous system differs with the practice of different hypnotizers. One of the characteristic methods of producing hypnosis is to require the subject to gaze at some bright object until a kind of partial stupor comes over him. He may then be aroused to activity through the sense of hearing. The ideas which he receives and the activities which he performs have, under these conditions, many of the characteristics of dissociation. Another way of producing hypnosis is to soothe the subject into a sleeplike condition. Stroking the forehead or the face is very commonly practiced by hypnotizers. Here again, the appeal to the subject, after the dormant condition has set in, is through the sense of hearing or even through the sense of vision.

Hypnosis more readily induced after it has once been established in a subject. When a subject has been frequently hypnotized, it is possible to reproduce the hypnotic condition without elaborate preliminaries. The subject acquires what may be called a habit of dissociation. A simple order from the hypnotizer is enough to throw the subject into the condition. Sometimes the habit is carried to such an ex-. tent that the subject is able to throw himself into the hyp- notic condition. Such self-induced hypnosis is known as auto-hypnosis. The ability to produce the hypnotic state in the subject does not depend upon any peculiar powers on the part of the hypnotizer; it depends rather upon his ability so to influence his subject that the condition of par- tial sleep described shall be induced. The essential condi- tion with which the subject himself must comply, in order to come under the influence of a hypnotizer, is that he con- centrate his attention. The only persons who cannot be hypnotized are young children, idiots, and insane persons, all of whom are unable to concentrate attention. This state- ment effectually disposes of the popular belief that only weak-minded persons can be hypnotized. The most effec- tive method of avoiding hypnosis is to scatter attention as much as possible over a great variety of objects. Concen- tration of attention is always favorable to hypnosis and allied conditions. The audience which gives close attention to a speaker or performer is susceptible to a species of hypnosis; while, on the other hand, there is no danger of hypnosis in a distracted audience. The methods of induc- ing hypnosis have been accidentally discovered from time to time by performers who are then able to give striking exhibitions of their discovery. Many oriental jugglers be- gin their performance, the success of which undoubtedly depends upon their hypnotic influence over their audiences, with a dance in which the body of the performer is moved with a gradually increasing speed, which inevitably induces a gradually increased concentration of attention on the part of the observer. When this dance grows more and more rapid and more and more engaging to the attention, the observer is completely mastered and the main performance may be undertaken. The hypnotic influence of such a dance is very frequently augmented by the burning of incense, which has more or less of a narcotic effect upon the observers. In like manner, certain animals are probably drawn into a hypnotic state by the movement of snakes. This has frequently been reported in the case of birds and monkeys.

Various characteristics of the hypnotized subject. When the hypnotic state has been produced, the phenomena exhibited are of two distinct types. First, there is a suspension of certain activities, and, second, there is an abnormal heightening of other activities. This may be seen with reference to the reception of sensory stimulations. Certain stimulations are no longer received by the hypnotized subject. For this reason the condition has sometimes been used by savage tribes for surgical purposes, exactly as in modern life we use drugs which will produce a dissociation of the nervous system and thus prevent pain from excessive external stimulation. On the other hand, certain other senses may be opened to stimulation. A hypnotized subject may be wholly anæsthetic in his skin, while still retaining the ability to receive impressions through certain of his other senses. Indeed, the concentration of nervous activity in certain particular senses results in such a heightening of their ability to receive impressions that the subject may perform most astonishing feats of sensory receptivity. He may hear very faint sounds ' or he may see remote visual objects. It is to be noted that this hyperæsthesia of the senses is not so extraordinary as it would at first sight seem to be. We all become hyperæsthetic when we concentrate attention in any direction. If one is listening for an important signal or watching for some object which is of great importance to him, he will be using his nervous energy in the emphasized direction and will be correspondingly impervious to impressions from other sources. The conditions in hypnosis are merely exaggerations of those which appear in ordinary life.

Ideas not subjected to criticism in hypnosis. Turning from the sensory processes to the central processes, we find again that certain activities are entirely in abeyance, while others are much intensified. If, for example, it is suggested to a hypnotized subject that he is an animal instead of a human being, the suggested idea may take such large possession of him as to command his whole attention and guide his activity. If a normal individual is told that he is an animal, he immediately brings to bear upon the suggested idea a great variety of incompatible experiences, which make it clear that the statement is false and unacceptable. In the case of the hypnotized subject, very much as in the case of the dreamer, the corrective ideas, which constitute the fabric of normal life, are absent, so that the single idea takes full possession of the mind and commands belief as the accepted content of consciousness. This credulousness of the hypnotic consciousness is described by saying that the subject is very open to suggestion. Anything that is said to him will be accepted, and any form of interpretation of experience which is offered to him will be taken up without serious question and without any effort on his part to criticize the ideas which have been given him by the hypnotizer. Suggestibility has very frequently been emphasized to the exclusion of the converse fact that the hypnotized subject is quite incapable of subjecting any ideas to critical comparison. So also the positive increase in sensitivity has been the impressive fact; the diminution of sensibility has often been overlooked. The negative considerations are, however, essential to a complete understanding of the case, just as the negative considerations are of importance if we would understand the credulousness exhibited in dreams.

Dual personalities in hypnosis. The central nervous conditions which are induced in hypnosis are sometimes sufficiently unstable to produce the most complex phenomena.

It is sometimes found that the dissociated parts of the cerebrum are not only dissociated from each other, but they are also, to a certain extent, capable of independent action. Thus, while one part of the cerebrum seems to be dealing with impressions received through the sense of hearing, another part may be engaged in responding to tactual impressions. Or, the case may be rendered even more complicated by the fact that the impressions coming from one ear seem to serve as stimulations for certain activities, while auditory impressions received on the opposite side of the body are effective in producing an entirely different set of experiences and responses. There result in such cases what are known as dual and multiple personalities. By personality, as the term is used in such cases, is meant any organized group or system of ideas and activities. The various groups of systematized activities and ideas which exist side by side in a hypnotized subject owe their separation to nervous and mental dissociation; each personality is, therefore, a relatively less complex system than that which exists when the whole cerebrum is acting as a single organ. The division of an individual into a number of systems of organization appears in other states than the hypnotic state, and it may result in certain permanent or certain temporary disruptions of personality, which have been noted in such stories as that of Dr. Jekyll and Mr. Hyde.

Dual personalities in other than hypnotic conditions. From time to time one reads of a case of lapse in memory which amounts to a dissociation of personality. A man forgets who he is or what business he has been following. He is sufficiently normal in his general organization to respond to a great variety of impressions in a regular fashion, but the complex structure of mental life breaks down and the man is only partly reconstructed in the second self. Tertiary and quaternary personalities may appear in all possible combinations. The secondary or tertiary personality may know its fellows, but may be itself quite forgotten. Several cases have been described in which personality B knows not only its own acts and emotions but also the acts and emotions of the other personality A. Sometimes B not only knows but heartily dislikes A. Sometimes two personalities exist simultaneously within the same body and seem to have separate lives and characters. The writer knew of a case of a young man who was the object of superstitious wonder in the village in which he lived, because he had two personalities. These two personalities knew each other and held long discussions with each other. Often, when they came to a turn in the road, they disagreed with each other as to the direction in which their body should move, and the passer-by could see the abnormal man mumbling an argument between his two selves.

Dual and multiple personalities analogous to the various selves of normal life. The details of such cases are baffling in the extreme, but nothing can be clearer from our earlier studies than the general formula of dissociation, with the added fact of partial organization around different centers. The matter becomes more intelligible if we remember that even in ordinary life there is a subdivision of experience into different systems. We distinguish, even in common parlance, between the business self, the social self, and so on. Each one of these selves is only partially related to the other systems of experience and forms of behavior. The man who is buried in the details of a business transaction is just as oblivious to considerations of a literary sort as the hypnotized subject is oblivious to a certain group of possible experiences. We do not call the ordinary absorption of the self in business a case of multiple personality, because the neglected personality in the case of the business man is not so remote but that it can be immediately called out, if he turns his attention to some literary considerations.

The normal individual is capable of transferring his attention and interest from center to center according as the external environment demands, while the hypnotized subject or abnormal person is, through dissociation, quite incapable of a rapid transfer of attention or of correlating the different phases of his experience.

Hypnosis a transient condition, insanity permanent. We shall return to the discussion of multiple personality under the general head of insanity, for the fundamental distinction between insanity and hypnosis is to be found in the degree of permanency which is attained in the former state, as contrasted with the more transient character of the hypnotic condition.

Movements sometimes normal in hypnosis, because the lower centers are not dissociated. In the meantime, it is necessary to add a few comments on the motor activities of hypnotized subjects. These motor activities frequently exhibit little or no departure from the ordinary coördinations of normal life. The hypnotized subject is capable of walking, often of writing or producing certain other complex forms of movement. Such continuation of the bodily coördinations is explicable on the ground that the lower centers of the nervous system are not dissociated by the changes that take place in the higher centers. Whenever the higher centers are able to send stimulations to the lower centers, these lower centers are capable of responding with their usual degree of coördination. The lack of organization is exhibited rather in the inability to maintain a normal balance between the various centers which call the lower centers into play. It is to be noted, however, that the movements of hypnotized subjects sometimes indicate by their clumsiness and lack of precision that the disintegrating force has affected certain of the motor channels as well as the central organizations. This is especially true when the attempted act involves a complicated coördination.

The after-effects of hypnosis tend to become permanent.
There is one group of facts in hypnosis which should
perhaps be made the subject of special comments. The
suggestions received by the hypnotized subject may, in
some cases, be carried over so as to become operative in a
later period, after the subject has apparently recovered from
the hypnotic trance. Such after-effects are known as post-
hypnotic effects, and the suggestions are described as
post-hypnotic suggestions. Even more significant is the fact
that after-effects of the hypnotic trance are of a general
kind. It is a fact that the effect of the hypnotic state is in
the direction of a perpetuation of dissociative tendencies.
Sleep is transient and leads to a more vigorous form of
activity after it is over. Hypnosis, on the other hand, tends
not to restore the nervous system to a more vigorous condition but to perpetuate dissociation. This is due to the fact
that sleep is negative, while hypnosis is positive in certain
of its phases, in that it trains certain centers to act without
reference to others. It therefore operates by virtue of its
positive phases toward permanent disorganization. It is for
such reasons as these that the use of hypnosis is in general
to be avoided. The disorganizing effects of hypnosis are of
the same general type as the disrupting tendencies of certain
drugs. The individual, who with sufficient frequency comes
under the influence of these drugs or of hypnosis, will
ultimately settle into a state of nervous disorganization from
which it will be quite impossible for him to recover, even
when recovery is demanded for the purposes of normal
life. Hypnosis is not utilized by reputable practitioners,
because its ultimate effects are not as readily controllable
as are the effects even of the narcotic drugs ; and there is
no justification whatever for the use of hypnosis as a means
of amusement, any more than there would be for using a
strong narcotic drug to bring an individual into a condition
which would make him a source of entertainment.

**Insanity a permanent form of disorganization, intro-
duced in many cases by dissociation and settling into an
abnormal reorganization.** As has been indicated in the
earlier paragraphs, insanity is a form of relatively permanent
dissociation. Certain forms of delirium, which have been
referred to before, furnish the best introduction to the study
of insanity. In delirium the subject is so highly excitable
that the normal avenues of stimulation and discharge are
for the time being completely disrupted, and the currents
of nervous activity and the corresponding facts of experience
are dissociated. As delirium disappears and gives place to
the usual intensity of nervous activity the individual may
return to the earlier normal condition or, on the other
hand, there may be left behind a permanent abnormal state,
because the earlier forms of organization are not fully
restored. One of the most characteristic symptoms of all
forms of insanity is found to be the existence of certain
hallucinations or fundamental abnormalities in the subject's
world of ideas. The insane person believes himself to be
Julius Cæsar or some Biblical character, or even some
divinity. There is no difficulty in recognizing the fact that
the idea of transferred identity may come into the mind of
any normal individual. It is, however, in the case of a
normal individual immediately criticized and abandoned,
because of its incompatibility with the person's general
knowledge of the world and his place in it. When the
compact organization which has been built up in normal
experiences has once given way, and the idea that one is
Julius Cæsar or some other character has presented itself
as a center of reconstruction in the midst of the resulting
chaos, there is a possibility of an abnormal reorganization
of experience. The individual is no longer restrained by
that system of ideas which has been laboriously built up
through contact with the world ; the result is that the whole
later ideational life of the individual loses its adaptation to

the real world. The characteristic fact in certain cases of insanity is, accordingly, not describable in simple terms of dissociation ; it is rather to be defined in terms of dissociation with an abnormal association or integration following upon the breaking down of the normal system. In other cases, disintegration is the more obvious fact. The individual simply loses control of his ideas, and his mind seems to be flooded with an incoherent mass of experience. His words reflect this incoherency of ideas, and his behavior indicates an absence of self-control. Such disintegrated forms of consciousness and behavior commonly appear in the last stages of almost every kind of insanity, even where there has been for a time reorganization about an abnormal center.

Melancholia as a typical form of dissociation. One of the very general forms of dissociative abnormality is that which appears in so-called melancholia. In melancholia there is a general reduction of all the bodily activities, including the activities in the nervous system. The subject becomes phlegmatic and depressed in all his functions. The whole feeling tone of experience takes on a marked disagreeable character, which can be explained in terms of our earlier discussion of feeling by saying that the individual does not arouse himself easily to respond to any form of stimulation, and when his nervous system is in any way aroused by powerful external excitation, the reaction upon the stimulus is so laborious and contrary to his tendencies and mood that he has a strong feeling tone of a disagreeable type. The ideas which such a subject has are often organized about each other in a way that furnishes a kind of false explanation of the subject's mood. The melancholic subject has certain grievances against the world. Sometimes these grievances are of a trivial character and make it clear that the grievance could not have been the exciting cause of the subject's condition. Sometimes the grievance is more real and furnishes an apparent ground for the condition.

Even in such a case it is to be said that the person's physical condition must have developed into one of general debility before the apparent cause of his mental conditions could have become the source of abnormal melancholia. The distinction between a passing case of depression in normal life and melancholia is that passing depression is temporary, and nature rebounds from it in such a way as to produce normal conditions after the depressing circumstances are past. In the case of melancholia the depressing tendencies become permanent, and it is this permanency rather than the fact of depression or its corresponding nervous conditions which constitutes the characteristic fact in insanity. Indeed, one can find almost every possible grade of transition from normal life to extreme abnormality. The result is that those who have made a special study of these transitions, and those whose attention is for the first time called to the possibility of such transition, are likely to indulge in the extravagant statement that all persons are at times or on certain subjects more or less insane. It is undoubtedly true that all persons do depart at times from the type of mental and bodily organization which constitutes normal life, but unless these states become fixed and lead to distorted and unadapted forms of behavior, they should not be classified as cases of insanity.

Excessive excitation as a second typical case of insanity. The opposite tendency to the melancholic condition just described appears in certain cases of excessive excitation. A person when abnormally excited is very frequently possessed of excessive bodily strength. This is not due to any change in the structure of his muscles, but rather to the fact that the nervous system which is in control of the muscles is sending to the active organs stimulations of excessive intensity. There are numerous cases in normal life which will help us to understand this fact. If an individual is fatigued, encouragement and stimulation from the outside world will appreciably increase his ability to execute muscular movements. In the same way an individual may be so stimulated by abnormal substances in the blood that his whole nervous behavior is raised to a high level of activity and the motor discharges are abnormally intense. The muscular activity of such a person is typical of his whole condition. His ideas come in an overwhelming flood and lead him into the most extravagant excesses of imagination and lack of self-control.

Fundamental disturbances of instinctive and emotional life. Of late much attention has been given to the fact that in all cases of dissociation the fundamental instincts assert themselves and play a leading part in the behavior and ideation of the abnormal individual. For example, there are types of fear which haunt a patient and distract him from all normal modes of thought and life. Or the sex instinct becomes dominant, or the food instinct leads to irregular or irrational behavior. The mode of treatment which is adopted in such cases aims in part to restore normal nutritive conditions and then proceeds on the assumption that the individual must be started on the road to a reconstruction of his mental world. Often the shortest route to this latter goal is to bring out in explicit detail some of the deep-seated dissociations. Thus, the person who is suffering from terror is made aware of the sources of his terror and is encouraged to reorganize his thinking and his attitudes toward the object of his dissociation. The abnormal state can be compared to physical clumsiness. The individual whose muscles will not coördinate must develop physical coöperation of the organs of his body by using them in a well-ordered, systematic fashion. So with the person suffering from mental incoördination, there must be a well-directed effort at mental recoördination.

Relation of psychiatry to psychology. These illustrations must suffice for our present purposes. There are all possible combinations of disintegration and reorganization exhibited in insanity. There is a science known as psychiatry which deals with these forms of dissociation and abnormal association, and there is a large field of practical observation and study open here to the trained scientist. The chief lesson for our general science is that the normal processes are processes of integration leading to forms of association which contribute to adaptation. There are frequently illustrations which throw light upon important principles of normal association, to be found by making a careful study of the facts of dissociation, but in general the explanation of abnormal states is made easier by a careful examination of normal processes rather than the reverse. It does not follow that dissociation will be along the same lines as association, and the effort to work out the details of one by the other often leads to fallacies. The general tendency of normal life is, however, obviously in the direction of adaptive organization ; the tendency of sleep, hypnosis, and insanity, on the other hand, is in the opposite direction. The particular path followed in each case can be defined only through empirical examination of the case.

CHAPTER XV

VOLUNTARY ACTION AND VOLUNTARY ATTENTION

Voluntary action a special form of behavior. Though the preceding chapters have discussed at length many of the relations between bodily activity and mental processes, they have not dealt specifically with that form of behavior which is described by the term "voluntary choice." One may reach out and pick up the book before him, or one may decide not to touch the book. One may take the pen and sign a contract, or one may refuse to sign. The whole personality enters into such a decision, and we recognize both in ordinary thought and in scientific consideration of the matter that the ability to choose, especially the ability to choose wisely and consistently, is the supreme power cultivated in the development of the individual. Our penal code recognizes the fact that an immature child is not responsible for his actions in the measure in which a full-grown man is responsible. Those who are mentally defective are exempt from the penalties of the law just in the degree in which they fall short of normal development. These and other illustrations of common practice show that voluntary choice is the fullest expression of the developed normal self.

Instinctive behavior different from voluntary action. The explanation of voluntary action depends on a series of distinctions which have been implied in earlier chapters. Thus instinctive acts are not forms of voluntary behavior. For example, the infant swallows not from deliberate choice but because nature has provided a nervous and muscular mechanism which responds promptly to the proper sensory stimulus.

One has only to think of the cases in adult experience where the swallowing reflex acts when the swallower would gladly check it. Furthermore, most people do not know that they cannot carry out the act of swallowing without a proper sensory stimulus. Let one try the experiment of swallowing five times in succession. All the saliva in the mouth will have been swallowed the second or third time the effort is made, and after that the mechanism refuses to work until more sensory stimulation is supplied. Instinctive acts are therefore different from volitions. Sometimes we can voluntarily check one of these acts, although here our powers are limited, and we can in some measure decide when an act provided by the inherited nervous mechanism shall be allowed to take place, but here again our control is limited as shown in the example given above.

Impulsive acts distinct from higher forms of voluntary action. If we follow the development of an individual from infancy, we find that there are other forms of behavior which resemble the instincts in that they are not fully under control. For this general class of acts we commonly use the term "impulsive acts." It is almost impossible not to imitate a yawn ; it is very difficult not to look around when one hears an unfamiliar noise. The impulse to take food when one is hungry is very strong ; the impulse to strike back when one is struck is so strong that the interpretation of responsibility is always based on an examination of provocation.

Impulsive acts as phases of general muscular tension. Impulsive acts can be explained by formulas which have been discussed at length in earlier chapters. It was there pointed out that the whole organism is constantly at a higher or lower level of tension. The muscles of a waking person are always on the stretch. There are internal activities of respiration and circulation and digestion which are not only in a state of tension but are in an actual state of continuous operation. The eyes are usually focused on some object ;

the hand is seldom at rest and still more seldom in a state of relaxation. This state of muscular tension and internal action is due to the continuous stream of nervous impulses which flow out to the active organs. The outgoing motor impulses are in turn the results of the sensory stimulations of the moment and the reverberations of sensory impressions which are circulating through the massive cerebrum.

Impulsive acts explicable through nervous organization. An impulsive act exhibits in its particular form the past experience and training of the individual. We often judge of a person's character and education by his impulsive acts. The spy who was betrayed by his impulsive and wholly uncontrolled response to a sudden military order to stand to attention exhibited his training by his very lack of voluntary control. One may guide his impulses in some measure by the slow process of changing his habits. If one tends to look up from his work every time a shadow passes over his desk, one may overcome this tendency by self-discipline; but in that case the inadvertent lapses into the old mode of looking up will furnish the strongest evidence of the difference between impulse and voluntary control.

Impulse comparable to involuntary attention. The term "impulse" as applied to behavior finds a parallel in certain terms which are used in describing strictly mental processes. One tends to look at any object that moves through the edge of the field of vision. This is an impulsive tendency. On the psychical side we describe this fact by saying that moving objects in the edge of the field of vision attract involuntary attention. Attention of the involuntary type is then contrasted with certain higher types of attention which are designated as voluntary. Thus, when one keeps his eyes fixed steadily on the signal which he is set to watch in spite of distracting appeals to his involuntary attention, we speak of his effort as an exhibition of voluntary choice or self-control.

Impulse and involuntary attention related to perception and habit. It is hardly necessary to elaborate here the matter of the relation of impulsive activity to perception and habit. Our earlier chapters have abundantly illustrated this relation and shown its importance. We have, however, reached the point where we must face the problem of the distinction between voluntary attention and all lower forms of perception and thought, and the problem of the distinction between voluntary action and impulse.

Simple case of choice. Perhaps the best method of making progress toward the solution of our problem is to analyze one of the simpler cases of volition. For this purpose let us consider choice in the presence of two clearly apprehended alternatives. There lies before the man who is out on a walk a fork in the road. Sometimes he will thoughtlessly strike out on that path which he has often followed, or because he is absorbed in thought he will be guided by mere accident. But in the case in which we are interested he sees the two roads clearly; each is inviting, and in terms of his experience and training, equally accessible; he may even pause a moment and then he turns to the left or right. We can explain this turning in a broad, loose way by using such phrases as "he decided," "he chose," "he selected." The impressive fact about each of these phrases is that it brings out the truth that we are in the presence of an explanation which includes and involves personality. We may speak of impulse in an impersonal way. One is led to do something when he acts under the spell of impulse, but one makes the decision himself when he chooses his road.

Behavior of the higher types dependent on ideas. The broad terms of our explanation do not satisfy the demand for a scientific account of the process of choice. We must go into greater detail. We can do this in some measure by pointing out that bodily activity is related to ideas no less than it is to percepts. One thinks of a tall object and, as we have seen in an earlier chapter, he tends to move his eye and his hand upward. One thinks over an offense which has been committed against him and he grows red with rage and tense for an attack. Ideas are related to actions because the nervous processes involved in the formation of ideas are, like all nervous processes, parts of a succession of processes leading to a motor discharge. In the association areas of the cerebrum there are complex nervous combinations and deposits of earlier excitations which are the immediate conditions of ideation and at the same time links in the chain of processes connecting the sense organs with the motor centers.

When as a result of experience an individual becomes mature enough so that his sensory impulses are taken up into a highly developed train of cerebral processes before they are allowed to go to the motor centers, we say of the individual that he acts on the basis of ideas. We mean by this statement that the instinctive tracts are relatively less and less important in this individual's life. We mean that the inner organization is more and more important. The inner organization of the cerebrum is, as we have seen, relatively remote from mere sensation. Hence, when the inner processes come more into control we find the explanation of individual conduct not in present impressions but in past experience. The first and most evident conclusion about voluntary choice is therefore that it depends on a high development of central paths and is related to the higher conscious processes.

Voluntary action and its complex background as contrasted with lower forms of behavior. The significance of the foregoing conclusion will be fully grasped only when it is recalled that the central or ideational conscious processes are complex as contrasted with mere perceptions and other conscious processes which involve only the lower elements of the nervous system and the lower phases of experience. An idea is a composite of experience. The general fact about ideational consciousness is that it brings into a single instant of experience a vast variety of elements. Conduct which is based on ideation is, accordingly, conduct which springs, not out of some simple single impression, but out of a combination of manifold impressions.

We have commented in earlier chapters on the advantage which comes to the individual from the possession of a world of ideas in which the whole of experience can be compactly represented and readily rearranged. We see now the advantage to conduct of ideational powers. The individual who has ideas can act on a broader basis than can the victim of mere impulse, or the undeveloped individual who has only the most immediate sensory motives for his comings and goings.

Decision a process of balancing ideas. Let us consider once more our individual who must choose at the fork of the road which branch he will follow. No outsider can fathom his choice. The inner world is the scene of a balancing and comparing, and out of this inner world comes a decision which turns the scale of muscular tension and results in a movement. If at the moment before decision an outsider would influence choice, he must appeal to the inner world; he must reach the thought process of the individual who is deciding.

Decision largely influenced by organization built out of past experiences. When we trace decision back into the inner world, we find justification for a second general conclusion. Volition is determined in very large measure by past experiences. All ideas, as we know, are explicable only in terms of organizations of experience which have been set up in the past. The choice which an individual makes to-day has its roots in the experiences of yesterday and of the earlier education before yesterday. To be sure, the present may bring into the mind a manifold of experiences out of which choice must issue, but this manifold will be arranged and organized in terms which comport with the past as well as with the present. We know in ordinary life that it is safe to assume that an individual who has made his decisions thus and so in the past will in the future exhibit like tendencies of choice.

The relation of choice to past experience is impressively illustrated by the fact that voluntary attention is controlled by what one has learned to think about. If one puts oneself through a series of experiences in which æsthetical objects are again and again examined and recorded in thought, it is safe to predict that æsthetic objects will in the future be centers of long concentrated attention. If one gives heed for years to matters of business to the exclusion of all other objects of thought, it is sure to be a great deal easier to fix attention on matters of this type in all future experience.

We come back to the formula with which our explanation began. Whatever enters into the personality of a man enters into his voluntary choice. When a man chooses, he expresses his personality. This is the essential fact about volition; choice is not an arbitrary, sudden mode of thought or action; it is, rather, the consummate expression of all that has entered into individual life.

The meaning of prevision. While emphasizing the importance of past experience in the development of voluntary control it is important that we should understand also the fact that volition looks by means of imagination into the future. One recombines ideas and foresees in this world of ideas certain consequences of this or that combination. Behavior is then dominated, not by present impressions or by habits alone, it is guided by the products of imagination. The thinker has tried out consequences in the world of thought and has the advantage in conduct of these purely mental trials. The power of imagination thus comes to be more important for human conduct than even habit or instinct.

For example, the general plans his movements with a map before him and with a thousand items of information in mind about the enemy and his own forces. His final orders are the results of his comparisons and mental experiments.

The power of choice becomes thus a matter of the relation of complex ideational processes to behavior. Conduct is related to ideas, and any elaborate process of combining ideas which results in a new idea will influence behavior.

The problem of the freedom of the will. We are now in a position to consider one of the problems which has long been a subject of hot debate among students of human life and conduct ; namely, the problem of the freedom of the will. It has been argued on the one side that in a given emergency an individual can follow any one of the various courses which lie before him. The five or six paths which he might follow all attract him, but he is free to follow the one which he chooses. So far we must agree. But the extremists seem to argue at times that the chooser is in no wise bound even by his own earlier experiences and training. The individual is free in the absolute sense, we are sometimes told. He may at this given moment strike out without reference to his past or to any other cause. His action is without determining cause. He is a wholly independent being, unguided by any outer or inner considerations except as he is willing in his sovereign independence to give heed to these considerations. This last statement of the doctrine has sometimes been called the doctrine of libertarianism. For this view there is no evidence. Personality is never free from its own past, even when it is producing new combinations of ideas through imagination. Personality is a product of organization. Personality is the name of that individual nature which has been developed out of the play and interplay of impressions and instincts and conscious comparisons and imaginations. Personality is never free from itself. Voluntary choice is an expression of personality, not of sheer caprice.

Voluntary choice guided by purposes. The conclusion to which we are thus led gives the largest emphasis to those reorganizations of experience which were discussed in the chapter on concepts. We saw in that chapter how a dominant inner purpose may control the organization of all thought. I may resolve to think about a geometrical proposition, and all my ideational processes will be rearranged and worked out in conformity with this central purpose. The rise in the mind of a dominant idea is therefore an important event, not merely in a vague, abstract sense, but in a practical sense as well. When some personality takes up with fixed purpose a definite line of thought, his own conduct and ultimately that of his social environment will be affected. This is what was meant by the statement that consciousness is a cause and a very potent cause in the world of affairs.

Behavior of a higher type is related to education. A text-book on the science of human mental processes is not the place for a homily on conduct, but it is so obvious an inference from what has been said that one can hardly refrain from recording the principle that all choice and all significant human influence in the world are dependent for their character on the growth of ideas. He who would influence his own conduct or that of others must therefore look to the roots of conduct in organized processes of ideation and thought.

It will be proper, therefore, for us to follow the study of voluntary behavior by a discussion of some of the more obvious devices by which human choices may be turned in the direction of fruitful and efficient developments.

Early scientific studies of behavior purely external. Before we apply the lessons we have learned, we owe it to the history of scientific method to comment briefly on the development of scientific studies of human behavior. The earliest scientific investigations of bodily activities were undertaken from a wholly external point of view. The specific method which was used for such investigations was devised by the astronomers who were interested in understanding the deficiencies of human movements when attempts were made to use these movements in recording the transit of stars through the field of the telescope. The astronomers found that the hand cannot be moved as soon as the eye sees a light. They therefore measured the interval which elapsed between visual impression and hand movement. They found further that different individuals have different personal equations, or periods of reaction. Evidently the observations of the astronomers are very suggestive as foundations for psychological investigations. The early psychological investigators, however, did not transform the method into a psychological method; they took it over unmodified. Their investigations of the active processes were not based upon any elaborate analysis. Certain simple movements were measured with reference to the time which elapsed between the stimulus and the muscular contraction, exactly as this time had been measured by the astronomers. The investigation of this time of reaction was treated as an indirect means of getting at the complexity of the nervous and conscious processes preceding the reaction. It was found, for example, that the length of time required for a simple reaction was appreciably shorter than the length of time required for a reaction which involved the discrimination of two simple colors from each other. Thus, if the reactor were required to move his finger as soon as possible after being stimulated by a flash of light, the measurement of this interval gave what was called a simple reaction time of about $\frac{180}{1000}$ of a second, or 180σ, the letter σ being used as the symbol for a thousandth of a second. If, on the other hand, the experiment was arranged in such a way that a number of different colors could be presented to the subject, and it was prescribed that he should react only after a clear recognition of one of these colors, then the clear recognition or discrimination added appreciably to the time which elapsed between the giving of the stimulus and the movement, sometimes as much as 60σ. This longer period of time was known as discrimination time. Again, if instead of reacting always with the same hand or finger the reactor was instructed to respond to one kind of stimulation with one movement and to another kind of stimulation with a second movement, the process involved not merely discrimination but also a simple choice of the organ to be moved. The reaction time in this case was called choice time.

Purely external investigations not productive. The earlier experimenters on reaction were satisfied to seek exact definitions of the lengths of these various kinds of reaction time. They paid little or no attention to introspection on the part of the reactor. The results of a large number of reactions were averaged, and the comparison between different simple mental processes was made in terms of these general averages. The outcome for psychology of these external studies was by no means large. There is very little contribution to the knowledge of human nature in the details of reaction times.

Recent investigations and their stress on introspection and analysis of movement. Recent investigations of reactions differ from the earlier external measurements in two respects. First, the effort has been made to find out, as far as possible, what are the conditions in the experience of the reactor during the reaction process. Attention has been called, for example, to the fact that if the reactor's attention is turned toward his hand, rather than toward the organ of sense which is to be stimulated, the time of reaction will for most individuals be shorter. A distinction may therefore be drawn between so-called muscular reactions and sensory reactions. The average difference in time corresponding to this introspective difference is often as great as 100σ. Again, the different types of discrimination and choice have been introspectively examined. The question of whether the content of consciousness before a choice reaction is an image of the movement to be executed, or a concentration of attention upon the sensation received, has been introspectively studied. The results of these introspective studies have done much to clear up the psychological doctrine of volition. Furthermore, the general outcome of a more careful examination of conscious correlates of reaction has shown how utterly formal was the gross averaging of all kinds of cases in the earlier investigations. It may be said that no introspective differences ever occur without some modification in the duration of the reaction process; hence, differences in duration are highly significant when supported by introspective observation and should not be eliminated by an arbitrary method of mathematical averaging.

Analysis of the form of movement. The second way in which recent reaction experiments have been elaborated is by analyzing the forms of the reaction movement. It was formerly assumed that the act of lifting the hand from a reaction key was so simple a process that it could be regarded as uniform in character throughout a long series of experiments. Recent investigations show that there is no such thing as an absolutely uniform series of movement processes. There are certain reactors, for example, who, when they make an effort to lift the hand as rapidly as possible, frequently go through a preliminary downward movement before beginning the upward movement. There are other preliminary phases of movement which prepare the way for the final reaction, and the relation between these preliminary movements and the final movement of the hand may be so complicated as to influence measurably the duration of the reaction period. The relation of these complexities of movement to nervous organization is most intimate. The studies in earlier chapters of the relation of perception and feeling to reaction have indicated the significance for psychology of the analysis of reactions. By way of criticism of the earlier studies, it may be said that they treated reactions as if they were merely uniform mechanical processes. The recent investigations have made it clear that the study of muscular behavior is productive only when it is related to a complete account of the introspective processes and the antecedent organizations which condition the particular form of movement.

Concept of organization as fundamental in all psychological studies. The study of movement has therefore brought us back to the consideration of principles of organization. Volition and impulse are merely the active correlates of organized forms of ideational and perceptual experience. The earlier studies of mental activity and the present study of behavior are mutually supplementary. We do not require any unique formulas or the recognition of any new factors. Behavior is a necessary and ever-present physical correlate of experience and, at the same time, a product of all those organizations which lie back of experience itself.

CHAPTER XVI

MENTAL HYGIENE

Hygiene a suggestive term for psychology. Just as there is a way of keeping one's physical organs in good condition through the adoption of rational principles of nutrition and exercise and sleep, so there is a way of organizing one's mental processes with a view to meeting most efficiently the demands of life.

Relation of psychological hygiene to physiological. The first maxim of mental hygiene is that the nervous system must be kept in a healthy condition. Indeed, physical hygiene here becomes an essential part of the application of psychology. If the nutrition of the body is defective, the nervous system suffers with the other organs, and the mental processes become abnormal. The same is true of sleep and the excretory processes. The body must be in good condition if the mind is to do its work.

Coördination of bodily activities. Assuming for the purposes of our discussion that the general physiological condition is favorable, the next maxim of mental hygiene is that all one's activities must be brought into harmonious coöperation, for the first function of the central nervous system is to control and coördinate the parts of the body. Thus, when muscles are contracting vigorously, there is a call for blood in the particular part of the body which is in action. The nervous system must distribute the blood supply of the body in such a way as to meet the strenuous local demand and at the same time keep all of the supporting organs properly supplied. The young child has to acquire the ability to do this. At first his organic activities are subject to all kinds of distractions and incoördinations. He is unprepared for any sustained effort because his body is not yet a well-coördinated system.

Perhaps the most striking illustration of the incoördination of a child's body is seen in the fact that excitement of any kind interferes with digestion. Digestion is in very large measure an active process. The glands are active in secretion, and the muscles of the digestive organs contract in rhythmical movements that are necessary in carrying the food through the alimentary tract. The elaborate system of organs thus involved in digestion must coöperate or the whole process will be disturbed. Suppose that all is going well, when suddenly a shock of violent stimulation comes to the nervous system. The flood of uncontrolled excitement will be discharged by the motor fibers into the inner muscular system, and digestion and circulation and respiration will be violently disturbed. It is one of the important results of training that disturbances of this type are overcome in increasing measure. The mature nervous system tends to check and distribute excitements so that the organism may not be disturbed in its fundamental activities.

Little children are very often disturbed by mere social excitements to an extent which seriously interferes with life. An adult, on the other hand, can receive the same kind and amount of stimulation and not be distracted from the inner activities of organic life. The training of one-self to receive all sorts of external stimulations without dislocating the inner machinery is one of the important lines of personal training.

Control of excessive stimulations. The formulas which can be adopted for such training are apparently contradictory. First, one should have regular habits of life. This will set up wholesome and balanced forms of action. Second, one should expose himself from time to time to irregular and exciting situations. Or, perhaps better put, one is sure, if he lives in the world with its various kinds of experience, to be drawn out of mere routine by forms of excitement which tend to break up his simple habits of life. Then one should aim to overcome the disturbance of inner life by deliberately controlling the excitement in order to give the organic habits an opportunity to reassert themselves. Control often means relaxation. Let an excited person take two or three long breaths; let him relax the jaw muscles or the muscles of the hands. Excitement which tightens up the muscles can often be overcome by these sheer physical devices. If the physical devices do not suffice, let there be an appeal to voluntary effort. If the excitement is one of fear, let the excited person face the problem and explore the source of the fear. Let one reason himself, if he can, into a less tense attitude. The fact is that every experienced adult has in the course of his life come to the point where he can deal more or less successfully with excitement. Ability to master excitement shows an internal state of coördination of a high type. The organism has acquired ability to undertake several kinds of action at once without interfering with its own life.

While emphasizing the importance of internal harmony, it may be well to refer once more to the disintegrating effects which follow chronic incoördination. All the dissociations which were discussed in an earlier chapter have in them elements of internal discord. The individual whose nervous system is sending out conflicting and discordant impulses is an unhappy individual in his conscious experience and an incoördinated individual in his active life.

Perceptual analysis. A third maxim of mental hygiene is one which relates to perception. All progress in perception and in muscular coördination results from particularization or concentration of attention on definite items of experience. It is worth the effort for everyone to learn to analyze the objects in his environment. Even if one is not going to use the details of information at the moment, it is valuable from the point of view of future adaptation to be able to concentrate attention and action on particular aspects of a situation. Most games illustrate this kind of demand. If a boy learns to catch a ball, he trains himself in concentration of attention and control of his muscles. In the animal world nature provides young animals with a play impulse through which the untrained individual is led into exploratory forms of behavior which in later life will be of use in nosing out real enemies and real prey.

As a practical measure of self-training, it may be urged that everyone ought always to analyze what he encounters. He should notice the details of behavior of those whom he meets ; he should note the contour of the objects he sees. If he gets a hint that there are details which he has overlooked, let him train himself to go back and find these details. The value of such self-control is not merely in the results gained at the moment, but in the conscious tendency to analyze. It was pointed out in an earlier chapter that perception is an active process initiated by the individual. The application of that lesson is that the individual must be active if he would perceive completely.

Perceptual synthesis. The counterpart of the foregoing demand for analysis is the demand that one cultivate the power of grasping many impressions at the same time. The observer should train himself to recognize at a glance as much as possible. It is said that the schools which train performers to give exhibitions of ability to recall a whole box full of trinkets after a single glance begin in childhood by exposing to the prospective performer for recognition, after a very brief exposure, three objects, then four, then five, and so on. The scope of attention is thus broadened.

All forms of expert observation involve this breadth of apprehension. The expertness cultivated in reading involves the power of recognizing at a glance a series of words. The child is limited in his ability to grasp words and only gradually reaches the stage where he can take in many at once. The poor reader is found to be one who has made little progress in the cultivation of a broad range of attention. Many an adult is seriously handicapped because he can recognize at a glance only one word. The individual who finds himself thus limited should train himself by going rapidly over familiar material. The familiarity will give the necessary clearness to details, for familiarity is likely to imply some earlier analysis. The rapid view of the familiar material will help to synthesize many elements into a single experience. The limits to which skill may be cultivated in this matter are described by saying that an expert reader can very often surpass by two or three hundred per cent an ordinary reader.

What is true of reading is true of other situations in which expertness can be cultivated. The person who draws learns not only to see minutely but to take in the totality of a situation. The architect sees many features of a building and shows a grasp of both detail and general appearance which the untrained individual can hardly comprehend. The skilled artisan sees more in every piece of work of the type which he knows than can an inexpert observer.

Dangers of specialization. There appears at this point one of the crucial difficulties in education. Perception is a process in which individual development is often highly specialized. For example, the skilled artisan may see much in the kind of materials with which he is used to dealing and be quite oblivious to other perceptual facts; the shoemaker sees the shoes which a passerby wears, but has no interest in his tailoring. The fact is that perception is closely related, as was shown in an earlier chapter, to special training in direct manipulation. The extension of experience to include many different kinds of percepts will therefore require deliberate effort on the part of the observer; otherwise he will fall into narrow modes of seeing only a small part of the world.

Control of perceptual attitudes. Not only so, but the limited range of ordinary perceptual experience is exhibited in the fact that our attitudes toward the objects about us are very often quite irrational. One dislikes a person whom one meets, for no better reason than that the stranger resembles an acquaintance whom the observer does not like. The child likes a color because he saw it first in an agreeable setting. If experience takes its course without supervision, these attitudes become fixed and the narrowness of perceptual interpretation passes into a lifelong habit.

Practical study of one's own attitudes ought to raise one above the level of accidental attitudes. It often requires time and effort to set aside one of the ready-made reactions which so easily attach to percepts. The person who is afraid of thunder and lightning may have to drill himself for years to overcome this attitude which has become second nature, but a new attitude can be cultivated by anyone who will set himself to the task.

Control of attitudes as a case of volition. In general, the types of training which have been advocated in the last two paragraphs are types which can be accomplished only through the domination of experience by higher mental processes. A man must know something of himself in an ideational way if he is deliberately to cultivate new ranges of perception and new attitudes. What he accomplishes through self-control will ultimately reach back into his perceptual life and will make him alert about many new opportunities to see and hear; it will also make his personal attitudes more rational. The result will be a richer perceptual life and a more wholesome series of attitudes. Perception will thus grow and overcome the inherent tendency toward specialization.

Rules of wholesome ideation. When one comes to memory and ideation, to language and abstraction, the field of applications in personal life is unbounded. A few particular maxims of mental hygiene in these fields may be selected, but the student will have to supply for his own case most of the rules which will insure success of his mental processes.

Economy of mental effort. One of the special problems of memory is the problem of economy of effort. If one has a passage of prose to learn by heart, how should he do it — by learning a line at a time or by taking in large units? The answer supplied by careful experimentation is that he should learn by large units. The reason why learning by large units is advantageous is not far to seek. If one reads to the end of a line and then goes back to the beginning of the line, he sets up an association between the two ends of the same line, whereas he ought to set up an association between the end of the first line and the beginning of the next.

The maxim that one should learn by large units can be amplified to include many cognate cases. The student translating a foreign word looks up the word in the vocabulary and glances through a long list of meanings, most of which he rejects. It would be economy of mental effort in the long run if he would master all the meanings, rejecting none but including all in a complete view of the word. The failure of the student to see this is due to the apparent ease of accomplishing the limited immediate purpose, whereas he ought to cultivate a broad, though more remote, purpose.

Preparation as aid to memory. Another general principle of memory is that even a very abstract scheme which prepares the mind in advance to retain experiences will make it possible to hold more in memory than can be taken in if the material is not arranged. This is illustrated by the man who prepared himself to remember long arbitrary lists of words by setting up in his mind a series of a hundred rooms, arranged in fixed order, in each of which was hung a single mental picture; then when the words to be remembered were given, he associated one with each successive mental room and picture. Later, by going through the rooms in order, he could recall the series of associated ideas. The prearranged mental scheme was the key to his power to retain.

Still better is a rational scheme. The student of science gets ultimately an outline of his subject in mind, and every new author whom he reads falls into this scheme and is classified in detail. A trained student thus cultivates a method of remembering a great body of opinion by classifying it.

If one wants to learn to remember what cards have been played in a card game, let him have a plan of arranging his own hand, and then the accidents of the game will be forced into an orderly scheme.

Organization the key to all correct thought. The general formula which emerges from all these examples is the formula of organization. Ideas should be arranged. When ideas are arranged, they can be carried in greater bulk than when they are isolated. Indeed, they can never be isolated in any absolute sense because some kind of association will always couple them together. Arrangement means, therefore, an association which is dominated by some clear purpose or plan.

The domination of thought by some leading idea. This general formula can be employed also in treating briefly some of the phases of abstraction. The world is for each individual rearranged in terms of personal interests and personal modes of abstraction. The man whose ambition is wealth selects out of everything that comes into his experience those elements which have to do with money. He comes ultimately to see the world from the one point of view. The man whose ambition is power sees men and things from an entirely different point of view. The man without ambition drifts about, looking at his world to-day from one point of view, to-morrow from another. Abstraction is the most subtle and pervasive fact in individual life. We all transform the worlds in which we live by the purposes which control us in life. So absorbed do we become in our personal points of view that it requires a serious jolt to bring us back to the point where we are willing to make revisions.

Language of great importance in furnishing central ideas. The importance of language as an instrument of social abstraction will be instantly recognized in the light of what has gone before. There are phrases current in language which dominate personal thought and make our thinking like that of our neighbors. Take such a word as " efficiency " ; the world is different to a man after he acquires that word as a part of his working vocabulary.

The ineffectiveness of a detached verbal idea. The meaning of these statements for individual development can hardly be misunderstood. The practices of the schools in making language subjects the center of the course of study can be defended in the light of a psychological study of language. To be sure there is danger in mere verbal reactions. Language subjects in the schools need to be brought back into relation with the practical activities of life in order to insure the use of words as instruments of real abstraction and social intercourse. Mere words may be trivial, but words as guides to thought and as instruments for the determination of abstractions are powerful factors in controlling personal thought and action.

To the student who spends most of his time dealing with books perhaps the warning in the last paragraph should be made somewhat clearer. The cerebrum is so complex in its structure that a tract may be established through its tissue, leading from the visual center directly to the speech center. Words read will be repeated, but if this short circuit alone is set in action, the process will have to be described as one of mere repetition.

Higher organization as a cure for verbalism. The remedy for mere verbalism is the development of larger systems of behavior. The eye may see a long stick and the hand may use this stick under the guidance of organized experience to pry up a weight. This reaction with the stick may not arouse at all the speech tract above described, even though the speech tract has been aroused by a textbook in physics to repeat a passage about a lever. The individual thus contains within his complex life one series which is a series of reactions with a real lever and another series which tells about levers. There is a possibility that these two tracts existing side by side will not affect each other in any way. The individual who is aware of this dangerous type of separation of relatable activities within himself will make a conscious effort to unite verbal reactions with practical reactions. He will aim to set up a higher internal organization including both speech and hand adjustment.

A neglect of this demand for complete internal development is one of the most serious dangers of our present-day education. The real trouble is not that words in themselves are bad or that handwork in itself is limited, but in the rush of modern life the two are cultivated side by side and neither gets the benefit of the other. What is needed is a higher type of organization which will include the verbal or theoretical discussion of levers and the illuminating experiences that come from having levers in the hand. This higher form of experience will bring to practical life all the advantages of abstraction and to abstract life all the advantages of concrete application. Both ends can be reached in one and the same individual.

Self-directed organization as the goal of the higher mental life. Again we find ourselves speaking in terms of higher forms of organization. Wherever the individual can comprehend in a single system of nervous or mental organization more elements, there the adaptations of life and experience will be broader and better. The lesson is clear. The individual must seek of his own initiative those higher forms of organization which will realize most fully the possibilities of his life.

The highest level of individual organization is reached when mental development becomes a matter of voluntary control. Under the definition of volition which was worked out in the last chapter it was seen that volition consists in a control of action through intellectual prevision of results. So it is also in the mental world. When the mind by self-study sees the goal which self-development should reach,' it is possible by voluntary effort to move toward this goal. Thus we have seen how knowledge of the nature of perceptual attitudes may guide one in modifying these attitudes. In like fashion, knowledge of the limitations of study of theory may guide one in cultivating applications. Knowledge of one's own limitations may lead to a persistent attack upon these limitations. In short, voluntary self-development means the cultivation of the broadest possible systems of behavior.

CHAPTER XVII

APPLICATIONS OF PSYCHOLOGY

Psychology a basis of scientific thinking about human conduct. There are many phases of practical and scientific thought regarding human activity which are illuminated by the study of psychology. Indeed, wherever human nature is a factor in any set of phenomena, there is need of a clear understanding of the human contribution to the situation, and this can be supplied in scientific form only by a study of psychology. The complete demonstration of the usefulness of psychology would require a series of supplementary chapters. It will be enough for our present purposes if the general outlines of some of these discussions are presented.

Design in art as a psychological fact. Our first illustration can be drawn from the field of the fine arts. This is a sphere in which the relations of the individual to his external environment are relatively free. When the artist paints a picture, he is guided, so far as the design of his production is concerned, by the laws of his own taste. Art grows out of the demand for subjective satisfactions, not out of any compulsion imposed by the physical world. It is for this reason that psychology draws many of its best illustrations from the sphere of art. If we find a general principle running through art, we are led at once to the conclusion that there is a corresponding tendency in human nature. Certain simple illustrations may be offered. Thus, there is a certain proportion between the long and short sides of rectangular figures which is pleasant to look at. The proportion can be expressed mathematically by saying that the long side is to the short side as the sum of both is to the long side. If we examine those objects which have been freely constructed without special external limitations, we shall find that a great many of them take on this proportion. For example, when an extensive series of measurements was made of the two legs of ornamental crosses, it was found that they maintain the proportion described. This fact can have no objective explanation and must have been dictated by human subjective attitudes.

Freedom in art. Again, certain of the types of symmetry in architecture are efforts to meet the demands of human nature rather than of external requirements. If we examine the forms of architecture which grew up in a period when men were free, so far as the external environment was concerned, to construct buildings of any size which they pleased, rather than to fit their constructions to the requirements of a city building lot, we find that the size and form of these free buildings assumed certain general proportions which were determined, not by the external conditions, but rather by the demands of taste. Indeed, one of the fundamental distinctions between ancient and modern architecture is a distinction which can be described by saying that the early builders followed their sense of proportion, while modern builders follow certain definite laws of mechanical construction. A Gothic cathedral of the pure type very commonly exhibits certain irregularities in the position and size of its columns, which yield in the mass an impression of solidity and symmetry that could not be obtained if every part of the building had been made to conform to exact mechanical rules. A modern building is constructed with definite reference to mathematical regularity of dimensions and with reference also to the strain which is to be placed upon every given part of its floors and walls. There is little tendency to use the material freely; there is much greater tendency to do only what is necessary to meet the simpler mechanical requirements. A column made of steel is designed to support a certain weight, and the size of the column used in a building is usually determined by the weight which it is to carry rather than by its appearance. The immediate effect of attention to such mechanical requirements is that we have many ugly buildings.

Architectural harmony analogous to musical rhythm and harmony. There are many indications in the earlier, freer architecture of the Greeks that they followed certain broad principles of rhythmical proportion which correspond so closely to what we find to be the principles of musical rhythm and harmony, that there is a suggestion of a common type of human organization lying back of both spheres of art. It has been pointed out, for example, that the height of a Greek column is an exact multiple of its diameter. Furthermore, the space between the columns always stands in definite relation to the diameter of the column. In details of construction also, as, for example, in the various portions of the decorations in the Ionic capital, the parts are related to each other in definite unit ratios, so that a constructive symmetry runs through the whole and gives the observer a feeling of composure and unity.

Literary art and psychological laws. What is true of architecture is much more obvious with reference to literary art. It is clear that the laws of literary composition must be laws of human nature, and the great artists have unquestionably followed with sufficient closeness the demands of human nature to leave their works as standards for future development and as expressions of the direction in which all individual development must tend.

Prose rhythms as related to the personal organization of writers. Some purely formal indications of the completeness with which great literature conforms to the demands of human nature may be found in the fact that there are even in prose compositions certain typical rhythms which give to these compositions a regular symmetry of character, which undoubtedly constitutes one of its charms. It is a striking example of the fact that art may outstrip science, that it is not yet possible to give any complete theoretical account of the prose rhythms of the best writers. Evidently those who have contributed the great works to literature have succeeded in utilizing the language in which they wrote in such a way as to express an internal organization of their own which was altogether appropriate to their theme and to the vernacular, and this they have done spontaneously and very often without complete theoretical recognition of what they were doing. When the student of such prose arrives by laborious analysis at some knowledge of the rhythms which it contains, he is not creating rhythms, but rather rediscovering by the tardy methods of scientific analysis a formula which has been achieved by the great writer through intuition.

Verse another example of the same type. If the forms of prose composition have exhibited complexity of structure, together with a fundamental regularity of form, it is even more true of verse that its masters have never followed rigid mechanical principles in their work. And yet they have adequately met the demands of human nature. Their conformity to a limited group of principles is seen in their adherence to certain regular forms which are sufficiently obvious to be imitated in gross outline by writers of less taste and power; but the full and effective use of verse forms has always involved a certain freedom of manipulation which has defied any complete theoretical account. Psychology must frankly admit in such a case as this that it follows in the steps of a complete adaptation, very far behind the adaptation itself. Nevertheless, the psychological problem is clear, and a general suggestion as to the explanation of these facts may be found in what has been said in an earlier connection regarding the nature of rhythm. Whatever the unknown details, rhythm is certainly in keeping with the natural demands of the nervous system. Because the nervous system is rhythmical in a complex way in its own functioning, it responds favorably to rhythms of impressions.

Literary content controlled by psychological laws. It is not alone in its form that literature expresses the demands of human nature ; the content may be studied from the same point of view. It is possible by a psychological analysis to throw much light on one case which has been the subject of much mystical speculation. It has often been suggested that human intuitions and vague feelings frequently bring us much nearer to that which afterward proves to be the truth than do our most elaborate processes of reasoning. The poet has always claimed for himself a higher position than he would allow to the scientist who is bound by the demands of rigid evidence. We often speak of the insights of the artist, and mean by this phrase that the artist sees beyond the ordinary facts of definite observation and clear vision to ranges of facts which are of importance, but are not open to our inspection.

Feeling and intuition. What has been said in an earlier chapter with regard to the nature of feelings will be of some assistance in clearing up the paradox which here appears. When explaining the feelings, we discovered that whatever runs counter to the organized nature of the individual will arouse a disagreeable feeling. Whatever is in fundamental agreement with nature will give pleasure. If now the experiences of life are in subtle agreement or disagreement with the organization of the individual, it does not follow that the individual will become clearly conscious of this fact in ideational or abstract terms, and yet he may be vividly aware of the disagreeable feeling imposed upon him by a certain experience. For example, as we have seen in earlier discussions, the organization of an animal may be such that certain color stimulations are fundamentally opposed to its natural organization. Feeling is, therefore, a kind of spontaneous adjustment with a practical value which often surpasses that of incomplete theoretical judgments. Feeling may be relied upon in those situations where the organization is simple enough or the response direct enough to give an unbiased reflection of the individual's relation to the impression. On the other hand, when life becomes complex, as it is in human beings, native instincts and native feelings are often overlaid by a series of developments so indirect that there comes to be a certain rivalry between the authority of feeling and the authority of abstract knowledge. There can be no doubt, for example, that the social selections by which one determines who shall be his friends are dependent in large measure on intuitions, but one does not need to be very old or worldly-wise to recognize that the complexities of social life are such that the instinctive feelings which we have in making the acquaintance of new individuals are not always safe guides in the development of social relations. What is true of social relations is true, undoubtedly, of artistic intuitions and of larger intuitions of universal truth. It is quite impossible to persuade one who regards a line of poetry as beautiful that it is not beautiful because it violates some rigid law of versification. It is quite impossible to convince one who enjoys a certain picture that the picture is deficient because it does not comply with certain canons of a certain school of art. On the other hand, it is frequently possible, by a series of educative contacts with better artistic and literary forms, gradually to modify an individual's organized feelings so that he shall completely change the character of his judgment. Intuition is, therefore, not a separate and distinct faculty of life ; it is rather an expression of that immediate form of recognition of congruity or incongruity which characterizes the feelings as distinguished from abstract theoretical knowledge. The statement made by the poet may express an attitude which is true to the facts and will later be fully explicated by the clearer ideational view cultivated in abstract thought. There is no ultimate opposition between feeling and thought.

Many of the social sciences predominantly objective in their methods. When we turn from the discussion of' art and feeling to certain more practical spheres of investigation involving human nature, — namely, those taken up in the social sciences and anthropology, — we find that the study of psychology is very direct in its application to these spheres of study and explanation. It has not always been fully recognized that psychology has a relation to the social sciences. Certain schools of social scientists have treated the institutions which they study merely as objective facts. To show this, we may take as an illustration one of the oldest of social sciences ; namely, the science which deals with language. Language is a product of human activity which has a sufficiently independent existence to make it an easy subject for examination and analysis. To trace the history of a word is to undertake an investigation which calls for little reference to the individuals who may have made use of this word. In like fashion, the study of a system of sounds and written symbols may result in the discovery of certain regularities and laws of phonetics without reference to the human beings who used this language and who were the ultimate sources of regularities in the language itself. The same historical and objective methods have been applied to the study of other institutions. For example, religious systems have been described and their uniformities and divergencies have been ascertained without more than a passing reference to the individuals who developed these systems or adhered to them.

Introspective psychology and its limited support to social science. The tendency to confine attention to an objective study of human institutions has been strengthened by the attitude which for a long time prevailed in psychology, when the chief method of investigation was the introspective method, according to which the individual attempted to discover the laws of mental life through an examination of his own immediate experience, and with very little reference to the modifying influence of his fellow beings or the secondary factors of his environment. When the problem of psychology is more broadly conceived, so that it is seen that the character of human mental life can be defined only by a more elaborate study of numerous examples and external relations, the spheres of institutional study and of psychological investigation are gradually brought nearer to each other.

Interrelation of psychology and social science. In the course of recent psychological study, much valuable illustrative material has been borrowed from the sciences which deal with language and from anthropology. Psychology has thus expanded under the influence of the new body of material which has been adopted into it. The methods of psychology have become more objective, and the results of individual introspection have been broadened. On the other hand, the scientific study of all other human beings must be based upon one's own personal experiences. One naturally thinks of primitive man in terms of his own mental experiences. If there is no scientific study of the matter, the student is likely to carry over analogies and apply them to cases where they do not illustrate, but rather obscure, the truth. Thus, as has been pointed out by a recent writer, there is a widespread tendency to describe the mental abilities of savages by means of a succession of negatives. Savages do not count, they do not have a full series of color terms, they do not paint pictures or write. All these negatives are mere expressions of the natural tendency to accept ourselves as standards. We should become sufficiently impersonal in our studies to recognize that savages probably have a nicety of space perception which is very much greater than ours. They may not select color qualities and name them, but for the finer grades of variation in plant and animal life as indicated by color they have the most highly developed discrimination. Not only the savage, but even our contemporaries in different civilizations from our own, are exceedingly baffling unless we make some study of their types of mental development. The institutions of Tibet, China, and Japan are obviously different from our own, but the character of the mental processes back of these institutions has been little thought of and little studied. The careful scientific study of the mental characteristics of different peoples is one of the most promising lines of extension of psychological study.

Human evolution psychical. So intimately is social organization bound up with the mental development of the individual that we are justified in the statement that psychology is the basis of any explanatory account of social institutions. There is one particular anthropological problem where the significance of psychological analysis can be made very clear. Anthropology has never succeeded in finding structural modifications in the human body which would at all adequately account for the great superiority of highly developed races over the more primitive tribes of mankind. Even the explanation of the crucial development by which man became differentiated from the animals is one of the obscure chapters in anthropology. It cannot be denied that the explanation of all these matters must be sought in terms which refer to the development of intelligence, especially the development of language and the use of tools, as has been indicated in an earlier discussion. The problem of anthropology is thus distinguished from the purely biological problem, where intelligence is not recognized as playing any part. How could a certain group of animals suddenly break away from the established type of evolution in which changes in structures played a large part and become animals characterized by intelligence, meeting the emergencies of their lives by a mental adaptation of themselves rather than by a purely physical adaptation?

Why should this group of animals turn to the development of all the instruments of civilization? The problem stated in this form becomes a problem of functional development rather than a problem of physical development. This animal must have been driven at some time into a situation where his development turned upon his ability to adopt a new type of behavior and a new mode of life. There can be no doubt that the scientific explanation of the breach between man and the animals depends upon the recognition of a transformation in the mode of behavior and mental life rather than upon any fact of gross bodily change. Put in another way, the statement may be made that we need no animal form to serve as a connecting link between man and the animals. The common structure, the common physical needs of man and the animals, are now made out so fully that what science requires is an explanation of the gap, rather than the link, between man and the animals. The doctrine of biological evolution has successfully established the principle of continuity. It remains for genetic psychology to explain the discontinuity which appears when intelligence begins to dominate, when sensory-motor adjustments of the reflex and instinctive type give place to habit acquired through individual intelligence and to the more elaborate forms of thought.

A hypothesis to explain the break between man and the animals. An interesting hypothesis has been suggested which illustrates the possibility of assuming a distinctly functional attitude toward the question of the evolution of man. This hypothesis suggests that the gradual changes in physical organization which characterize all of the different species of primates lead up to the appearance of man only because at one time a number of these primates were forced, probably by the emergencies of a glacial climate in certain quarters in which they were confined, to adopt a mode of life which brought them down out of the trees and forced upon them types of activity which led to their construction of artificial shelters and to the preparation of forms of food which had not been previously utilized by their race. The change here assumed depends on the rise of a powerful motive for new ways of behavior. Whatever change there was in the individual consisted in the opening of new paths in the central nervous system. This change in the trend of evolution, when once it appeared, was so important that the further history of the group of animals which succeeded in effecting it was in the direction of adaptation through intelligence and nervous organization rather than through gross changes in bodily structures. Whether we give any credence to this hypothesis or not, it expresses admirably the functional attitude in the explanation of human evolution. It expresses clearly the fact that the nature of mental and functional adaptation is the significant problem for anthropology rather than the mere search for changes in physical organization; it gives to anthropology a definite impetus in the direction of the study of mental organization, as distinguished from the study of bodily structures.

Spencer's application of psychology to sociology. Another illustration from a later period of human development which will also emphasize the significance of psychological study for anthropology is to be found in Spencer's discussions, in which he calls attention to the fact that the growth of civilization depends upon the broadening of the individual's mental horizon. He points out the fact that the savage who had interest in only a small range of territory and the present enjoyment of objects immediately about him gradually developed into the semicivilized man interested in a larger territory, a larger number of individuals, and a longer period of time. The planting of crops and the erection of permanent buildings cannot be explained by objective conditions as has sometimes been attempted in the history of civilization. There must be ideas and imaginations in the mind of some active being before the future can be anticipated sufficiently to lead to the planting of the crop or the erection of the building.

Relation of educational practices to scientific psychology. Conspicuous among the social institutions to which psychology may be applied in a direct and practical fashion is the institution of education. Here again is a type of adaptation which has grown in an unscientific way to a high degree of maturity. This statement implies no disposition to deny the effectiveness of many of the practices of educational institutions. They may be effective without being scientific. They are the outgrowth of a need which has been felt by every generation, and the educational institutions which have been developed in response to this general need have been refined and modified in view of experience, until finally they express with a high degree of perfection the final judgment of many generations upon important questions connected with the training of the younger generation. Yet there are obvious reasons why these historical institutions should be reëxamined. Some of the uncritical methods of education are found to be wasteful; again, the educational practices of different peoples or different sections of the same nation are found to be inharmonious. There arises, therefore, a demand for a careful analysis of the whole situation and the establishment of those practices which scientific analysis can justify. It is true that many hold the same attitude with regard to education that they do with regard to art; namely, that it is safer to rely upon the intuitions of human feeling than to attempt to formulate an abstract system of education. Those who adopt this position with regard to the advantages of intuition in education have justification for their position, in so far as educational practices are refined to a point beyond our knowledge of the laws of human development. The most acceptable plea for a scientific study of education which could be presented to such persons would consist in a plea for a more complete knowledge of the same sort which they have in their native intuitions. It might be said, for example, that the study of educational methods involves nothing more than the bringing together of the individual experiences and practices of all those who have become skilled in educational practice. A comparative study would help to eliminate those individual intuitions which are incorrect, because they are based upon too narrow experience.

Psychology as a preparation for the intelligent diagnosis of particular situations which arise in educational practice. The final examination of educational practices must go much further, however, than is implied in this appeal for a comparative study of intuitions. Attention must be called to the fact that much of our devotion to traditional educational practices is nothing more or less than a deliberate confession of our ignorance of the way in which the human mind develops. When a teacher is confronted by children who are unable to comprehend the lesson which has been set, he very commonly can make no analysis of the child's difficulty. He then covers up his ignorance of the step which should be taken by requiring repeated efforts on the child's part, until in some unknown fashion the difficulties are mastered. It does not follow that the particular difficulty encountered in any given case would have been recognizable if the teacher had made a study of human development in other individuals, but the probability that the trained teacher will be able to make a scientific analysis of the difficult situation at hand is increased if he becomes acquainted with the principles and results of scientific psychology. Intuition should therefore be supplemented by as full an account as can be given of the way in which mental processes go on and of the methods by which these processes may be examined.

A few illustrations may serve to make clear the place and value of the psychological study of educational problems. First, a number of investigations have recently been undertaken with a view to defining in detail the course of development of certain habits. Broadly stated, the conclusions of these studies show that no habit develops in all of its stages at a uniform rate. There is at the outset a period during which improvement is relatively very rapid ; this is followed by a period of slow development, which in turn gives way to successive periods of rapid and slow growth.

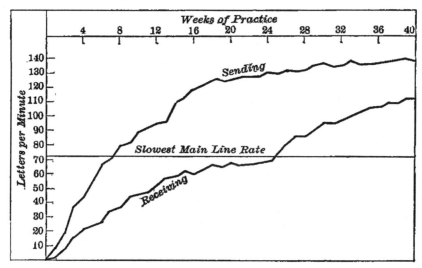

FIG. 60. Curves for sending and receiving telegraphic messages

The curve is published by Bryan and Harter. The number of weeks of practice is indicated in the upper part of the figure. The number of letters which can be received and sent in a minute is represented in the vertical. The figure is divided by a horizontal line, which shows the standard rate

A curve illustrating the process of learning. One of the earliest investigations of the way in which an individual learns may be described in detail. This investigation was undertaken to determine the rate at which a learner acquired the ability to send and receive telegraphic messages. The selection of this particular case for the test was due to the ease with which measurements of proficiency could be made and to the maturity of the persons investigated, which made it easy to subject them to a series of tests. In Fig. 60 the results of the investigation are represented in a curve. Along the top of the figure are marked the successive weeks during which the investigation was carried on ; along the vertical line at the left the number of letters which could be received or sent in a minute. A single point on the curve represents, accordingly, both a stage in the practice series and the number of letters which could be received or sent during a minute at this stage of development. The curves taken in their entirety represent the gradual increase in the ability of the subject. It will be noticed, in the first place, that the improvement in sending and in receiving messages followed an entirely different course, both with reference to rate of improvement and also with reference to the successive stages of development. Concentrating attention for the moment upon the curve which records improvement in receiving, we see that the development is at first rapid and then for a long time practically stationary. After the stationary period, or plateau as the authors called this part of the figure, came a second rapid rise in the curve.

Significance of a " plateau " in development. In Fig. 61 a second curve of the same sort is shown, which makes it possible to explain the pause, or plateau, in development. The lowest curve in this second diagram represents the development of proficiency in recognizing isolated letters. The second curve represents the development of proficiency in receiving isolated words which did not unite into sentences, and the full curve represents, as before, the development of efficiency in receiving words which constituted sentences. It will be noticed that the ability to receive isolated letters and the ability to receive isolated words developed rapidly for a time, until they reached their maxima, and then they continued indefinitely at the same level. This level is so related to the plateau in the total curve that the plateau can safely be defined as the period during which the subject was in the word stage of development, rather than in the sentence stage. Only after the ability to receive single words had been thoroughly matured was a new type of development possible.'

Other examples of the same type of development. Such an analysis as this of a case of learning shows much with regard to the psychological character of the process. It also

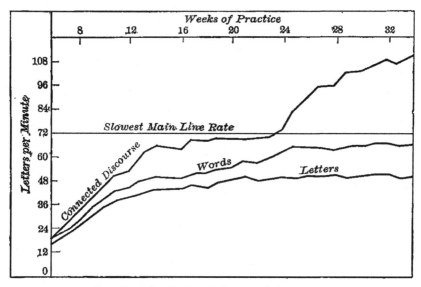

FIG. 61. Analysis of the receiving curve

This figure is similar to Fig. 60. For further discussion, see text (p. 339)

suggests the possibility of including the process of mental development under certain broad laws of development. There are many analogous cases in general evolution where it has been noted again and again that periods of rapid development are followed by long periods of assimilation. It is a well-known fact of bodily growth that the enlargement of the body is most marked at certain periods in the year and at certain well-defined periods in the child's life. After one of the sudden enlargements of the body, there follows a period of gradual assimilation of the new developments, during which the body remains stationary in its size for a considerable time. The facts of organic evolution on a larger scale are of the same type. During certain periods the animal kingdom has advanced rapidly by the production of new forms, after which long stationary periods appear, during which these new forms are more completely adjusted to their environment without being in any important sense modified. Such statements as these make clear the distinction between assimilation and acquisition in both the physical and mental worlds.

The fact that certain forms of mental development are periodic rather than continuous is illustrated in many cases where quantitative tests have not been made. It has often been casually observed that a mature subject learns a foreign language, not with uniform rapidity, but in a way analogous to that shown in the curves given above. At first there is rapid acquisition of the words and grammatical constructions of the new language, but after a time the power to acquire new phases of the language seems to be brought to a standstill; and the period of discouragement which follows is often felt by the learner to be a period of no development, while in reality it is a period of assimilation and preparation for the later stages of growth. When the later development into the full use of the language comes, it is so sudden and striking in its character that it has been noted time and time again as a period of astonishing mental achievement.

Motor habits intermittent. Many habits of action exhibit the same type of intermittent development. If one learns some manual art, he finds that the incoördinations with which he begins are only gradually eliminated; but finally he learns the combination which is advantageous, and from that point on the improvement seems for a time to be very rapid. It is sometimes advantageous in a course of training to give up practice for a time in order that the various elements of the coördination may have an opportunity to readjust themselves and in order that the new efforts at development may begin at a new level. Professor James has made the striking remark that we learn to skate during the summer and to swim during the winter. The significance of this observation is that it recognizes the intermittent character of the development of habit and the advantage of a period of assimilation, sometimes even of a period of complete cessation of the activity in question.

School training in its relation to the stage of development attained by the mind. From the point of view of practical education, it is obvious that the types of training which should be given at the different periods in mental development are by no means the same. During a period of rapid acquirement of new material, one sort of training is appropriate; during a period of delayed assimilation, that form of training is most appropriate which is technically known in the schools as drill. The ordinary unscientific education has recognized vaguely that there is a difference in the kinds of training demanded at different times; but the adjustment of these different types of training to the demands of individual mental development is an intricate problem which can be worked out satisfactorily only when a careful study is made of educational practice.

Significance of scientific studies often indirect. The value of scientific studies of habits and of forms of training is shown by such considerations as the foregoing. It also becomes evident that such studies do not necessarily change the subjects of instruction nor even the general methods established by tradition, but serve rather to refine our knowledge of the process of mental growth and make it possible for us to deal with different stages of the educational process with much greater precision. To justify scientific investigations which seem at first sight remote from school problems, it may be well to point out that the solution of one problem in mental development makes it possible to attack all other problems of a similar kind more intelligently. If one knows with scientific precision that a period of assimilation occurs in one case of mental development, he will be better prepared to discover and understand a similar period in other cases where it may be less easy to make an exact scientific study. For example, we get useful suggestions to guide us in understanding children's reading from the study reported above on learning telegraphy. The mastery of the word elements in ordinary reading is similar to the mastery of these same elements in the case of the telegrapher.

Expression as an essential condition of mental life. Another concrete illustration of educational progress may be found in the fact that there is a general disposition among educators to-day to recognize the importance and value of expressive activities in all educational processes. The early type of education was that in which sensation processes were emphasized almost to the exclusion of activities. Whether the educational practice which emphasized impressions can be attributed to the sensation psychology which was contemporary with it, or whether the sensation psychology was the outgrowth of a false educational theory, is a question which need not be discussed here. Certain it is that the limited view of mental life and the false principle of education, both of which emphasized impressions rather than expression, existed for a long period side by side. It may have been the growing experience of practical teachers which led to the discovery of the fallacy in the doctrine that mind is conditioned primarily by impressions. It may have been the insight of scientific students which gradually made it clear that human activity must always be recognized in discussing the processes of mental development; or it may be that the two lines of thought and practice grew up together. In any case, it is certain that a transformation of educational practice and a corresponding transformation of psychology have been going on for a generation, until now we have in both an emphasis on bodily activities.

Psychology historically a part of philosophy. Turning from these practical applications of psychology to education, it remains for us to discuss one of the applications of psychology which has always been recognized in the historical development of this science ; namely, the relation of psychology to the philosophical disciplines. Indeed, it may be said that psychology was not only applied to the problems of philosophy ; it was originally devoted to the discussion of these problems to such an extent that it was regarded as an integral part of philosophy, not as an independent science. Philosophy deals with the ultimate nature of matter and mind, with the fundamental laws of reality and the relation of reality to human experience, with the ultimate nature of truth, goodness, and beauty. There have been times, for example during the medieval period, when the interest in such ultimate problems ran so high that there was little or no attention given to the special problems of science. The time came, however, with the development of modern thought when these larger problems receded into the background and men began to concern themselves with the phenomena in the world rather than with the ultimate realities underlying these phenomena. It is characteristic of the present scientific period that the special sciences neglect to as great an extent as possible the questions of ultimate reality. The student of psychology participates to a very large extent in this tendency to omit from his discussion questions relating to the ultimate nature of mind. He cannot, however, accept as final this aloofness from the broader questions, for he finds himself, more than his neighbor who deals exclusively with the natural sciences, led to ultimate problems.

Relation of psychology to philosophy closer than that of any of the special sciences. When, for example, one points out that a sensation is related to a fact of external energy indirectly through the organs of sense, or when one points out that space is a definite form of perception on the one hand, and of arrangement· of objects on the other, the psychologist is driven to consider the relation between consciousness and the external world more than the student of the other particular sciences. The student of natural science uses in every act of observation the relation between subjective experience and the physical world; he exercises his mind in trying to know the world, but his interests are always centered on the relations between things, never on the relation between things and consciousness. Hence the student of natural science easily avoids questions relating to the ultimate interaction between himself and the physical world. The student of psychology cannot escape these questions. His study of sensation pushes him in the direction of an examination of this relation. Furthermore, when the student of psychology finds that the construction of concepts is an elaborate mental activity, he is immediately led to ask not only what are the laws which control such conceptual activity, but also what are the relations of scientific ideas to external reality, and what are the laws which determine the validity or lack of validity of these concepts. It is true that psychology cannot answer all of these questions, and it has been our purpose in the foregoing discussions to adhere as closely as possible to the sphere of strict psychological inquiry, postponing these ultimate questions or entirely omitting them. It is, therefore, very appropriate that we should call attention at the end of our inquiry to the disciplines which deal with these more elaborate inquiries, and that we should define their relation to psychology.

Psychology and logic. Logic attempts to formulate the laws of valid reasoning. To be sure, logical principles can be worked out without the aid of psychology, through repeated efforts to reason correctly, but the clear definition of logical relations waits on the psychological descriptions of the mental processes involved in reasoning.

Psychology and æsthetics. The second branch of philosophy is æsthetics. In earlier chapters reference has been made repeatedly to the underlying principles which control the recognition of symmetry and regularity of form, and it was pointed out in earlier paragraphs of this chapter that the canons of architecture and painting are directly related to certain fundamental principles of human feeling and recognition. There still remain a large number of special analyses and special considerations which must be worked out in order to define fully the canons of taste in each field of art and the general canons of taste which underlie all forms of art. Such considerations of the canons of art constitute a legitimate development of the general psychological studies which have been suggested, and constitute the special discipline of æsthetics.

Psychology and ethics. When we turn to the third of the special philosophical disciplines, namely ethics, we find again a natural relation to psychology, though it is perhaps proper to emphasize here more than in the case of logic or æsthetics the independence of ethical canons from purely subjective organizations. The rightness or wrongness of human behavior is not understood primarily through an analysis of the processes of behavior themselves. The rightness or wrongness of behavior depends upon certain broad considerations involving the social interrelationships of the active individual. It is necessary, therefore, to make a study of the extra-mental or social relations of the individual in order to establish the canons of ethical conduct. One does not need to discuss the extra-mental relations to anything like the same extent when he attempts to define the laws of reasoning in logic or the laws of appreciation in æsthetics. It is true that the individual's modes of behavior, as they have been worked out in the course of social life, come to embody much of the social interrelationship which determines their ethical validity. The individual who has grown up in a social group ultimately conforms in his modes of thought and internal organization to those social demands which are imposed upon him by the community in which he lives. It is probably true, therefore, that in the last analysis the fundamental truths of ethics are expressed in the internal organization of the individual as well as in the forms which are approved under the canons of social life, but the development of ethical laws lies somewhat beyond the application of psychology. We come to ethics chiefly through the study of the applications of psychology to the sciences of social institutions.

Psychology and metaphysics. When we turn from the special philosophical disciplines to the broader field of metaphysics, or the general theory of reality, we find that the relation of psychology to these broader types of consideration is relatively indirect. Metaphysics takes up the results of natural science which deals with matter and of psychological science which deals with consciousness, and attempts to formulate some general principles of the relations between all forms of reality. To this general discussion psychology cannot contribute final answers any more than could the special sciences of physics or chemistry. Psychology can only present its conclusions after it has carried out as complete an analysis of consciousness as possible, and must leave it for metaphysics to make an ultimate comparison of these facts with the physical facts. The student who finds that an empirical analysis of consciousness conflicts with any of the established views which constitute a part of his general theory of the world should recognize that it is not the function of any single science to reconstruct his total theory of the world. He will have to accept the results of empirical analysis in all the different spheres of exact research and work out a general view which will include all of these results. The conclusions of psychology need to be generalized exactly as do the conclusions of physics and chemistry. No generalization will be finally valid which does not comprehend the empirical analysis of each one of these sciences. Furthermore, it should not be forgotten that there are many types of consideration which forced themselves upon human attention long before the various forms of scientific analysis could be worked out, and these considerations must also be recognized in the construction of a broad philosophy of life. The generalizations which were reached before the development of the special sciences require revision in order to include the results of these sciences. This fact should not disturb the mind of any student and need not lead him to ignore many nonscientific types of experience. The training in scientific inference which he has received in the study of empirical psychology should lead him to recognize that all generalizations are subjective constructs built up from a great variety of experiences, many of which are superficially in disagreement with each other. The subjective construct is not to be discarded as invalid, because it changes with the acquisition of new knowledge; one's theory of the world must change in order to fulfill its function as a complete, organized expression of the manifold experiences which enter into life. Psychology, more than any other science, should lead to a recognition of this demand for a constantly progressing enlargement of philosophic view. While, therefore, modern psychology as a science has freed itself from the obligation of dealing with the broad philosophical questions, it continues, when rightly understood, not only to contribute material for philosophic thought, but also to urge the student to the rational reconstruction of his general abstract views. It is therefore introductory, not merely to the special philosophical disciplines but also to the more remote discussions of metaphysics itself.

INDEX

ANNOUNCEMENTS

METHODS OF TEACHING IN HIGH SCHOOLS

By SAMUEL CHESTER PARKER, The University of Chicago

xxv + 529 pages, illustrated, $1.50

A CAREFUL study of the principles which underlie classroom instruction in high-school subjects forms the basis of this interesting book, which concerns itself primarily with the actual class work of high-school teachers and only in a minor degree with the curriculum and organization of high schools. The following chapter titles are suggestive of some of the lines pursued by the book : Economy in Classroom Management ; Reflective Thinking ; The Use of Books ; Conversational Methods ; Laboratory Methods ; The Art of Questioning ; Practice Teaching and Lesson-Planning ; Measuring the Results of Teaching. As a volume for reading and for general reference the book will be invaluable to high-school teachers.

THE PSYCHOLOGY OF HIGH-SCHOOL SUBJECTS

By CHARLES HUBBARD JUDD, The University of Chicago

515 pages, $1.50

A VOLUME which analyzes psychologically the mental processes which each subject in the high-school curriculum develops in the student. From these analyses come the solutions of many problems of value and method, and it is from this viewpoint that the author discusses these problems. Each discussion is introduced by a summary of the psychological facts relating to it. Problems of discipline are treated in a new and suggestive way, and the characteristics of the adolescent period are described in their relation to the stages of mental growth. The book is well worth the consideration and thought of all who are interested in educational problems.

204

GINN AND COMPANY PUBLISHERS

ELEMENTARY PSYCHOLOGY

SUGGESTIONS FOR THE INTERPRETATION OF HUMAN LIFE

By D. E. PHILLIPS, University of Denver

12mo, cloth, xi + 352 pages, illustrated, $1.20

IN this volume the author connects psychology as a science with life and conduct in such a vital way as to create a wide and permanent interest in psychology. Among the chapters that contribute to a larger view of the practical applications of the science and that touch on problems of contemporary interest are : Suggestion and Mental Healing, Magic and Spiritualism, Relation of Psychology to Evolution, Problems of Heredity and Environment, Social Psychology, and Psychology in Literature and Art.

The subject is developed inductively through the use of abundant examples and illustrations. Feeling, instinct, imitation, habit, etc. are presented simply and are treated as the springs of human conduct and the basis for explaining the more formal and technical part of psychology. Every chapter contains great moral lessons and demonstrates the intricate network of all human conduct.

The book is admirably adapted for an introductory course with students in normal schools and colleges. It provides interesting material, also, for teachers and reading circles and for the general reader.

192 b

GINN AND COMPANY PUBLISHERS

AN
INTRODUCTORY PSYCHOLOGY

With Some Educational Applications

By MELBOURNE STUART READ, Professor of Psychology and
Education in Colgate University

12mo, cloth, 309 pages, illustrated, $1.00

THE aim of the book is to present to the reader the main truths of the science of psychology in a simple, direct, and interesting fashion. It is the normal development and workings of the reader's own mental experience which the book attempts to help him understand, the mind being conceived as a part of a psychophysical organism, adjusting itself to the conditions of its life.

The main topics taken up are the following: The nature and problems of psychology; the general nature of consciousness; the nervous system; the simple adaptive processes, — impulse, instinct, and habit; the simple and the complex processes of sense stimulation, — sensation and perception; attention and interest; association; the simpler and the more complex affective processes, — affection, feeling, emotion, and sentiment; the ideational processes, — memory, imagination, conception, and thought; and the processes of complex conscious adaptation, — the will.

Considerable space has been given to practical applications, as they help decidedly in making clear and in fixing in mind the principles involved. Applications of psychology are, of course, especially useful to the teacher, and the learning and teaching processes have received much attention.

As its title indicates, this is a first book in psychology. It is especially designed for use as a text in normal schools, teachers' training classes in high schools, and in elementary courses in colleges.

192 a

GINN AND COMPANY Publishers

TWO BOOKS BY
LESTER F. WARD

APPLIED SOCIOLOGY

384 pages, with charts, $2.50

THE author's purpose in this volume is to point out how the obstacles to human progress may be overcome by the application of the principles of social science, and how the human race may be brought into the full fruition of its powers.

The argument is supported by historical facts, and the work is to a considerable extent statistical. It is illustrated by colored maps, charts, and tabular exhibits.

The clearness, brilliancy, and vigorous defense of some pronounced doctrine which we have learned to expect from Professor Ward are characteristic of this book. It concerns real facts, not verbal distinctions; it delights by its cleverness of thought and style. — *Science*

THE PSYCHIC FACTORS OF CIVILI-
ZATION (Second Edition)

xxi + 369 pages, $2.00

THIS work is an original contribution to both psychology and sociology, and is, in fact, a combination of these two departments of science. It shows in a systematic and fundamental way the workings of mind in social phenomena.

The work is divided into three parts — the subjective factors, the objective factors, and the social synthesis of the factors; and appeals especially to the following classes of readers: psychologists, sociologists, economists, philosophers and thinkers, biologists and naturalists, also to socialists and to social and political reformers.

It is impossible to indicate in a brief notice the variety of interest in the content of Professor Ward's book, which boldly correlates still disputed doctrines from psychology and evolutionary science, and connects with them a theory of rational and aggressive social action, based upon the primary egotistic forces — "believing that neither meliorism nor sociocracy is dependent upon altruistic props for its support."— *Philosophical Review*

GINN AND COMPANY PUBLISHERS

ImTheStory.com

Personalized Classic Books in many genre's

Unique gift for kids, partners, friends, colleagues

Customize:

- Character Names
- Upload your own front/back cover images (optional)
- Inscribe a personal message/dedication on the
  inside page (optional)

Customize many titles Including
- Alice in Wonderland
- Romeo and Juliet
- The Wizard of Oz
- A Christmas Carol
- Dracula
- Dr. Jekyll & Mr. Hyde
- And more...

Lightning Source UK Ltd.
Milton Keynes UK
UKOW06f0628210217

294911UK00015B/222/P